My Mother's Southern Entertaining

OTHER BOOKS BY
JAMES VILLAS

My Mother's Southern Desserts
(with Martha Pearl Villas) (1998)

Stews, Bogs, and Burgoos:
Recipes from the Great American Stewpot (1997)

My Mother's Southern Kitchen
(with Martha Pearl Villas) (1994)

The French Country Kitchen (1992)

James Villas' Country Cooking (1988)

Villas at Table
(1988, reissued 1998)

Town & Country Cookbook (1985)

American Taste
(1982, reissued 1997)

My Mother's Southern Entertaining

James Villas

with

Martha Pearl Villas

WILLIAM MORROW
An Imprint of HarperCollins*Publishers*

HarperCollins books may be purchased for educational, business, or sales promotional use. For information please write: Special Markets Department, HarperCollins Publishers Inc., 10 East 53rd Street, New York, NY 10022.

FIRST EDITION

Designed by Richard Oriolo

Photographs © 2000 by Dennis Gottlieb
Food styling by A. J. Battifarano

Printed on acid-free paper

Library of Congress Cataloging-in-Publication Data has been applied for.

ISBN 0-688-17184-2

00 01 02 03 04 FF 10 9 8 7 6 5 4 3 2 1

FOR ANN SCARBOROUGH

A proud Mississippi belle, a great cook who
understands cornbread like no other Southerner,
and a most loving and beloved friend

Acknowledgments

For the third time, a grateful salute to our gifted editor at William Morrow, Pam Hoenig, for once again embracing "the Southern cause" and teaching us for the umpteenth time what recipe precision is all about. Respectful thanks also to Kate Heddings for her keen eye at editorial coordination; to Gary Crain and Jim Smith, two other Southern gents whose generous help in the final stages of the book has been invaluable; and to a certain kind lady in Southampton, New York, for her gracious hospitality.

Contents

Introduction

"Honey, if I couldn't find a legitimate excuse to throw a party, I'd invent one."

I'd like to have a nickel for every time I've heard my mother make that statement, a proclamation that is as valid today as when I was a child in North Carolina and one that explains why there's no season of the year that doesn't provide Mother with numerous excuses to entertain in the graceful Southern tradition. No sooner, for example, has the first frost of fall turned the last tomato plants a sickly brown than she begins to plan her annual jack-o'-lantern celebration, an elaborate Thanksgiving feast, a series of after-shopping and gift-making lunches with "the gals," and her ritualistic spend-the-day fruitcake party. The cold months of winter warrant not only all types of festive holiday meals but any number of low-keyed, quaint social teas and get-togethers. By the time the yellow bells (forsythia to you non-Southerners) of spring are in bloom and fresh asparagus fills the markets, her thoughts shift to an Easter egg picnic for children and adults alike, a large, formal cocktail supper, and her special Low Country "perloo" party. And when the summer temperature soars enough to ripen fat strawberries, fuzzy peaches, and thick-skinned tomatoes, Mother has already prepared who knows how many casual beach dinners, fired up the grill for an authentic Carolina pork barbecue, and sent out invitations to a neighborhood church supper.

Mother is no longer the young lady who, as a teenager, prepared and served frozen fruit salad and creamed chicken in fancy pastry cups at her first bridge club, or the budding bride who hosted her first Super Bowl buffet to impress my father. But don't remind her of that, not unless you're ready for a stern lecture on how age has not dimmed her passion for entertaining and how she still has a thing or two to teach the younger generation. "I learned from my mama, who learned from her mother," she informs, "and I suppose you could say that I consider it a duty to continue gathering folks together in Old Southern style and trying to make them happy."

And I think it's safe to say that entertaining is a veritable way of life with Mother, whether it involves orchestrating a lavish Christmas Eve dinner, or serving a special meal for friends' children graduating from high school or college just the way she did when my sister and I were students, or sponsoring a home-style bereavement buffet to celebrate the life of a deceased family member or friend. No matter the occasion, Mother handles it like the expert she is, making all the planning and organization and cooking appear to be easy as pie and carrying out all aspects with the good taste expected of any Southern hostess. "What some people might not realize," she says enthusiastically, "is that I honestly and truly love this sort of activity. I mean, it's plain down fun for me, as it should be for everybody else."

If anything characterizes my mother's style of entertaining, no doubt the utter absence of pretension would be the key element. Don't get me wrong: she's as capable of displaying stunning decorations, and using the finest silver and china, and serving the most elegant Southern dishes as any serious hostess. But to suggest that Mother strives "to put on the dog" at most of her affairs is as absurd as proposing that she add sugar to her buttermilk biscuits. Those who come to Mother's house always know what to expect in the way of overall decorum and style of food. There may be a different handmade runner on the dining table, special flower arrangements and name cards to fit the occasion, or any number of new dishes on the buffet, but never is there any visible or culinary nonsense that might make guests feel anything but comfortable, relaxed, and "at home."

I've witnessed for decades the ways Mother entertains, ways that are outlined in detail throughout this book and that often differ from my own perceptions and methods. Oh yes, we do argue and cajole when I get into the act, just as things can get pretty hairy when we cook together. I express my own ideas about how certain Southern dishes should be prepared, and Mother typically admonishes that I don't have a grain of common sense, and that I fiddle around too much with food, and that I've just lived Up North too long. Of course, ribbing is part of the extremely close bond that has been established between us over the years, but, well, it does hurt and humiliate when, over and over, I realize and am forced to admit that, damnit, she's always right.

Perhaps one of the most enlightening and valuable aspects of this book are dozens of Mother's tips on entertaining and cooking scattered throughout the text, pithy statements of wise advice that reflect a lifetime of rich experience and should facilitate the efforts of hosts and hostesses in both the dining room and kitchen. As for the actual recipes, some are Mother's renditions of sacred Southern classics, others are dishes procured by exchange from close friends and family members, while still others are her own unique creations. All (even those with a bit of our Greek and Swedish heritage) have the basic proud look, aroma, and flavor of the South, and all serve as just testimony to a gracious lady who provides joy to so many and remains for me the most wonderful mother on earth.

My Mother's Southern Entertaining

Fall

Fall arrives late in the South, which means that Mother can usually entertain inside or outside throughout September and often well into October. It also means that she can still depend on lots of fresh summer produce (late peaches, tomatoes, berries, and the like) to stretch the warmer months, an important consideration given her obsession with seasonal ingredients. Come the first frost, however, and her thoughts shift to pecans arriving in the mail from Georgia, finding the first fresh cranberries and field pumpkins, driving to the mountains to choose a couple of well-aged country hams, making fruitcakes and gifts for the upcoming major holidays, and, to be sure, entertaining in ways that best celebrate the nippy fall days.

Mother's fall entertaining revolves partly around traditional holidays and seasonal observances, but equally important to her are the many social get-togethers intended to benefit a local charity, fulfill one project or another, and begin the preparation of various special Christmas foods. It's almost a nonstop routine: a big family dinner, a working luncheon for "the girls," a fruitcake party, a housewarming for new neighbors, a "do" primarily for the kids—there always seems to be a reason to invite people over, and at the center of all the activity are Mother's distinctive Southern dishes that welcome the arrival of autumn.

An Old-Fashioned Farm Supper

WHEN MOTHER WAS FIRST MARRIED DURING THE
Depression, one of the highlights of her and Daddy's weekends was driving out
on Saturday nights to a close relative's working farm for an elaborate Southern
supper prepared by her brother-in-law's mother and served at a large table on the
porch. "Mrs. Theiling would invite every soul in the family," Mother remembers,
"and you never saw such a spread of good Southern food: big hams and roasts,
three or four types of vegetables, baskets of fresh cornbread and biscuits, all sorts
of relishes and pickles, at least two rich desserts, pitchers of iced tea—and those
were hard times!"

Mother never forgot those copious farm suppers, and they were the main
inspiration behind the ones she still loves to prepare for relatives and neighbors
throughout the early fall months when the weather is rarely too hot or cold to
eat outside. This is the time she takes down her rustic Jugtown pottery serving
platters and bowls collected from the sandhills of North Carolina, decorates
the table with clusters of nandina berries and dried corn and okra stalks in big
ceramic jugs, and uses everyday knives and forks, oversize iced-tea glasses,
and kitchen salt and pepper shakers. The food is served and eaten boarding
house style—genuine, no-nonsense fare that illustrates to non-Southerners
what Rebs love to eat when they're really hungry and craving old-fashioned
fellowship and fun.

Martha Pearl Advises

At sit-down meals, I like to place candles of different heights on the table and surround the bases with simple garden flowers.

Menu

Twice-Stuffed Baked Potatoes

Company Meat Loaf

White Turnip and Onion Soufflé

Apple and Kumquat Chutney

Cracklin Biscuits

Nutty Collard Greens

Peach Brown Betty

Iced Tea

Twice-Stuffed Baked Potatoes

Don't ask me why Mother has always called these "twice-stuffed" and not "twice-baked"
potatoes. Even she can't explain it: "That's just what I and lots of other Southerners
call them," she waves disinterestedly. Her use of both Parmesan and cheddar cheeses,
however, is unusual and utterly delectable, and the first items to be grabbed and eaten
at one of her farm suppers are the crunchy potato skins.

8 medium-size Idaho potatoes, scrubbed well and dried

3 large eggs, beaten

¼ cup milk

¼ cup freshly grated Parmesan cheese

3 tablespoons butter, softened

2 tablespoons finely chopped onion

2 teaspoons minced garlic

Salt and black pepper to taste

⅓ cup finely grated sharp cheddar cheese

Preheat the oven to 450°F.

Bake the potatoes (*not* wrapped in aluminum foil) till fork-tender, about 45 minutes, and transfer to a working surface. Reduce the oven temperature to 350°F.

Slice off the top quarter of each potato, scoop the pulp from the tops into a large mixing bowl, and set the skins aside. Quickly but carefully scoop most of the pulp from the potatoes into the bowl and position the shells on a heavy baking sheet.

Add the eggs, milk, Parmesan, butter, onion, garlic, and salt and pepper to the pulp and beat with an electric mixer till the cheese and butter have melted and the mixture is smooth. Spoon equal amounts of the mixture back into the potato shells, sprinkle the top of each with the cheddar, place the reserved skins on the baking sheet, and bake till the potatoes are golden on top and the skins crunchy, 20 to 30 minutes.

8 SERVINGS

Company Meat Loaf

Understand one thing: so finicky is my mother about meat loaf and what all might be in it that she refuses to eat any that either she or her cronies don't prepare—and certainly none in a restaurant or cafeteria. Her regular meat loaf is a pretty simple affair, but when she goes all out for a special dinner such as this, using three types of ground meat (ground twice for more refined texture), mushrooms, and any variety of herbs— plus a sauce—the results are nothing less than sensational and give a whole new meaning to the idea of meat loaf. Mother never bakes meat loaf in a loaf pan, adamant in her conviction that only a free-form loaf can shed its grease and cook and brown evenly.

FOR THE MEAT LOAF

3 tablespoons butter

1 large onion, minced

2 tablespoons seeded and minced green bell pepper

2 garlic cloves, minced

¼ cup finely chopped mushrooms

2 pounds lean beef (rump or round), ground twice

1 pound veal shoulder, ground twice

1 pound fatty pork (shoulder or fresh ham), ground twice

3 sprigs fresh parsley, finely chopped

¼ teaspoon dried thyme

¼ teaspoon dried summer savory

Salt and black pepper to taste

¼ cup catsup

2 large eggs, beaten

3 tablespoons heavy cream

1 cup dry bread crumbs

4 strips bacon

3 tablespoons catsup

2 tablespoons Dijon mustard

3 tablespoons beef stock or bouillon

1 small garlic clove, minced

Tabasco sauce to taste

In a medium-size skillet, heat the butter over moderate heat, then add the onion, bell pepper, garlic, and mushrooms and cook for 3 minutes, stirring.

Preheat the oven to 350°F.

In a large mixing bowl, combine the three meats, the mushroom mixture, parsley, thyme, summer savory, and salt and pepper and mix till well blended. Add the catsup, eggs, heavy cream, and bread crumbs and continue mixing till the mixture is smooth and well blended. Form the mixture into a firm loaf with your hands, place it in the middle of a shallow baking dish, arrange the bacon strips over the top, and bake for 45 minutes.

Meanwhile, in a small mixing bowl, combine all the ingredients for the basting sauce and mix till well blended.

Holding the meat loaf in place with a heavy spatula, pour most of the fat from the baking dish and remove and discard the bacon from the loaf. Baste the loaf with the sauce, return it to the oven, and bake for about 15 minutes longer, basting once more. Let the loaf stand for 10 minutes before cutting into slices and serving with a little of the sauce.

8   SERVINGS

Martha Pearl Advises

Especially when using several kinds of meat for meat loaf, I have my butcher grind it twice for ideal mixing and texture. And I always mix my meat loaf with my hands to get just the consistency I want.

White Turnip and Onion Soufflé

Correct or not, a Southern "soufflé" is simply any baked vegetable dish that contains eggs, and never has Mother's imagination yielded more sumptuous results than when she came up with this homage to the common turnip—"a vegetable that I love and that is disgracefully misunderstood and neglected these days," she huffs. To prevent the turnips from darkening, never use metal cooking vessels for this dish, and don't over-bake it.

2½ pounds (about 8 medium-size) white turnips, peeled and diced
2 large onions, diced
3 tablespoons bacon drippings
¼ cup (½ stick) butter, softened and cut into pieces
2 teaspoons salt
2 teaspoons black pepper
1½ teaspoons sugar
½ teaspoon dry mustard
3 large eggs
1 cup fresh bread crumbs
1 teaspoon fresh lemon juice

Preheat the oven to 375°F. Butter a medium-size glass or ceramic casserole and set aside.

In a large stainless steel or enameled pot, combine the turnips, onions, and bacon drippings and add enough water to cover. Bring to a boil, reduce the heat to moderate, cover, and boil till the turnips are soft, about 25 minutes. Drain the turnips and onions in a colander, then transfer to a large mixing bowl. Add the butter, salt, pepper, sugar, and mustard and beat with an electric mixer till smooth. Add the eggs one at a time, beating till well blended. Add the bread crumbs and lemon juice, stir till well blended, pour into the prepared casserole, and bake till a knife inserted into the center comes out clean but the soufflé is still moist, about 50 minutes.

8 SERVINGS

Apple and Kumquat Chutney

Mother loves to make various chutneys to serve on special, rather prodigious occasions, and none is more appropriate and unusual than this seasonal one made with tiny, tart kumquats, eaten skin and all. When shopping for kumquats, look for heavy, unshriveled fruit and, since this chutney is good year-round with so many meat dishes, you might double or even triple the recipe and preserve lots of jars the way Mother usually does.

1½ pounds kumquats
1½ pounds (5 to 6) Granny Smith apples, peeled, cored, and coarsely diced
1 large lemon, cut in half, seeded, and coarsely diced
4 medium-size onions, coarsely chopped
2 cups light seedless raisins
2 cups firmly packed dark brown sugar
1 cup cider vinegar
1 cup dry white wine
1 tablespoon mustard seeds, finely crushed
1 teaspoon pickling spice
½ teaspoon ground ginger

Remove the stems and leaves from the kumquats, wash and rinse the fruit well, cut into quarters, scrape out and discard the seeds, and place in a large, heavy stainless-steel or enameled pot. Add the remaining ingredients and stir till well blended. Slowly bring the mixture to a simmer and cook at a slow simmer till nicely thickened, about 2 hours, stirring from time to time to prevent sticking.

Spoon the chutney into clean jars, let cool, and refrigerate till ready to use, or spoon it into hot sterilized jars and seal. (Unsealed chutney keeps, covered, up to 2 months in the refrigerator.)

ABOUT 3 PINTS

Cracklin Biscuits

½ cup finely diced salt pork
2½ cups all-purpose flour
1 teaspoon salt
1¼ tablespoons baking powder
¼ cup plus 1 teaspoon Crisco vegetable shortening
1 cup milk

Preheat the oven to 450°F.

In a heavy skillet, fry the salt pork over moderate heat till golden brown and crisp, about 8 minutes, then remove with a slotted spoon and drain on paper towels.

Into a large mixing bowl, sift together the flour, salt, and baking powder. Add the shortening and work it into the flour mixture with your fingertips till the particles of shortening are about the size of oatmeal flakes. Add the pork cracklins and continue to mix with your fingers. Add the milk and stir quickly with a fork just long enough to dampen the flour.

Transfer the dough to a lightly floured work surface, knead for no more than 10 seconds, and pat out to ½ inch thick. Cut the dough into rounds with a 2½-inch biscuit cutter or small juice glass, gathering up the scraps, repatting them together, and cutting into rounds. Place the rounds on one or two ungreased baking sheets and bake till golden on top, about 12 minutes.

20 TO 24 BISCUITS

Martha Pearl Advises

Metal biscuit cutters come in various sizes, but the one I use the most measures 2½ inches in diameter. In a bind, a small juice glass could be substituted to cut out biscuits, but since biscuits must be cut evenly without twisting the cutter, nothing equals the metal ones—and they're not expensive.

Nutty Collard Greens

3½ pounds collard greens
1 chunk streak-o'-lean (lean salt pork)
1 tablespoon salt
1½ teaspoons sugar
¼ cup (½ stick) butter
1 cup chopped pecans
1 cup finely chopped onions
½ cup cider vinegar

Remove and discard all stems from the greens, rinse them thoroughly under running water, place in a large pot, and add enough water to half-cover. Add the cooking meat, salt, and sugar and bring to a boil. Reduce the heat to low, cover, and simmer the greens for 1½ hours.

In a small skillet, heat the butter over moderately low heat, add the pecans, and stir till nicely glazed and slightly browned, about 10 minutes.

Drain the greens well in a colander, remove and discard the cooking meat, and place the greens in a large serving bowl. Add the pecans, onions, and vinegar, toss quickly, and serve immediately.

8 SERVINGS

Peach Brown Betty

Southerners prepare brown Bettys, cobblers, crisps, and crumbles with every fruit imaginable, but never does the classic concept reach such glorious heights as in Mother's luscious peach brown Betty made with the season's last, almost overly ripe Elbertas. For a really crispy surface, be sure to use stale bread crumbs, and make note that this dessert is just as appealing cold as hot.

continued

1½ cups stale bread crumbs

⅓ cup butter, melted

1 cup firmly packed light brown sugar

1 teaspoon ground cinnamon

½ teaspoon ground nutmeg

½ teaspoon ground allspice

Pinch of ground cloves

1 teaspoon grated lemon rind

3 pounds (about 9) ripe peaches, peeled, pitted, and sliced ½ inch thick

¼ cup apple cider

Vanilla ice cream

Preheat the oven to 375°F. Butter a large baking dish and set aside.

In a small mixing bowl, combine the bread crumbs and butter, toss well, and set aside. In another small mixing bowl, combine the brown sugar, cinnamon, nutmeg, allspice, cloves, and lemon rind and set aside.

Scatter a few tablespoons of the buttered bread crumbs over the bottom of the prepared dish, arrange half the peaches on top, sprinkle with one-half the spice mixture, and scatter about one-third of the remaining buttered crumbs over the top. Repeat the layers, ending with the crumbs. Pour the cider over the top and bake till the peaches are soft and the top nicely browned, about 30 minutes. Transfer the brown Betty to a wire rack to cool briefly and serve in bowls topped with scoops of ice cream.

8 SERVINGS

Martha Pearl Advises

In most recipes for peaches and mangoes, the two fruits can be used interchangeably with great success.

Gumbo Night

MOTHER ORIGINALLY GOT THE IDEA FOR THIS annual event years ago when old friends outside New Orleans invited Daddy and her one fall evening for seafood gumbo (simmered outdoors in a big black pot), garlic French bread, avocado salad, and bread pudding in the backyard of their gracious antebellum house. Since the weather in the South is still relatively warm even into October, she really prefers to make this a very rustic, casual outside dinner with small lanterns suspended from the oak branches and a guest list that can stretch to a dozen or more friends and neighbors. I know she'd love to cook this gumbo over an open fire, but given that impracticability, she fixes it in the kitchen, positions the iron pot (ideally nestled on a bed of Spanish moss or fall leaves) in the middle of a large picnic table set with a red-checkered cloth, huge dishcloth napkins, wide ceramic bowls, and the other dishes on the menu, and just lets guests dig in. Of course everybody drinks beer, kept cold in an ice-packed tub on the grass, and, depending on how many Sazeracs have been consumed beforehand, things can get pretty . . . festive. And if you want to see Mother really chafe, just let the temperature turn too chilly or there be a forecast of rain. (Personally, I throw similar gumbo, as well as Brunswick stew, parties on the open deck of my house, and I think my friends have just as much fun.)

Menu

Miss Ella's Sazeracs

Tangy Pimento Cheese Dip

Creole Shrimp and Oyster Gumbo

Savannah Red Rice

Big Mary's Pineapple Slaw

Clabber Biscuits

Jefferson Davis Pie

Beer

Miss Ella's Sazeracs

Miss Ella is none other than Ella Brennan, the legendary force behind Commander's Palace in New Orleans, an old friend and, in Mother's opinion, the world's greatest authority on the Sazerac. I hate to guess how many of these potent libations we've sipped with Ella and her family in the restaurant's enchanting garden before swaying inside for bowls of seafood gumbo and other delectable Creole dishes. Do make the effort to find a bottle of distinctive Peychaud's bitters, available in most specialty food shops.

FOR BAR SYRUP

1 cup water

2 cups sugar

FOR EACH COCKTAIL

1 ounce Pernod

1½ ounces bourbon

⅓ ounce bar syrup

4 dashes Peychaud's bitters

2 dashes Angostura bitters

Crushed ice

1 lemon twist

To make the bar syrup, combine the water and sugar in a small saucepan and stir well. Bring to a boil, reduce the heat to low, and simmer for 5 minutes. Let the mixture cool and pour into a jar. Store the syrup in the refrigerator till ready to use. (It keeps indefinitely.)

To make a cocktail, pour the Pernod into a chilled old-fashioned glass, roll the glass around till the sides are well coated with it, and pour off any excess Pernod. In a cocktail shaker, combine the bourbon, bar syrup, both bitters, and ice, stir quickly till very cold, and strain into the prepared glass. Garnish the syrup with the lemon twist and serve.

Tangy Pimento Cheese Dip

This is one of Mother's most amazing dips—totally different from her regular pimento cheese spread. For years, she made the dip with ordinary, aged, extra-sharp cheddar, then she discovered white Vermont cheddar ("a really exceptional Yankee product") and now swears by it. "And don't cheat by using plain old tomato juice instead of V-8 or other such vegetable juice," she emphasizes.

6 ounces white Vermont cheddar cheese

One 4-ounce jar pimentos (see Martha Pearl Advises, page 205), drained and finely chopped

One 2-ounce can finely chopped chili peppers, drained

1 tablespoon finely chopped fresh chives

One 3-ounce package cream cheese, softened

½ cup sour cream

½ cup V-8 juice

Grate the cheese finely into a medium-size mixing bowl, add the pimentos, chili peppers, and chives, and stir well. Add the cream cheese, sour cream, and V-8 juice and beat with an electric mixer till light and smooth. Scrape the mixture into a crock or attractive bowl, cover with plastic wrap, and chill at least 2 hours before serving with crackers or raw vegetables.

2 CUPS

Creole Shrimp and Oyster Gumbo

Although this is not a classic gumbo by virtue of its having no roux or filé powder, to Mother's way of thinking it (like her chicken gumbo) qualifies simply on the basis of okra used as a thickening agent. In any case, this stew plays the leading role at her annual gumbo dinner, and guests always rave about it. Remember not to overcook the shrimp and oysters.

⅓ cup butter

2 tablespoons vegetable oil

1 large onion, finely chopped

1 celery rib, finely chopped

½ green bell pepper, seeded and finely chopped

½ pound fresh okra (or 10-ounce package frozen okra, defrosted), stem ends trimmed and
  chopped

1 garlic clove, minced

2 tablespoons all-purpose flour

4 cups chicken stock or broth

4 ripe tomatoes, chopped, or 2 cups chopped canned tomatoes, drained

½ teaspoon dried thyme

1 bay leaf

2 teaspoons salt

2 teaspoons black pepper

1½ pounds medium-size fresh shrimp, shelled and deveined

1½ dozen oysters, shucked and liquor reserved

2 teaspoons Worcestershire sauce

Tabasco sauce to taste

2 cups or more cooked rice

In a large, heavy casserole, heat the butter and vegetable oil together over moderate heat, then add the onion, celery, bell pepper, okra, and garlic and cook for 5 minutes, stirring. Sprinkle the flour on top and cook for 3 minutes, stirring. Slowly add the broth, stirring, then the tomatoes, thyme, bay leaf, salt, and pepper. Bring to a boil, reduce the heat to low, cover, and simmer for 45 minutes.

continued

Add the shrimp, return the heat to a simmer, and cook for 5 minutes. Add the oysters plus the reserved liquor, return to a simmer, and cook till the oysters curl, about 3 minutes. Add the Worcestershire and Tabasco, stir well, check and correct the seasonings, and serve the gumbo over small amounts of rice in soup bowls.

AT LEAST 8 SERVINGS

Savannah Red Rice

Red rice harks back to Low Country plantation days, and Mother has loved it ever since her family first visited friends in Savannah when she was a young girl and she watched the black cook prepare it in a special steamer. The sugar gives the rice part of its distinctive taste, as does the bacon grease. But two types of rice at one meal? You bet—at least in the South.

½ pound lean sliced bacon

2 medium-size onions, finely chopped

One 6-ounce can tomato paste

2 cups water

3 teaspoons salt

2 teaspoons sugar

Black pepper and Tabasco sauce to taste

2 cups long-grain rice

In a large skillet, fry the bacon strips till crisp and drain on paper towels. Pour off half the grease and reserve.

Add the onions to the remaining bacon grease in the skillet and cook over moderate heat for 3 minutes, stirring. Add the tomato paste, water, salt, sugar, pepper, and Tabasco, stir well, and cook for 10 minutes, stirring once or twice. Transfer the contents of the skillet to a large saucepan, add the reserved bacon grease, and bring to a boil. Add the rice, reduce the heat to low, stir once, cover, and cook till the rice has absorbed most of the liquid, about 25 minutes.

Remove the pan from the heat, crumble the bacon and add to the rice, stir well, and let the rice stand, uncovered, for 5 minutes to dry slightly.

6 TO 8 SERVINGS

Martha Pearl Advises

Baked, steamed, fried, and used in soups, stews, breads, stuffed peppers, meat loaves, and puddings, long-grain rice is a major staple in my kitchen. I often automatically put a big bowl of buttered rice on any buffet table, not only because all Southerners love it but because it's something I'm always sure that children will eat (plain or topped with other foods they might otherwise reject).

To reheat cooked long-grain rice (unlike wild rice), place it in a colander over (not in) simmering water for about 10 minutes and cover with a paper towel. Don't ask me why a paper towel; I just know it works best.

Big Mary's Pineapple Slaw

Mother visits me frequently in East Hampton and, as is her habit, she once got on intimate terms with the very portly gal who used to work behind the counter of my favorite deli and actually made all the cole slaw for sale. "Honey," Mother said to Big Mary one day, "that's the best cole slaw I ever put in my mouth, and if you don't tell me your secret, I'm gonna go crazy." Willingly, Mary revealed that finely chopped pineapple was what made the difference, so Mother began adding just a suggestion, then more, and eventually a half cup. Today, the slaw's a staple at her gumbo party—and I must say it is out of this world.

5 cups cored and finely shredded green cabbage (1 small head)

1 small carrot, scraped and finely shredded

½ cup finely chopped pineapple

2 teaspoons celery seeds

Salt and black pepper to taste

3 tablespoons mayonnaise (Mother prefers Hellmann's)

2 tablespoons cider vinegar

3 teaspoons sugar

In a large mixing bowl, combine the cabbage, carrot, pineapple, and celery seeds, season with salt and pepper, and toss till well blended. In a small mixing bowl, combine the mayonnaise, vinegar, and sugar, stir till well blended, and pour over the cabbage mixture. Mix till well blended, cover with plastic wrap, and refrigerate till ready to use.

6 TO 8 SERVINGS

Clabber Biscuits

"Whew!" I've heard Mother exclaim a thousand times when testing milk kept too long in the refrigerator. "That's almost clabber!" The irony being, of course, that nobody in this world loves buttermilk more than my mother, the same residual liquid derived from semisolid sour milk that's been called clabber in the South since the seventeenth century and used to make all sorts of breads and desserts. Real clabber is hard to come by these days, but these biscuits made with sour cream at least approximate the ones made regularly by my maternal grandmother and great-grandmother.

2$\frac{1}{2}$ cups all-purpose flour
4 teaspoons baking powder
1 teaspoon baking soda
1 teaspoon salt
$\frac{1}{3}$ cup butter, chilled and cut into pieces
1$\frac{1}{2}$ cups sour cream

Preheat the oven to 425°F.

Into a large mixing bowl, sift together the flour, baking powder, baking soda, and salt. Add the butter and cut it in with a pastry cutter or two knives till the mixture is mealy. Add the sour cream and stir with a wooden spoon till the dough is soft, adding a little more sour cream if necessary. Transfer the dough to a floured work surface and knead very gently with five or six strokes. Press the dough out to a $\frac{1}{4}$-inch thickness, cut straight down into even rounds with a biscuit cutter, and place the rounds $\frac{1}{2}$ inch apart on one or two ungreased baking sheets. Gather up the scraps of dough and repeat the procedure. Bake the biscuits till lightly browned on top, about 15 minutes.

ABOUT 2 DOZEN BISCUITS

Jefferson Davis Pie

Legends abound about when, where, and how this great Southern pie named after the president of the Confederacy originated (probably during the actual War Between the States) and evolved, but whatever the truth, it's for sure that the pie remains an expected highlight at Mother's gumbo bash. In some respects, it appears to be a spicy, overdressed first cousin of another renowned Southern specialty, chess (or 'jes) pie, and Mother says she's even eaten it in Mississippi with chopped dates and crystallized fruits—"which I think is really stretching things a bit." In any case, Jeff Davis pie has as many versions throughout the South as does brown Betty.

FOR ONE UNBAKED 9- OR 10-INCH BASIC
PIE OR TART SHELL

1½ cups all-purpose flour

½ teaspoon salt

½ cup Crisco vegetable shortening

4 to 5 tablespoons ice water, as needed

FOR THE FILLING

½ cup (1 stick) butter, softened

¾ cup granulated sugar

½ cup firmly packed dark brown sugar

1 tablespoon all-purpose flour

2 large eggs, beaten

1 cup half-and-half

1 tablespoon bourbon

½ teaspoon ground cinnamon

½ teaspoon ground allspice

½ teaspoon pure vanilla extract

⅔ cup seedless golden raisins

To make the pastry, combine the flour and salt in a large mixing bowl, then cut in the shortening with a pastry cutter or two knives till the mixture resembles coarse meal. Stirring with a wooden spoon, gradually add enough of the water so that a ball of dough is formed. Wrap the dough in plastic wrap and chill for 1 hour. Grease a 9- or 10-inch pie plate or tart pan and set aside.

Place the chilled dough on a lightly floured work surface and roll it out from the center (not to and fro) with a lightly floured rolling pin to a ⅛-inch thickness. Carefully fold the pastry in half, lay the fold across the center of the prepared plate or pan, unfold it, and press it loosely into the bottom and sides of the plate or pan. Prick the bottom and sides with a fork, trim and crimp the edges, place on a heavy baking sheet, and set aside.

Preheat the oven to 425°F.

To make the filling, cream together the butter and two sugars with an electric mixer at medium speed in a large mixing bowl till fluffy, then add the flour and eggs and beat till well blended. Add the half-and-half, bourbon, cinnamon, allspice, and vanilla and continue to beat till well blended and smooth. Stir in the raisins, scrape the mixture into the prepared pie shell, and bake for 10 minutes. Reduce the oven temperature to 350°F and continue baking till a knife inserted into the center comes out clean, about 30 minutes. Transfer the pie to a wire rack and let cool to room temperature. Serve in wedges at room temperature or chilled.

ONE 9- OR 10-INCH PIE;
AT LEAST 8 SERVINGS

Martha Pearl Advises

To bake a pie shell, preheat the oven to 425°F, place the dough on a lightly floured surface, and roll it out from the center (not to and fro) with a lightly floured rolling pin to a ⅛-inch thickness. Carefully fold the pastry in half, lay the fold across the center of a greased pie plate or pan, unfold it, and press it loosely into the bottom and sides of the plate or pan. Prick the bottom and sides with a fork, trim and crimp the edges, place on a heavy baking sheet, and bake till the shell browns evenly, 12 to 15 minutes.

An After-Shopping Brunch

ONE OF MOTHER'S MAJOR SOCIAL AND CIVIC activities has always been work connected with her Charity League, a group of local ladies dedicated to helping and supporting about thirty underprivileged preschool children who attend the Sunshine Day Nursery. All during the fall months, Mother and "the girls" periodically shop for toys and necessities, after which they gather (usually at Mother's place) to discuss the nursery and chat casually, come up with suggestions for improvements, and, indeed, share a nice semiformal, two-hour brunch served course-by-course on white lace place mats with fine silver, delicate linen napkins, and crystal white-wine glasses. I've witnessed the scenario once and can only liken it to scenes from John Berendt's *Midnight in the Garden of Good and Evil* where six very proper Southern ladies of Savannah gather weekly to drink, eat, and gossip. "The key to entertaining like this," Mother says, "is to have a menu where every single dish can be prepared in advance and ready to serve." If she doesn't have help, she prepares and serves the individual plates herself, "and let me tell you, those gals eat every morsel put in front of them."

Menu

Sassy Shrimp Rémoulade

The Original Vidalia Onion Pie

Molded Avocado Salad with Herb Mayonnaise

Cheddar Pimento Cornbread

Coconut Buttermilk Pie

California Chardonnay

Sassy Shrimp Rémoulade

Mother's always said that the shrimp rémoulade served at Galatoire's in New Orleans is in a class by itself, reason enough for her to ask for the recipe years ago. "Of course, I know they didn't give me the exact receipt," she still complains, "but sometimes I think my sassy version tastes even better than the original." One of the keys to any great shrimp rémoulade is not to overcook the shrimp, so watch them carefully (if the shells start to curl too much, dash the shrimp under cold water).

1½ **pounds medium-size fresh shrimp**
4 green onions (green tops included), chopped
1 large celery rib, chopped
8 sprigs fresh parsley, chopped
2 garlic cloves, minced
6 tablespoons Creole mustard
1½ **tablespoons prepared horseradish**
½ **cup white vinegar**
Salt and black pepper to taste
Tabasco Sauce to taste
1 cup extra-virgin olive oil
Shredded lettuce

Place the shrimp in a large pot with enough water to cover and bring to a boil. Remove from the heat, cover, and let stand till the shrimp are just firm, about 1 minute. Drain in a colander and, when cool enough to handle, shell and devein them and set aside.

In a blender or food processor, combine the green onions, celery, parsley, and garlic, blend to a coarse puree, and scrape into a large mixing bowl. Add the mustard, horseradish, and vinegar, season with salt and pepper and Tabasco, and stir till well blended. In a slow stream, add the olive oil, whisking till emulsified. Add the shrimp, toss to coat thoroughly with the dressing, cover the bowl with plastic wrap, and chill at least 2 hours before serving.

Line salad plates with the lettuce and mound equal amounts of shrimp in the center of each.

6 SERVINGS

The Original Vidalia Onion Pie

Long before Vidalia onions became so fashionable all over the country, Mother and other Southerners were using the sweet onions to make all sorts of delectable dishes, including this proud Georgia specialty. Today we've noticed a tendency to overload the pie filling with so much cheese that the subtle flavor of the onions is virtually lost. The original pie as Mother remembers it in and around Macon had only a little Parmesan sprinkled over the top—not mixed into the filling—and this does make a big difference in flavor and texture. Serve the pie hot or at room temperature.

½ cup (1 stick) butter
2 pounds (about 6) Vidalia onions, thinly sliced
1 unbaked 9-inch Basic Pie Shell (page 23)
3 large eggs
1 cup half-and-half
½ teaspoon salt
½ teaspoon black pepper
Cayenne pepper to taste
½ cup finely grated Parmesan cheese

Preheat the oven to 400°F.

In a large, deep, heavy skillet, heat the butter over moderately low heat, then add the onions and cook, stirring, till just soft and slightly golden, about 10 minutes. Scrape the onions into the pie shell evenly and set aside.

In a medium-size mixing bowl, combine the eggs, half-and-half, salt, pepper, and cayenne and whisk till well blended. Pour the mixture over the onions, sprinkle the cheese over the top, and bake 15 minutes. Reduce the oven temperature to 350°F and continue to bake till the pie is puffy in the center and the top golden brown, about 25 minutes.

ONE 9-INCH PIE; 6 SERVINGS

Martha Pearl Advises

When cooking most hot dishes with Parmesan cheese, I find some of the commercial ready-grated just as acceptable as the imported product, but for delicate hot pastries, cold salads, and chilled vegetable preparations, I use only genuine Parmigiano-Reggiano.

Most people don't realize that Vidalia onions deteriorate relatively quickly—especially if they touch one another. I store mine in a clean nylon hose, knotted between each onion, in a cool area.

Molded Avocado Salad with Herb Mayonnaise

FOR THE SALAD

One 3-ounce package lemon-flavored Jell-O

1¾ cups boiling water

¼ teaspoon salt

2 tablespoons fresh lemon juice

1 tablespoon prepared horseradish

1 teaspoon grated onion

2 ripe avocados, peeled, pitted, and diced

½ cup finely diced celery

Bibb lettuce leaves

Pimento strips for garnish

FOR THE HERB MAYONNAISE

1 cup mayonnaise (Mother prefers Hellmann's)

1 garlic clove, minced

¼ cup finely chopped fresh parsley leaves

1 tablespoon minced fresh chives

1 tablespoon drained and chopped capers

1 teaspoon finely chopped fresh dill

½ teaspoon fresh lemon juice

¼ teaspoon salt

Dash of Worcestershire sauce

¼ cup sour cream

Oil a 4-cup salad mold and set aside.

To make the salad, dissolve the Jell-O in the boiling water in a medium-size mixing bowl. Stir in the salt, lemon juice, horseradish, and onion and chill till partially set, about 30 minutes. Beat the mixture with an electric mixer till smooth, fold in the avocados and celery, scrape the mixture into the prepared mold, and refrigerate till firm, about 2 hours.

To make the mayonnaise, combine all the ingredients except the sour cream in a small mixing bowl and stir till well blended. Fold in the sour cream till the mixture is well blended and smooth.

Arrange the lettuce leaves around a large serving plate or on small salad plates and either unmold the salad on the large plate or divide it among the individual plates. Decorate the top or tops with crisscrossed or chopped pimentos and serve the salad with the mayonnaise.

6 SERVINGS

Cheddar Pimento Cornbread

I think Mother could eat cornbread at every meal every day, and she's forever coming up with different versions, this being her latest. "If cheese and pimento biscuits are so good," she reasons, "why not the same with cornbread?" Do note that this is a loaf bread (not a traditional pan bread) made with sifted cornmeal and intended to be carefully sliced and served at room temperature. Although canned pimentos are not the same as red bell peppers, the latter can be roasted, peeled, seeded, finely chopped, and used as a substitute in this bread.

¼ cup (½ stick) butter
8 green onions, finely chopped
2 cups yellow cornmeal
1 cup all-purpose flour
1 tablespoon baking powder
1 teaspoon salt
2 cups milk
2 large eggs
3 cups (about 12 ounces) finely grated sharp cheddar cheese
3 ounces pimentos (see Martha Pearl Advises, page 205), well drained and chopped

continued

Preheat the oven to 400°F. Grease and flour a medium-size loaf pan, tapping out the excess flour, and set aside.

In a small skillet, heat the butter over moderately low heat, then add the green onions and cook, stirring, till just soft and slightly golden, about 10 minutes. Set aside.

Into a large mixing bowl, sift together the cornmeal, flour, baking powder, and salt and stir till well blended. In a medium-size mixing bowl, whisk together the milk and eggs till frothy, add to the cornmeal mixture, and stir till finely blended. Stir in the cheese and pimentos till well blended, scrape the batter into the prepared pan, and bake till a knife inserted into the center comes out clean, 45 to 50 minutes. Turn the bread out on a wire rack to cool completely, then cut crosswise into thin slices.

1 LOAF; 6 SERVINGS

Martha Pearl Advises

Always store ground cornmeal in a tightly sealed plastic bag in the refrigerator to prevent its losing its flavor—and to avoid mealybugs.

Cornbread, cut in wedges and stored in sealed plastic bags, freezes beautifully up to about 2 weeks, and I always have some on hand to reheat in emergencies and serve with any hot food—including last-minute chili. Ditto for small corn sticks, which are great with any soup or stew and just wonderful toasted and buttered for breakfast.

Coconut Buttermilk Pie

In the South, buttermilk is used to make breads, pancakes, crusts, and Lord knows what else, but perhaps its greatest legacy are our sublime, mellow, rich buttermilk pies that can taste almost like cheesecake. Mother often incorporates cherries, grapes, berries, and even raisins in her pies for added dimension, but none is more memorable than this one with grated coconut (preferably fresh).

1½ cups sugar
3 tablespoons all-purpose flour
¼ teaspoon salt
3 large eggs, beaten
2 tablespoons butter, melted
1½ cups buttermilk
1 teaspoon pure vanilla extract
½ teaspoon pure lemon extract
½ teaspoon finely grated orange rind
1 cup unsweetened grated coconut (fresh or frozen)
1 unbaked 9-inch Basic Pie Shell (page 23)

Preheat the oven to 350°F.

In a large mixing bowl, combine the sugar, flour, and salt and mix till well blended. Add the eggs one at a time, beating well with an electric mixer after each addition, then beat in the melted butter, buttermilk, extracts, and orange rind till well blended and smooth. Stir in the coconut, scrape the batter into the pie shell, and bake till a knife inserted into the center comes out clean, about 35 minutes. Transfer the pie to a wire rack to cool and serve at room temperature or chilled.

ONE 9-INCH PIE; 6 SERVINGS

A Jack-O'-Lantern Celebration

EVEN AT HER RIPE AGE, MOTHER IS STILL AS MUCH
a child at Halloween as when she donned a spooky black cat outfit some eighty-
odd years ago in Macon, Georgia. Some today might play down Halloween as a
bother and inconvenience, but for my mother, fall just wouldn't be fall without
throwing her traditional jack-o'-lantern festivity with costumed children trick-
or-treating, small pumpkins with votive candles lighting the path, a canopy of
orange and black crepe at the doorway, and, to be sure, a giant pumpkin full of
smoky pumpkin soup ladled into small pumpkin "bowls." Typically, adult guests
take turns each year (and they must also wear a costume) escorting the children
around the neighborhood at dusk, and Mother always has prizes on hand (tiny
goblin, ghost, and witch toys or colorful baskets filled with candy corn) for the
most original costumes and the largest number of gathered "treats." The kids
play various games while the grown-ups wash down beer cheese with mulled
cider. Names are inscribed in gold on fall leaves as place cards, napkins are tied
with black and orange ribbons, and the sideboard buffet is filled with dishes to
be eaten at random after the ceremonial soup. One neighbor loves to terrify
the children by dressing up very convincingly as a ghost and rattling a bag of
"bones," but most fright is relieved when Mother passes out to the younguns
small gift packages of fresh gingerbread figures and her crazy chocolate

Halloween "spiders" to take home. Everybody has loads of fun, the adults relish Mother's classic Southern dishes, and for those children who still refuse to touch pumpkin, spoonbread, and the like, she also fries a few chicken drumettes and makes potato salad.

Menu

Kentucky Beer Cheese

Smoky Pumpkin Soup in a Pumpkin

Mulled Apple Cider

Country Ham Spoonbread

Gingered Grapefruit, Orange, and Cranberry Salad

Onion Corn Sticks

Old-Fashioned Goober Pie

Beer

Gifts for Adults: Brandied Pumpkin Loaves; Cranberry Relish

Gifts for Children: Halloween Spiders; Gingerbread Men

Kentucky Beer Cheese

Supposedly created around the turn of the century in a Louisville, Kentucky, saloon and served with crackers at bars to any customer ordering a 5-cent lager, beer cheese is one of the South's greatest appetizer spreads. Over the years, Mother has added and subtracted all sorts of ingredients (onion, hot peppers, celery, chives, different mustards, a little Parmesan), so feel free to experiment—sensibly. And to transform the spread into a simple dip, just add a little more beer. Either way, the concoction is delectable—and also ideal as a snack.

2 pounds extra-sharp aged cheddar cheese, at room temperature

2 garlic cloves, minced

2 tablespoons minced fresh chives

1 teaspoon dry mustard

2 tablespoons Worcestershire sauce

Tabasco Sauce to taste

$\frac{1}{2}$ teaspoon salt

$1\frac{1}{2}$ cups lager beer

Shred the cheese finely into a large mixing bowl. Add the garlic, chives, mustard, Worcestershire, Tabasco, and salt and beat with an electric mixer till well blended. Gradually add the beer, beating till the spread is smooth. (To transform the spread into a dip, beat in about $\frac{1}{4}$ cup more beer.) Scrape into a crock, cover tightly, and chill overnight.

Serve the spread with toast points (see Martha Pearl Advises, page 38), crackers, or rye bread rounds (or, as a dip, with raw vegetables).

ABOUT 5 CUPS

I'm never without plenty of toast points to serve with spreads, dips, oysters, creamed chicken, salads, and the like. To make them, trim the crusts from loaves of thin sandwich bread, cut each slice into 4 triangles, and brown on an ungreased baking sheet in a toaster oven or under the broiler for about 2 minutes. The toast can be kept up to a month in sealed plastic bags.

⟪⟨⟩ Smoky Pumpkin Soup in a Pumpkin

Don't even think about making this luscious soup with any rum except a superior dark one like Myers's. "If you don't have a bottle of good dark rum in the house," I've heard Mother advise curtly, "go out and buy one."

One 6- to 7-pound pumpkin
5 strips bacon
2 medium-size onions, chopped
2 garlic cloves, minced
1 teaspoon dried ground sage
Tabasco Sauce to taste
Salt and black pepper to taste
4 cups chicken stock or broth
3 cups half-and-half
2 to 3 tablespoons dark rum, to your taste

Cut a wide, deep circle around the stem of the pumpkin and remove the lid. Scrape the seeds and membranes from the pumpkin and its lid with a large, heavy spoon and discard, then very carefully scrape out most of the flesh remaining in the pumpkin shell and on the lid, reserving both the pumpkin and the lid. Coarsely chop enough of the flesh to measure 4 cups and reserve the remaining flesh for another use.

In a large skillet, fry the bacon till crisp, drain on paper towels, and set aside. Add the onions and garlic to the skillet and cook over moderate heat for 3 minutes, stirring. Add the chopped pumpkin and sage, season with Tabasco, salt, and pepper, and stir. Add the stock, stir, cover the skillet, and simmer over moderately low heat till the pumpkin is tender, about 30 minutes. Remove from the heat and let cool to room temperature.

Transfer the contents of the skillet to a blender or food processor (in batches), reduce to a puree, and transfer the puree to a large saucepan. Add the half-and-half and rum, stir well, and heat till very hot but not boiling.

When ready to serve, pour the soup into the prepared pumpkin shell, crumble the reserved bacon and sprinkle over the top, and place the lid back on the pumpkin. Serve directly from the shell.

8 SERVINGS

Mulled Apple Cider

1½ cups water
¼ cup firmly packed light brown sugar
8 allspice berries
8 cloves
Ten 3-inch-long cinnamon sticks
1½ quarts apple cider

In a large saucepan, combine the water, brown sugar, allspice, cloves, and 2 of the cinnamon sticks, bring to a boil, reduce the heat to low, and simmer for 10 minutes. Strain the mixture into another large saucepan, add the cider, and simmer for 5 minutes. Pour the mulled cider into a covered container and let sit overnight.

When ready to serve, pour the mulled cider into mugs and garnish each mug with a cinnamon stick.

8 DRINKS

Country Ham Spoonbread

Mother makes spoonbread with everything from cheese to bourbon, from bacon to nuts, but never is the dish more sumptuous than when she uses leftover pieces of one of our cured country hams from the North Carolina mountains. Most Southerners make spoonbread with yellow cornmeal; Mother believes firmly that white produces a much finer dish. Nor would she ever dream of adding sugar to spoonbread any more than to cornbread—as so many others do. Since genuine country ham is so salty (and we never soak our hams), no salt is needed.

3 cups milk

1½ cups white cornmeal

½ cup (1 stick) butter, softened and cut into pieces

2 teaspoons baking powder

5 large eggs, separated

1 cup diced cooked country ham

Preheat the oven to 350°F. Butter a medium-size casserole or baking dish and set aside.

In a large saucepan, bring the milk to a boil and gradually add the cornmeal, stirring rapidly with a spoon as you slowly pour it in. Reduce the heat to low and cook, stirring constantly, till the mixture is thick, about 10 minutes. Remove the pan from the heat, add the butter and baking powder, stir till the butter has melted, and set aside to cool.

In a small bowl, beat the egg yolks with a fork till light, then stir them into the cooled cornmeal mixture. Add the country ham and stir till well blended. In a large bowl, beat the egg whites with an electric mixer till stiff peaks form, then fold them into the mixture till all traces of white have disappeared. Scrape the mixture into the prepared casserole and bake till a knife inserted into the center comes out clean, about 40 minutes. Serve hot.

6 TO 8 SERVINGS

Gingered Grapefruit, Orange, and Cranberry Salad

One 12-ounce bag fresh cranberries, picked over for stems

1 cup sugar

1 cup water

2 grapefruits

2 oranges

½ cup orange-flavored liqueur (like Contreau or Grand Marnier)

1 sliver fresh ginger, peeled

In a large saucepan, combine the cranberries, sugar, and water, bring to a boil, reduce the heat to moderate, and cook till the cranberries pop, 3 to 5 minutes. Remove the pan from the heat, let the cranberries cool, then transfer them to a large serving bowl.

Cut the grapefruits in half, carefully remove the sections with a citrus or serrated paring knife, and add the sections to the cranberries. Peel the oranges, remove and discard as much white pith as possible, and add the sections to the cranberries and grapefruit. Pour the liqueur over the fruits, toss with two large spoons to mix thoroughly, cover the bowl with plastic wrap, and let stand for 1 hour in the refrigerator. When ready to serve, grate the ginger over the top.

6 TO 8 SERVINGS

Onion Corn Sticks

For years, Mother refused to add any major secondary ingredients to her corn sticks. Then, when she realized that the "perfect" hush puppies we discovered one summer in a fishing pier restaurant at Carolina Beach, North Carolina, contained a few finely minced onions, she decided to do the same with her corn sticks. To make truly memorable corn sticks, you must use cast-iron molds for even heat distribution, and remember to heat the molds till scorching hot before spooning in the batter.

2 cups yellow cornmeal
1 cup all-purpose flour
1 tablespoon baking powder
1 teaspoon baking soda
1 teaspoon salt
2 large eggs
1 cup buttermilk
¼ cup Crisco vegetable shortening, heated slightly
1 medium-size onion, minced

In a large mixing bowl, combine the cornmeal, flour, baking powder, baking soda, and salt and stir till well blended. Add the eggs one at a time, beating the mixture well after each addition. Add the buttermilk and stir till well blended, then add the shortening and onion and stir till well blended and smooth. Cover the bowl with plastic wrap and refrigerate for 1 hour.

Preheat the oven to 500°F.

Grease two or three cast-iron corn-stick molds and set in the oven till the molds are very hot. Spoon the batter into the molds and bake till the tops are golden and crisp, 10 to 12 minutes.

ABOUT SIXTEEN 5-INCH-LONG CORN STICKS

Old-Fashioned Goober Pie

For those who don't know, Southerners often call peanuts "goobers," and for Georgia Crackers who don't know, the greatest peanuts in the world are the large, oily, full-flavored goobers of lower Virginia and upper North Carolina on which are fed many of the hogs destined to become superior country hams. Once you've tasted these goobers, all others pale by comparison, reason enough for Mother and me to order 2-pound bags of raw, shelled, skinless beauties from the Original Nut House in Wakefield, Virginia (phone: 1-800-803-1309) every fall to be simply roasted with butter and salt or used to make breads, candies, soups, and delicious goober pie. The pie is not unlike pecan pie, the main difference being a more brittle crust—produced by the molasses. Don't you dare overcook this pie—it's done when the center is just soft.

4 large eggs
1 cup sugar
$\frac{1}{2}$ cup Karo light corn syrup
$\frac{1}{2}$ cup molasses
$\frac{1}{4}$ cup ($\frac{1}{2}$ stick) butter, melted
1 teaspoon all-purpose flour
$\frac{1}{4}$ teaspoon ground cinnamon
$\frac{1}{4}$ teaspoon salt
1 teaspoon pure vanilla extract
$2\frac{1}{2}$ cups roasted peanuts, roughly chopped
1 unbaked 9-inch Basic Pie Shell (page 23)
Whipped cream (optional)

Preheat the oven to 350°F.

In a large mixing bowl, beat the eggs with an electric mixer till frothy, then add the sugar, corn syrup, molasses, melted butter, flour, cinnamon, salt, and vanilla and beat till well blended and smooth. Add the peanuts and stir till the nuts are evenly distributed.

Scrape the mixture into the pie shell and bake till the filling is just soft in the center and the crust is golden brown, 50 to 60 minutes. Cool the pie completely on a wire rack and serve at room temperature with dollops of whipped cream, if desired.

ONE 9-INCH PIE; 6 TO 8 SERVINGS

Brandied Pumpkin Loaves

As gifts for guests, Mother wraps these aromatic loaves in colored plastic wrap
(available in four colors in supermarkets).

4 large eggs
2¾ cups sugar
1 cup vegetable oil
One 16-ounce can pumpkin puree
3½ cups all-purpose flour
1 teaspoon baking soda
1 teaspoon salt
1 teaspoon ground cinnamon
1 teaspoon ground nutmeg
1 teaspoon ground allspice
⅔ cup brandy
1 cup chopped pitted dates (see Martha Pearl Advises, page 45)
1 cup chopped nuts (pecans, walnuts, or hazelnuts)

Preheat the oven to 350°F. Grease and flour three medium-size loaf pans and set aside.

In a large mixing bowl, beat the eggs with an electric mixer till frothy, then gradually add the sugar, beating till thick. Gradually beat in the oil, then add the pumpkin and beat till well blended.

Into a medium-size mixing bowl, sift together the flour, baking soda, salt, and spices, then add the flour mixture alternately with the brandy to the egg mixture, beating till well blended. Fold the dates and nuts into the pumpkin mixture, scrape equal amounts of the batter into the prepared pans, and bake till a knife inserted into the centers comes out clean, about 1 hour. Turn the loaves out onto a wire rack to cool completely before slicing.

3 LOAVES FOR GIFTS

To cut raisins, dates, and other sticky foods, use kitchen shears or scissors dipped in water.

Cranberry Relish

Since fresh cranberries (even frozen) are difficult to find out of season, Mother makes plenty of this relish and stores it for future use in any jars not given as gifts during the holidays. As gifts for guests, she ties small paper lace doilies over the jar lids with colorful ribbons.

2 pounds fresh cranberries, rinsed and picked over for stems
3¼ pounds sugar
1 pound light raisins
2 oranges, rinsed, seeded, and finely chopped (rind and juice included)
1 tablespoon fresh lemon juice
1 tablespoon grated lemon rind
1 cup apple cider vinegar
2 teaspoons ground cinnamon
½ teaspoon ground cloves

In a large, heavy pot, combine all the ingredients, stir till thoroughly mixed, and bring to a boil over moderate heat, stirring. Reduce the heat to low and cook, uncovered, till the mixture is soft, about 30 minutes. Ladle the relish into sterilized jars and seal. Let cool completely.

TEN ½-PINT JARS

Halloween Spiders

Leave it to Mother to come up with something spooky like these leggy spiders, which she makes as an exciting gift for children. She buys the Chinese noodles in 8-ounce cellophane packages at the supermarket. Sometimes she passes out extra spiders to trick-or-treaters, which means she's the most popular lady in the neighborhood. Be sure to keep the spiders well chilled till ready to serve.

1½ **cups semisweet chocolate chips**
5 **ounces Chinese noodles**
1 **cup miniature marshmallows**

Grease one or two baking sheets and set aside.

Place the chocolate in the top of a double boiler over boiling water, reduce the heat to low, and stir constantly till the chocolate melts completely. Break up the noodles, add them to the chocolate, and stir till they're well coated. Remove the pan from the heat, add the marshmallows, and stir till well coated.

Drop the spiders by teaspoons onto the prepared baking sheet. Let them cool completely, then chill at least 6 hours. As a gift, pack the spiders loosely in colored plastic wrap in tins or small boxes.

ABOUT 3 DOZEN SPIDERS

Gingerbread Men

Mother is forever looking for different types of metal cutters to make these gift cookies for children—goblins, witches, various animals—but the forms that are most readily available in kitchen shops and hardware stores are in the shape of tiny men. Use whichever ones you can find. Typically, she arranges the cookies in small, colorful tins or boxes and always warns the kids "not to crush the goodies." The irony is that the adults love the cookies as much as the children—I certainly do.

½ cup (1 stick) butter or margarine, softened

½ cup firmly packed light brown sugar

1 cup molasses

2 teaspoons cider vinegar

4 cups all-purpose flour

1 tablespoon ground cinnamon

1 teaspoon ground ginger

½ teaspoon ground cloves

1 teaspoon salt

Dark seedless raisins for decorating

Small candies (like M&M's) for decorating

Preheat the oven to 350°F. Lightly grease one or two baking sheets and set aside.

In a large mixing bowl, cream together the butter, brown sugar, molasses, and vinegar till well blended and smooth. Into another large mixing bowl, sift together the flour, spices, and salt and stir till well blended. Gradually add the creamed mixture by large spoonfuls to the dry ingredients, mixing well with a wooden spoon and kneading if necessary to make the dough hold together. (It will be very stiff.) Wrap the dough in plastic wrap and chill for 30 minutes.

On a lightly floured work surface, roll out the dough with a floured rolling pin to a ⅛- to ¼-inch thickness. Cut out gingerbread men with a 3½-inch cutter, lift them carefully to the prepared baking sheet, and, using raisins and candies for eyes, noses, and buttons, decorate the cookies. Bake the cookies till lightly browned, 12 to 15 minutes, let cool on the pan a minute or so, then transfer to a wire rack to cool completely.

ABOUT 3 DOZEN COOKIES

The Golden Gobbler Feast

I SIMPLY CAN'T IMAGINE ANYONE ANYWHERE holding a more elaborate Thanksgiving feast than the one to which Mother has been treating family and friends for as long as I can remember. In Old Southern tradition, the dinner takes place fairly early in the afternoon, after everybody has attended church, and Mother's decorations are almost mind-boggling: a bundle of dried corn on the front door; a huge ceramic turkey on the table bursting with yellow and bronze mums and fall leaves; small flowering cabbages, miniature pumpkins, Pilgrim figurines, and vases of goldenrod placed on ledges and side tables; and heaven knows how many dips and desserts and food gifts and children's favors displayed on various counters. She even sets a separate small table for the children graced with the same type of linen tablecloth, heavy silver, and cutout turkey place cards as for the adults. Champagne cocktails are a ritual at this formal dinner (for the kids, she has cranberry punch), and while Mother prefers to limit the guests to eight grown-ups, more than once she's told me to lug out an extra leaf for the mahogany table when, for one reason or another, more people are included—and believe me, there's always plenty of extra champagne and food.

Of course, no Thanksgiving dinner of Mother's would be complete without her fixing small paper plates of leftover turkey for guests to take home for sandwiches, and when she prepared a Thanksgiving feast a couple of times at my home in East Hampton, the first thing that none other than Craig Claiborne would announce upon arrival was, "Martha, don't you dare forget to pack me a little white turkey." And what guest would not be disappointed upon leaving if not presented with a gift of Mother's homemade bread, or cookies, or relish, or fruit preserves? "Who knows when hunger might strike?" she quips as guests almost stagger out the door.

Menu

Hot Seafood Dip

Champagne Cocktails

Roast Turkey with Oyster and Almond Stuffing

Sweet Potato and Apple Gratin

Streak-O'-Lean Snappies with Pecan Butter

Congealed Cranberry, Orange, and Pineapple Salad

Plantation Rice Bread

Southern Comfort Ambrosia

Holiday Bourbon Cake

California Chardonnay

Hot Seafood Dip

Typically, Mother doubles this recipe for her Thanksgiving feast no matter the number of guests, since "people always eat more of the dip with cocktails than they really should," and, besides, it keeps well covered in the fridge for a couple of days and can be reheated for another cocktail party.

½ cup (1 stick) butter

½ cup all-purpose flour

1 cup milk

¼ cup evaporated milk

2 teaspoons mild paprika

½ teaspoon black pepper

Salt to taste

2 tablespoons dry sherry

1 tablespoon Worcestershire sauce

Dash of cayenne

½ pound fresh lump crabmeat (see Martha Pearl Advises, page 52), picked over for shells
and cartilage

½ pound shelled cooked shrimp, coarsely chopped

¼ pound fresh mushrooms, stems trimmed, sautéed in 1 tablespoon butter over moderate
heat until tender, and finely chopped

1 cup finely chopped fresh parsley

In a medium-size heavy saucepan, melt the butter over moderate heat, then add the flour and whisk till well blended. Gradually add the regular milk and evaporated milk, whisking constantly till the mixture is thickened and smooth. Add the paprika, black pepper, and salt and whisk till well blended.

Remove the pan from the heat, add the sherry, Worcestershire, and cayenne, and stir well. Fold in the crabmeat, shrimp, and mushrooms, mixing gently but well. Add the parsley, stir till well blended, and heat gently over low heat. Transfer the dip to a small chafing dish and serve with Melba toast rounds.

AT LEAST 8 SERVINGS

Champagne Cocktails

FOR EACH COCKTAIL

1 teaspoon superfine sugar

5 dashes Angostura bitters

1 ounce cognac

3 ounces well-chilled champagne

1 maraschino cherry

Place the sugar in a champagne glass, add the bitters, and stir till well blended. Add the cognac and champagne and garnish with the cherry.

Roast Turkey with Oyster and Almond Stuffing

Mother loves cooking with almonds almost as much as with pecans, but when one year she decided to stuff her turkey with this unorthodox oyster and almond dressing instead of a more traditional combination of sagey cornbread and sausage or simple oysters and herbs, I raised an eyebrow. Suffice it to say that the stuffing was a revelation, and I've since enhanced it (in my opinion but not Mother's) with a few tablespoons of dry sherry. The stuffing is also great baked by itself.

FOR THE STUFFING

¾ **cup (1½ sticks) butter**

1½ **cups chopped onions**

1½ **cups chopped celery**

1 cup chopped almonds

7 cups coarse fresh bread crumbs

1 tablespoon salt

1 teaspoon black pepper

¼ **teaspoon ground nutmeg**

1 pint shucked oysters, drained (liquor reserved) and chopped

2 large eggs, beaten

Milk as needed

FOR THE TURKEY

One 12- to 14-pound turkey, giblets included

Salt and black pepper to taste

1 cup water

To make the stuffing, melt the butter in a large, heavy skillet over moderately low heat, then add the onions, celery, and almonds and cook, stirring, till the vegetables are soft, about 10 minutes. Transfer the contents of the skillet to a large mixing bowl, add the bread crumbs, salt, pepper, nutmeg, oysters, and eggs, and mix with your hands till well blended. Add the reserved oyster liquor, mix well, then add just enough milk to fully moisten the stuffing, taking care not to make it too wet.

Preheat the oven to 325°F.

Season the turkey inside and out with the salt and pepper, stuff the cavity loosely with the stuffing, and truss the bird. (Place any additional stuffing in a buttered baking dish. Keep it refrigerated until the last 45 minutes of roasting and place it in the oven.) Position the turkey breast side up on a rack in a large roasting pan, pour the water into the pan, cover, and cook 2½ hours, basting from time to time. Remove the cover and continue roasting till the turkey is golden, 15 to 20 minutes longer. Transfer to a large serving platter, remove the trussing, and cover the bird loosely with aluminum foil till ready to carve.

To serve, spoon the stuffing into a heated bowl, carve the turkey, and, if desired, serve with giblet gravy (see note below).

AT LEAST 8 SERVINGS

Martha Pearl Advises

To make giblet gravy, while the turkey is roasting, place the giblets in a large saucepan with about 2½ cups of water and simmer, covered, 1 hour. Transfer the giblets to a chopping board, chop coarsely, and reserve the cooking liquid.

When the turkey has finished roasting, place the pan over moderately high heat and cook down the drippings till nearly burned, scraping the pan. Gradually add the cooking liquid from the giblets, stirring and scraping, till the gravy is slightly thickened. Stir in the chopped giblets, season with salt and pepper to taste, heat well, and pour the gravy into a sauceboat.

Jimmy roasts his turkey with a little water in the pan to keep it moist. I never do. If a turkey is roasted slowly and basted well, it renders plenty of its own juices, and it's these undiluted juices I use to make perfect natural gravy. Of course, I can't ever tell Jimmy anything.

Sweet Potato and Apple Gratin

Mother and I both are nuts about anything gratinéed, and this variation on ordinary baked sweet potatoes (or yams) is one of the best she's ever come up with. Since the gratin is part of an elaborate meal involving many flavors, Mother had kept the dish simple, but for other occasions, try adding a cup of seedless raisins or various spices. Do watch carefully to make sure the gratin doesn't dry out.

3 large sweet potatoes, peeled and cut into rounds ⅛ inch thick

2 large Golden Delicious apples, peeled, cored, and cut into rounds ⅛ inch thick

1 large onion, finely chopped

2 garlic cloves, minced

Salt and black pepper to taste

1 cup half-and-half, or more as needed

⅓ cup fine dry bread crumbs

3 tablespoons butter, cut into pieces

Preheat the oven to 350°F.

In a large, well-buttered gratin dish, arrange a layer of slightly overlapping sweet potatoes, then a layer of apples. Sprinkle some of the onion and garlic over the top, season with salt and pepper, and continue building layers of sweet potatoes and apples, adding to each a little onion, garlic, and salt and pepper, until all are used up. Pour the half-and-half around the sides and bake till the sweet potatoes are tender, about 50 minutes.

Remove the dish from the oven and baste the top with the cooking liquid, adding a little more half-and-half if the sweet potatoes seem too dry. Sprinkle the bread crumbs on top, dot with the butter, and continue baking till the top is nicely browned, about 15 minutes.

8 SERVINGS

Streak-O'-Lean Snappies with Pecan Butter

"Snappies" is a Southern term that originally applied to pole beans with tough strings that had to be removed before the beans were snapped for cooking. Although real string beans are a rare commodity these days, even in the South (and their flavor is inimitable), Mother still calls all green beans snappies and, quite literally, she will not eat (or serve) any that are not simmered with cooking meat for at least 45 minutes—"for flavor, flavor, flavor," she harks. Southern pecan butter is not a "butter" at all, simply crushed pecans that are glazed in butter and used to enhance all sorts of vegetables and broiled or grilled fish. It's exquisite.

FOR THE BEANS
2 pounds fresh green beans (not thin French style)
1 medium-size onion, finely chopped
One 1-inch-thick chunk streak-o'-lean (lean salt pork) cooking meat
Salt and black pepper to taste
FOR THE PECAN BUTTER
½ cup (1 stick) butter
⅔ cup roughly crushed pecans
Salt to taste

To cook the beans, pinch off the ends, snap the beans into 1½-inch pieces, rinse well in a colander, and transfer to a large pot. Add the onion, cooking meat, salt and pepper, and enough water to cover by 1 inch. Bring to a boil, reduce the heat to low, cover, and simmer the beans slowly for 45 minutes.

Shortly before the beans are cooked, make the pecan butter by melting the butter in a small, heavy skillet over moderate heat. Add the pecans, stir till they are well coated, and cook, stirring, till the pecans are golden brown, about 10 minutes. Season with salt and stir again.

To serve, drain the beans, discard the cooking meat, and place in a large serving bowl. Pour the pecan butter over the top, toss gently, and serve immediately.

8 SERVINGS

Congealed Cranberry, Orange, and Pineapple Salad

One 3-ounce package lemon-flavored Jell-O
1 cup boiling water
One 16-ounce can whole cranberry sauce
Two 11-ounce cans mandarin oranges, drained
One 8-ounce can crushed pineapple, drained
1 cup chopped pecans or hazelnuts, toasted (see Martha Pearl Advises, page 119)
Lettuce cups

In a large mixing bowl, combine the Jell-O and boiling water and stir till dissolved. Add the cranberry sauce, oranges, pineapple, and nuts and stir till well blended. Transfer the mixture to a large mold, cover with plastic wrap, and chill till firm, at least 3 hours.

Serve the salad in lettuce cups.

8 SERVINGS

Plantation Rice Bread

Mother is one of the few Southern cooks left who still makes old-fashioned rice bread or, as it was often called in the Carolina and Georgia Low Country during plantation days, "philpy" bread. A lot like cornbread, rice bread can also be made with rice flour for a smoother texture. Either way, serve it with plenty of butter.

2 cups long-grain rice, boiled until soft
1 cup buttermilk
2 large eggs, beaten
1½ cups all-purpose flour
1 teaspoon baking powder
1 teaspoon baking soda
1 teaspoon salt

Preheat the oven to 425°F. Grease two 9-inch loaf pans and set them aside.

In a large mixing bowl, combine the boiled rice, buttermilk, and eggs and mash the mixture with a potato masher till well blended and smooth. In a small mixing bowl, combine the flour, baking powder, baking soda, and salt and stir till well blended. Add the dry mixture to the rice mixture, stir till well blended and smooth, and scrape equal amounts of batter into the prepared pans. Bake till almost golden brown, about 30 minutes.

Turn the loaves out and serve hot.

2 LOAVES

Southern Comfort Ambrosia

Generally, Mother is an absolute purist about ambrosia, insisting fervently that the dessert be made with only oranges, fresh coconut, sugar, and perhaps a little orange juice, and served only at Christmas. Her one concession was made when I once took it upon myself to add grapefruit and a little Southern Comfort. At first she protested sternly, but the following year at our Thanksgiving feast, she announced half-apologetically to guests that "This is Jimmy's ambrosia, and I guess it's okay." Then, the next year she served it again. Quietly, I claim a small victory.

8 seedless oranges

2 grapefruits

2 cups unsweetened shredded coconut (preferably fresh; if using frozen, defrost it)

¼ cup sugar

2 to 3 tablespoons Southern Comfort, to your taste

Cut the oranges and grapefruits in half, cut out the sections carefully with a citrus or serrated paring knife (removing all the white pith), and place the sections in a large glass serving bowl. Squeeze juice from the orange and grapefruit shells over the sections, add the coconut, sugar, and Southern Comfort, and toss lightly but thoroughly. Cover the bowl with plastic wrap and refrigerate at least 1 hour before serving with a slotted spoon.

8 SERVINGS

Holiday Bourbon Cake

This is one of Mother's most ceremonial cakes and one that goes perfectly with any type of ambrosia. Sometimes she enriches it even more with a half-cup of molasses or maple syrup, and she might add more spices or use different nuts. Here is a glorious cake that reeks of grand Southern entertaining.

½ cup (1 stick) butter, softened
½ cup granulated sugar
½ cup firmly packed dark brown sugar
3 large eggs
2½ cups all-purpose flour
2 teaspoons baking powder
1 teaspoon ground cinnamon
1 teaspoon ground allspice
½ teaspoon salt
¾ cup bourbon
1 cup chopped walnuts
Confectioners' sugar for sprinkling

Preheat the oven to 350°F. Butter a 10-inch Bundt or tube pan and set aside.

In a large mixing bowl, cream the butter and two sugars together with an electric mixer, then add the eggs one at a time, beating till the mixture is well blended and smooth. Into a medium-size mixing bowl, sift together the flour, baking powder, cinnamon, allspice, and salt. Add the flour mixture alternately with the bourbon to the creamed mixture, beating till well blended and smooth. Stir in the walnuts till well blended, then scrape the batter into the prepared pan and bake till a knife inserted into the middle comes out clean, about 1 hour.

Let the cake cool for 10 minutes on a wire rack, then turn out on the rack to cool completely. Sprinkle the top with confectioners' sugar before serving.

ONE 10-INCH BUNDT OR TUBE CAKE;
AT LEAST 8 SERVINGS

A Housewarming Basket

FOR MANY YEARS, MOTHER HAD GENEROUSLY prepared and carried or mailed food (or "friendship gifts") to people in the hospital, shut-ins, or simply someone she has reason to thank. When, however, friends move from a house to a condo, or a new family arrives in the neighborhood, she makes a royal production over entertaining them with one of her "basket meals" intended to make them feel at home and lessen the pressures of having to cook.

Typically, she sprays one of her large peach baskets (saved from a summer trip to the peach farm) a pastel color, lines it with an oversize tea towel big enough to extend over the sides, packs it with attractive paper plates and napkins, plastic tableware and wineglasses, and prepared food, and ties a billowy bow on the handle. In one corner she then tucks a small bunch of flowers, and, if other neighbors care to contribute to the housewarming, she somehow finds room in the basket for maybe a jar of relish or an extra box of cookies. Bottles of good wine are then tied with ribbons and carried separately. Sometimes, Mother (and perhaps some of her pals) simply leaves the basket with each dish labeled and cooking instructions included, but more often than not, the newcomers insist that she stay, in which case she virtually takes over in the kitchen as only my headstrong mother is fully capable of doing. And people wonder how she has so many friends!

Menu

Tidewater Pickled Shrimp

Sausage and Mushroom Strata

Parmesan Chicken Wings

Banana Buttermilk Muffins

Pecan Coconut Brownies

California Chenin Blanc

California Merlot

Tidewater Pickled Shrimp

Since Mother seems to make a different marinade every time she pickles these shrimp, feel free to experiment with other herbs and seasonings. To transfer the shrimp to a housewarming or other locale, be sure to drain them first and transfer to a plastic container—keeping them chilled till the last minute.

2 pounds medium-size shrimp

2 medium-size onions, thinly sliced

1 cup vegetable oil

½ cup cider vinegar

3 tablespoons fresh lemon juice

1 tablespoon sugar

1 tablespoon Worcestershire sauce

1 teaspoon dry mustard

1 teaspoon salt

Freshly ground black pepper to taste

Pinch of cayenne pepper

2 bay leaves, crushed

2 tablespoons finely chopped fresh parsley leaves

2 teaspoons finely chopped fresh dill

Place the shrimp in a large saucepan with enough water to cover. Bring to a boil, remove from the heat, cover, and let stand for 1 minute. Drain the shrimp, let cool, then peel and devein them.

Layer the shrimp and onions in a large glass baking dish. In a large mixing bowl, combine the oil, vinegar, and lemon juice and whisk together till frothy. Add the remaining ingredients, whisk till well blended, and pour over the shrimp and onions. Cover with plastic wrap and chill at least 12 hours.

Remove the shrimp from the marinade and serve with toothpicks.

6 TO 8 SERVINGS

Sausage and Mushroom Strata

I have no earthly idea when and how the term "strata" entered the Southern culinary vernacular, but it's obviously a distortion of "stratification" and always refers to a layered casserole. Some stratas can be pretty awful, but this one, which Mother considers ideal for housewarmings since it is partially baked in advance, is remarkably delicious—and filling.

4 to 5 slices white bread, crusts trimmed away
1 pound bulk pork sausage, broken up
½ pound mushrooms, finely chopped
1 medium-size onion, finely chopped
2 teaspoons Dijon mustard
1 cup finely shredded genuine Swiss (Emmentaler) cheese
2 cups half-and-half
3 large eggs, beaten
1 teaspoon Worcestershire sauce
Salt and black pepper to taste
Tabasco Sauce to taste

Grease a medium-size casserole, arrange the bread slices across the bottom in a single layer, and set aside.

In a large skillet, brown the sausage over moderate heat, drain on paper towels, and pour off all but about 2 tablespoons of the grease. Add the mushrooms and onion to the skillet and cook, stirring, over moderate heat till soft, about 10 minutes. Return the sausage to the skillet, add the mustard, and stir till well blended.

Spoon the sausage mixture evenly over the bread in the casserole and sprinkle the cheese over the top. In a medium-size mixing bowl, combine the half-and-half, eggs, and Worcestershire, season with salt, pepper, and Tabasco, whisk till well blended, and pour over the cheese. Cover the strata with plastic wrap and refrigerate at least 2 hours.

Preheat the oven to 350°F, then bake the strata till just set, about 30 minutes. When ready to serve, bake an additional 15 to 20 minutes.

6 TO 8 SERVINGS

Parmesan Chicken Wings

*Mother's favorite part of any chicken has always been the wings ("the sweetest meat,"
she exclaims), which is why she has so many chicken wing recipes. This latest one, created for old friends who'd finally moved from their large Colonial house to a more sensible condo, is utterly delectable and perfect for a housewarming—or picnic, cookout,
or elaborate cocktail buffet.*

3 pounds chicken wings
1 cup finely grated Parmesan cheese
2 tablespoons finely chopped fresh parsley leaves
1 teaspoon dried tarragon
1 teaspoon dried marjoram
1 teaspoon mild Hungarian paprika
Salt and black pepper to taste
Pinch of cayenne pepper
$\frac{1}{2}$ cup (1 stick) butter, melted

Preheat the oven to 375°F. Grease a large, heavy baking sheet and set aside.

Disjoint the chicken wings and cut off and discard the tips. On a large plate, combine the
cheese, parsley, tarragon, marjoram, paprika, salt and black pepper, and cayenne and stir till
well blended. Dip each chicken piece into the melted butter, dredge lightly in the cheese
mixture, tapping off any excess, place on the prepared baking sheet, and bake till golden
brown and crispy, about 1 hour. Serve the wings hot or at room temperature.

6 TO 8 SERVINGS

Banana Buttermilk Muffins

1 cup all-purpose flour
$\frac{1}{2}$ teaspoon salt
$\frac{1}{2}$ teaspoon baking soda
$\frac{1}{4}$ cup ($\frac{1}{2}$ stick) butter, softened
$\frac{1}{4}$ cup granulated sugar
$\frac{1}{4}$ cup firmly packed light brown sugar
2 large eggs
$\frac{1}{2}$ cup buttermilk
2 very ripe bananas, peeled and mashed
1 teaspoon ground cinnamon

Preheat the oven to 375°F. Grease an 8-cup muffin tin and set aside.

Into a large mixing bowl, sift together the flour, salt, and baking soda. In another large bowl, cream together the butter and two sugars with an electric mixer, then add the eggs and buttermilk and beat till well blended. Stir in the bananas and cinnamon. Add the banana mixture to the flour mixture and stir just till blended, or your muffins will end up being tough.

Spoon the batter equally into the prepared muffin cups, filling each about two-thirds full, and bake till golden brown, about 25 minutes. Let the tin cool on a wire rack for 5 minutes, then unmold the muffins onto the rack to cool completely.

8 MUFFINS

Martha Pearl Advises

To prevent the scorching and discoloring of unused cups in a muffin tin while baking, fill them about half full of water.

Pecan Coconut Brownies

Whether people realize it or not, the combination of chocolate and coconut is one of those sacred culinary marriages, as these unusual brownies illustrate. They are drier than Mother's regular fudgy brownies and thus ideal for packing and transporting to another location. It's not obligatory, but do try to use fresh coconut for ideal results.

Three 1-ounce squares unsweetened chocolate
⅔ cup butter, cut into pieces
3 large eggs
1½ cups sugar
1 teaspoon pure vanilla extract
1½ cups all-purpose flour
½ teaspoon baking powder
1 cup chopped pecans
½ cup unsweetened shredded coconut (fresh, or defrosted if frozen)

In a medium-size, heavy saucepan, combine the chocolate and butter and stir over low heat till the chocolate is melted and the mixture is smooth. Remove the pan from the heat and let cool to room temperature.

Preheat the oven to 325°F. Grease a 10-inch-square baking pan and set aside.

In a large mixing bowl, beat the eggs, sugar, and vanilla with an electric mixer till well blended. Add the cooled chocolate mixture and beat till well blended. Stir in the flour and baking powder till well blended, add the pecans and coconut, and stir till well blended and smooth. Scrape the mixture into the prepared pan and bake till the cake is just soft, about 30 minutes. Let the cake cool in the pan on a wire rack, then cut out square brownies.

ABOUT 2 DOZEN BROWNIES

Spend-the-Day Fruitcake Party

MY MATERNAL GREAT-GRANDMOTHER, SWEET MAA, did it; my grandmother, Maw Maw, did it; and Mother has been sponsoring her annual spend-the-day fruitcake party since I was a child. Thanksgiving is over, one of the "girls" calls to inform that the supermarket finally has crystallized fruit, Mother gets her first shipment of pecans from Atwell Pecan Company in Wrens, Georgia, so it's time to make fruitcakes. Each lady brings her own ingredients and large plastic containers, Mother supplies the chopping boards, kitchen shears, sharp knives, measuring cups, and scales, and after early morning coffee and homemade coffeecake, they each take their special places in the kitchen and begin cutting and chopping and dicing and mixing all the fruits and nuts. The banter never stops: this year the cherries are unusually nice, large, and juicy; the pineapple looks and feels a little dry; the pecans are meaty and full-flavored.

Time to break for traditional apple slushes and pâté in the living room, followed by lunch which Mother has prepared well in advance and has ready to serve on the dining room table already decorated with a colorful felt runner, the season's first holly and poinsettias, and various holiday ornaments and figurines. A molded salad, spiced fruit, homemade bread, a rich cake, and lots of wine and recipe talk before heading back into the kitchen to drizzle brandy or rum or bourbon all over the fruits and nuts, pack mixtures in airtight containers, and return to the respective homes to bake fruitcakes the following day. The ritual never changes, and when, sadly, a participant goes to meet her maker, she's replaced by another lady ready and eager to sustain a Southern tradition that's as sacred to Mother as church barbecues and putting up pickles and preserves.

Menu

Apple Slushes

Last-Minute Chicken Pâté

Molded Salmon Salad

Spiced Cherries

Pecan Bread

Caramel Pound Cake

French Chablis

Apple Slushes

1 quart apple juice

2 ounces frozen orange juice concentrate

5 ounces vodka

In a blender, combine all the ingredients, blend to a smooth slush, and pour into crystal cocktail glasses.

4 TO 6 DRINKS

Last-Minute Chicken Pâté

Mother collects and freezes chicken livers year-round, so she always has plenty on hand when there's leftover cooked chicken in the refrigerator to turn into this quick pâté for any type of social get-together. Even when frozen hard, the livers can be easily separated and sautéed (though the cooking time over low heat must be increased). Sometimes she also adds a little ground nutmeg or mace to this pâté, but what really makes the spread so Southern is the cream cheese.

3 tablespoons butter

2 green onions (white part only), finely chopped

1 small garlic clove, minced

¼ pound chicken livers, trimmed of membranes and cut in half

2 cups skinned and shredded cooked chicken legs or thighs

One 3-ounce package cream cheese, softened

1 teaspoon finely chopped fresh tarragon leaves or ¼ teaspoon dried tarragon

½ teaspoon salt

¼ teaspoon black pepper

2 tablespoons brandy

continued

In a small skillet, melt the butter over moderately low heat, then add the onions, garlic, and livers and cook, stirring, till the onions are soft and the livers just cooked through. Remove from the heat and let cool slightly, then transfer to a blender or food processor, add the remaining ingredients, and blend till very smooth. Scrape the pâté into a crock or bowl, cover with plastic wrap, and chill for 2 hours.

Serve with crackers or toast points (see Martha Pearl Advises, page 38).

4 TO 6 SERVINGS

Molded Salmon Salad

"Don't be uppity about using canned salmon if you don't have fresh," Mother advises. *"You really can't tell the difference."* Same with the dill.

2 envelopes unflavored gelatin

1 cup water

1 cup mayonnaise (Mother prefers Hellmann's)

½ cup half-and-half

1 tablespoon fresh lemon juice

½ teaspoon dry mustard

1 tablespoon snipped fresh dill or ½ teaspoon dried dill

Black pepper to taste

2 cups flaked cooked salmon (fresh or canned that's been drained and picked over)

½ cup finely chopped celery

3 tablespoons seeded and finely chopped green bell pepper

1 tablespoon minced onion

4 to 6 lettuce leaves

Grease an 8-cup ring or fish-shaped salad mold and set aside.

In a small saucepan, soften the gelatin in the water for 5 minutes, then place over low heat, stirring till the gelatin is dissolved. Remove from the heat and let cool.

In a large mixing bowl, combine the mayonnaise, half-and-half, lemon juice, mustard, dill, and pepper and stir till well blended. Add the gelatin to the mixture and stir till well blended and smooth. Add the salmon, celery, bell pepper, and onion and stir till well blended. Scrape the mixture into the prepared mold, cover with plastic wrap, and chill till firm, at least 3 hours.

Serve the salad on top of lettuce leaves.

4 TO 6 SERVINGS

Spiced Cherries

These cherries are always a special highlight of Mother's fruitcake party, but I also love to serve them with pork and game dishes. Since the cherry juice is essential, I don't advise trying to spice fresh cherries—as I once did, stupidly substituting a little Madeira, with weird results.

One 1-pound, 1-ounce can pitted dark cherries, drained and juice reserved
¼ **cup white vinegar**
¼ **cup sugar**
2 strips orange rind
1 small cinnamon stick
3 whole cloves
¼ **teaspoon salt**

In a medium-size saucepan, combine 1 cup of the reserved cherry juice, the vinegar, sugar, orange rind, cinnamon stick, cloves, and salt and stir. Bring to a boil, reduce the heat to low, cover, and simmer for 10 minutes. Remove the pan from the heat and let cool slightly.

Place the cherries in a ceramic or glass bowl, strain the spiced liquid over the top, and let cool completely. Cover the bowl with plastic wrap and chill overnight.

With a slotted spoon, transfer the cherries to a deep glass serving dish or store in the refrigerator in a tightly sealed jar up to 3 days.

4 TO 6 SERVINGS

Pecan Bread

There are no fruits or overly assertive flavorings in this rather delicate bread, the idea being (as Mother is forever reminding others) to really emphasize the wonderful taste of the pecans.

2½ cups all-purpose flour
2 teaspoons baking powder
½ teaspoon baking soda
1 teaspoon salt
⅓ cup butter, softened
1 cup sugar
2 large eggs
½ teaspoon pure vanilla extract
1 cup milk
1 cup finely chopped pecans

Preheat the oven to 325°F. Butter a medium-size loaf pan and set aside.

Into a medium-size mixing bowl, sift together the flour, baking powder, baking soda, and ½ teaspoon salt and set aside. In large mixing bowl, cream together the butter and sugar with an electric mixer, then add the eggs, vanilla, and remaining ½ teaspoon salt and beat till well blended and smooth. Alternately, add the flour mixture and milk to the creamed mixture and stir till well blended and smooth. Fold in the pecans, then scrape the batter into the prepared pan. Bake till the loaf is springy to the touch and the top golden brown, about 1¼ hours. Let the bread cool in the pan for 10 minutes, then turn it out on a wire rack to cool completely before slicing.

1 LOAF

Caramel Pound Cake

I'm not saying that this platonic pound cake is better than Mother's Satan chocolate one, but it comes in a very close second—an opinion I expressed while observing all the action at her last fruitcake party. "It's almost just like a plain old caramel cake," she dismissed my ecstatic ravings. Yeah, and her dark fruitcakes are almost just like the mail-order ones! And, oh yes, this sensational cake, wrapped tightly in foil, keeps literally for weeks in the refrigerator.

FOR THE CAKE

3$\frac{1}{2}$ cups all-purpose flour

1 teaspoon baking powder

$\frac{1}{2}$ teaspoon salt

2 cups firmly packed light brown sugar

1$\frac{1}{4}$ cups granulated sugar

1$\frac{1}{2}$ cups (3 sticks) butter, softened

6 large eggs

1$\frac{1}{4}$ cups milk

FOR THE FROSTING

$\frac{1}{2}$ cup (1 stick) butter

1 cup firmly packed dark brown sugar

$\frac{1}{2}$ cup milk

$\frac{1}{2}$ teaspoon pure vanilla extract

4 cups confectioners' sugar, sifted

Preheat the oven to 325°F. Grease a 10-inch tube or Bundt pan and set aside.

To make the cake, sift the flour, baking powder, and salt together into a medium-size mixing bowl and set aside. In a large mixing bowl, cream together the two sugars and butter with an electric mixer, then add the eggs one at a time, beating after each addition till well blended. Alternately, add the flour mixture and milk to the creamed mixture and beat till well blended and smooth. Scrape the batter into the prepared pan and bake till a knife inserted into the cake comes out almost clean, about 1 hour (be careful not to overbake). Transfer the cake to a wire rack, let cool for 10 minutes, then turn it out onto the rack to cool completely.

To make the frosting, melt the butter in a large, heavy saucepan over low heat, then add the brown sugar and milk and, stirring, bring the mixture almost to a boil. Remove from the heat and let cool. Stir in the vanilla, then gradually add the confectioners' sugar and stir till well blended and very smooth.

Transfer the cake to a cake plate and frost the top and sides using a heavy knife or rubber spatula. Let the cake stand for at least 1 hour before serving.

ONE 10-INCH TUBE OR BUNDT CAKE;
AT LEAST 10 SERVINGS

Martha Pearl Advises

If frosting begins to harden while being spread on cakes or other confections, simply dip the knife or spatula into a glass of hot water.

A Holiday Gift-Making Luncheon

"HOPE SOMEBODY'S BROUGHT THE PINK FELT FOR Santa's face," Mother announces joyfully as a half-dozen or more of her friends arrive not long after Thanksgiving to begin making by hand Christmas tree skirts and stockings, table runners, elves, snowmen, sleds, and teddy bears from yards and yards of bright fabrics, spool after spool of colored threads, and thousands of sequins and beads. First, Mother serves cups of cider tea from the mahogany trolley in the living room, then the ladies cut, stuff, sew, pin on, and do whatever else is necessary to produce exquisite gifts for special friends, family members, holiday bazaars, and church benefits. "It's hard work," Mother declares, "but it's a labor of love and a wonderful way to share creative ideas and skills. And I must add proudly that every gift is one of a kind and that not a single ounce of glue is ever used."

At noon sharp, everybody stops the serious work for a first glass of Mother's favorite Gewürztraminer (Alsatian) wine and a little social gossip, followed by mugs of hot soup. Since every table in the house is filled with gifts in the making, Mother next serves a relatively simple lunch of salad, her beloved vegetable sandwiches, and dessert on handsome trays picked up in the kitchen and carried to the living room or den, after which the work (and wine sipping) continues till well into the afternoon. "We're pretty tired by the time supplies are packed up," she confesses, "but when we sit back, and admire what all we've accomplished, and think about how happy we'll make some people come Christmas, we know it's worth every bit of effort."

Menu

Virginia Peanut Soup

Get-Together Vegetable Finger Sandwiches

Autumn Seafood Salad with Poppy Seed Dressing

Pumpkin Cheesecake

Alsatian Gewürztraminer

Spiced Cider Tea

Virginia Peanut Soup

Unlike Mother's Georgia peanut soup, this Virginia version has no cream and depends mainly on fresh chicken stock and a surprising touch of tomato sauce—not to mention genuine Virginia peanuts (see the headnote to Old-Fashioned Goober Pie on page 43 for a mail-order source)—for its distinction. The procedure requires a bit of effort, but, believe me, the smooth, almost silky results justify following the directions to the letter. The soup, topped with a dollop of whipped cream, is also delicious cold.

2 cups roasted Virginia peanuts

6 cups chicken stock or broth

3 tablespoons peanut oil

1 medium-size onion, chopped

2 celery ribs (including leaves), chopped

2 garlic cloves, chopped

2 tablespoons all-purpose flour mixed with 2 tablespoons cold water into a paste

1 tablespoon canned tomato sauce

½ teaspoon Worcestershire sauce

5 drops Tabasco Sauce

Salt and black pepper to taste

In a blender or food processor, combine 1 cup of the peanuts with 1 cup of the stock and blend to a puree. Add the remaining nuts and another cup of stock and blend again till very smooth, then strain the mixture through a fine sieve into a bowl and set aside.

In a medium-size skillet, heat the peanut oil over moderately low heat, then add the onion, celery, and garlic and cook for 5 minutes, stirring. Transfer the sautéed vegetables to the blender or food processor, add another cup of stock, reduce to a puree, and scrape the mixture into a large, heavy saucepan over moderate heat. Add the flour paste to the vegetable puree, stir, and cook for 5 minutes, stirring. Add the remaining 3 cups stock, the strained peanut mixture, tomato sauce, Worcestershire, and Tabasco, season with salt and pepper, stir well, and continue to cook till the soup is velvety smooth, about 5 minutes.

6 TO 8 SERVINGS

Get-Together Vegetable Finger Sandwiches

Mother has been making these elegant sandwiches for as long as I can remember, keeping them covered tightly with waxed paper in a large plastic container till ready to serve and storing any unused spread in the refrigerator for up to a week. To prevent sogginess, be sure to use day-old bread that's not too soft, and don't fail to trim the crusts and serve the sandwiches with alternating colors facing up. (I personally like to keep a container of the spread in the fridge for snack crackers.)

10 slices day-old white loaf bread

10 slices day-old brown loaf bread

2 medium-size ripe tomatoes, cored and peeled

1 small green bell pepper, seeded

1 medium-size onion, peeled

1 medium-size cucumber, peeled

1½ cups mayonnaise (Mother prefers Hellmann's)

1 teaspoon salt

Black pepper to taste

1 tablespoon unflavored gelatin

¼ cup water

Trim off the edges of both breads and set the slices aside.

On a cutting board, finely chop the tomatoes, bell pepper, onion, and cucumber and combine well. Drain the vegetables in a colander for about 15 minutes, then transfer to a large mixing bowl, add the mayonnaise, salt, and pepper, and mix well.

In a small saucepan, combine the gelatin and water, stir, and dissolve over low heat. Add the dissolved gelatin to the vegetables, stir till well blended, and chill till firm, about 2 hours.

To make the sandwiches, spread ¼ cup of vegetable filling over each slice of white bread, top each with a slice of brown bread, and cut each sandwich into thirds. Arrange the finger sandwiches on a tray with alternate bread colors facing up, cover tightly with waxed paper or plastic wrap, and chill till ready to serve. (Or store the sandwiches, chilled, up to 2 days in a tightly covered plastic container.)

30 FINGER SANDWICHES

Martha Pearl Advises

None of my food is more practical (and delicious) than my vegetable sandwiches. I serve them at teas, luncheons, and bereavements; I take them to picnics, shut-ins, and new neighbors; and nothing makes a nicer gift than a small tub of the spread— which keeps a good week in the refrigerator. I chop all the vegetables by hand; if you use a blender or food processor, the spread tends to be soupy.

Autumn Seafood Salad with Poppy Seed Dressing

Since mangoes are now available almost year-round (and Mother's convinced they're riper in fall than in summer), it's just as feasible to make this salad for the holidays as for warm-weather occasions. If you can't find beautiful mangoes, substitute two oranges. Likewise, Mother also loves this salad made with flaked fresh salmon. The dressing is equally good over any fresh fruit salad.

FOR THE SALAD

1 pound medium-size fresh shrimp

½ pound fresh lump crabmeat (see **Martha Pearl Advises, page 52**), picked over for shells and cartilage

1 large celery rib, finely chopped

3 tablespoons minced fresh chives

2 tablespoons seeded and finely chopped red bell pepper

1 ripe mango (see **Martha Pearl Advises, page 309**), peeled, seeded, and cut into small chunks

Bibb lettuce leaves

FOR THE DRESSING

¼ cup sugar

3 tablespoons cider vinegar

2 teaspoons grated onion

Pinch of dry mustard

Salt and black pepper to taste

1 cup vegetable oil

2 tablespoons poppy seeds

Place the shrimp in a large saucepan and add enough water to cover. Bring to a boil, remove from the heat, cover, let stand 1 minute, and drain. When cool enough to handle, shell and devein the shrimp and place in a large mixing bowl. Add the crabmeat, celery, chives, bell pepper, and mango, stir, cover the bowl with plastic wrap, and chill the salad for 1 hour.

To make the dressing, combine the sugar, vinegar, onion, and mustard in an electric blender, season with salt and pepper, and blend well. With the blender running, very slowly add the oil till the emulsion is thick. Add the poppy seeds and stir till well blended.

Pour the dressing over the salad, toss to coat the ingredients, and mound the salad over lettuce leaves on a serving platter or on individual salad plates.

6 TO 8 SERVINGS

Pumpkin Cheesecake

FOR THE CRUST

1¼ cups finely crushed graham crackers

¼ cup (½ stick) butter, softened

3 tablespoons granulated sugar

FOR THE FILLING

One 16-ounce can pumpkin puree

2 cups granulated sugar

4 large eggs

1 tablespoon ground cinnamon

1 teaspoon ground nutmeg

1 teaspoon ground ginger

½ teaspoon salt

Two 8-ounce packages cream cheese, softened

½ cup heavy cream

1 teaspoon pure vanilla extract

TO FINISH

Confectioners' sugar for dusting

To make the crust, combine the crushed graham crackers, butter, and sugar in a small mixing bowl and, using a fork, mix till well blended. Transfer the mixture to a 9-inch springform pan, press it onto the bottom of pan, and chill the crust for 30 minutes.

Preheat the oven to 375°F. Bake the crust for 10 minutes, transfer the pan to a wire rack, and let cool. Increase the oven temperature to 400°F.

continued

To make the filling, combine in a medium-size mixing bowl the pumpkin puree, 1 cup of the sugar, the eggs, cinnamon, nutmeg, ginger, and salt and stir till well blended. In a large mixing bowl, combine the cream cheese, heavy cream, vanilla, and the remaining 1 cup sugar and beat well with an electric mixer till smooth.

Fold the pumpkin mixture into the cream cheese mixture, scrape the filling into the prepared crust, and bake for 10 minutes. Reduce the oven temperature to 300°F and bake the cheesecake till a knife inserted into the center comes out almost clean, about 1¼ hours.

Transfer the pan to a wire rack, loosen the cake from the sides of the pan with a small knife, and let cool completely. Cover the cake lightly with plastic wrap and chill at least 4 hours before serving. Remove the sides of the pan and sprinkle the top of the cheesecake with confectioners' sugar.

ONE 9-INCH CAKE; AT LEAST 10 SERVINGS

Spiced Cider Tea

6 to 8 tea bags

6 whole cloves

1 small cinnamon stick

3 to 4 cups boiling water, to your taste

3 to 4 cups hot apple cider, to your taste

2 to 3 tablespoons sugar, to your taste

Place the tea bags, cloves, and cinnamon stick in a large china teapot, pour on the boiling water, cover the pot, and let steep for 5 minutes. Remove and discard the tea bags, add the hot cider and the sugar, stir well, and let stand for 2 minutes longer. Pour the tea through a strainer into teacups.

6 TO 8 CUPS

Winter

A Christmas Eve Country Ham Buffet

A Classic Southern Christmas
Breakfast

A Yuletide Sandwich Tea

A Tots' Jingle Bell Party

A New Year's Good Luck Supper

A Super Bowl Sports Buffet

A Southern Greek Dinner

The week after Thanksgiving, Mother begins decorating for Christmas and planning her entertainment, not just for the holidays but for the entire winter season. Up goes the big, twinkling spruce in the living room; out come the handmade tree skirt, antique ornaments, gift-filled wooden reindeer for the fireplace, special red-and-green kitchen and bathroom towels, and the miniature ceramic Christmas tree for the dining room table; and she waits anxiously for the first poinsettias and elaborate wreaths and colorful wrappings for food gifts to come on the market. For Mother, Christmas is a continual religious and social celebration conducted in the exact same manner it was when I was a child. Others of her generation might have toned down all the festivities once family have dispersed and friends passed on, but not my mother, who is never without some excuse to sponsor a get-together for plenty of old and new acquaintances eager to share her exceptional holiday spirit and food. The activity is, of course, most vibrant during the Christmas season itself, but then there's New Year's, and the bowl games, and Valentine's Day, and Mardi Gras, and, to be sure, her very special Southern-accented nod in March to Charlotte's proud Greek-American community and my Greek heritage. "For most people, wintertime is viewed as a dull social season, but I don't buy that," she proclaims.

Mother's kitchen from early December to March is almost an embarrassment, every spare cabinet, shelf, and surface, not to mention refrigerator/freezer, being literally filled with homemade foods intended for various aspects of her entertaining and gift-giving: multiple tins of ripening fruitcakes; huge plastic containers of cookies and cakes and delicate finger sandwiches; canisters of conserved and macerated fruits; jars of jams and pickles; all sorts of biscuits, muffins, and candies; and bags of frozen appetizers ready to pop into the oven. "I like to be prepared," she quips, "not only for all my planned teas and brunches and buffets but for what we in the South call 'drop-ins.' "

A Christmas Eve Country Ham Buffet

CHRISTMAS EVE HAS ALWAYS BEEN THE HIGH POINT in all of Mother's holiday entertaining, a truly festive occasion for eight to ten close family members and old friends that begins around six P.M. and continues till most dishes on the groaning buffet have been virtually wiped clean and the time comes for everybody to go home and await Santa Claus. (Today, this is strictly an adult affair, but how well I remember my grandfather scaring the life out of us children by shaking a concealed strap of sleigh bells and warning that we'd better get to bed.)

The first thing guests see upon arrival is a huge red heart on the front door with "Enter with Christmas in Your Heart" printed in bold letters across the front. Inside, Mother's Christmas decorations are almost staggering: poinsettias everywhere; wreaths with big ribbons on every door; a mantel graced with various figurines and handmade stockings for everyone (including dogs and cats); candles in all the windows; and, in addition to the large spruce positioned on a handsome tree skirt and draped with tiny take-home gifts, the same small, lighted, ceramic Christmas tree on the buffet table that she used when I was a child. In typical Southern fashion, the gents come dressed in colorful jackets and neckties and the ladies in elegant embroided and sequined sweaters, and on the CD player is continuous Christmas music.

All the fun begins in the den around Mother's elaborately decorated punch bowl full of potent bourbon wassail, after which guests take bamboo trays set with lace linen place mats and fine silver, make a first round of the buffet, and eat at small tables in the living room. Of course, the highlight of this feast is the aged country ham that Mother travels many miles to procure in the mountains of North Carolina, a noble joint that is cut just so to display a frilly bone and decorated with tiny ceramic pigs. And how do these Rebels eat their country ham? Between split buttermilk biscuits, of course.

Then, to top off the celebration, every guest leaves with one of Mother's homemade food gifts: a jar of preserves, a box of cookies, delicate candies, a miniature fruitcake—tendered with "Just in case you have a sweet-tooth attack while getting ready for Santa."

Martha Pearl Advises

At formal buffets, after dessert I place a large electric coffee urn on the table flanked by bottles of after-dinner liqueurs and bowls of whipped cream, sugar crystals, candied ginger, orange, and lemon peels, bittersweet chocolate bits, and other flavorings for coffee.

Menu

Bourbon Wassail

Toasted Orange Pecans

Jezebel

Country Ham Braised in Cider and Molasses

Party Potatoes Beverly

Winter Squash Casserole

Holiday Seven-Layer Salad

Glazed Cranberry and Apple Tart

Missy's Buttermilk Biscuits

Bourbon Wassail

4 cups apple cider
4 cups pineapple juice
1 cup orange juice
1 cup apricot nectar (available in cans or jars)
2 cinnamon sticks
2 teaspoons whole cloves
1 whole nutmeg
Bourbon to taste

In a large, nonreactive pot, combine the cider and juices and stir. Tie the spices up in cheese-cloth, add to the juices, and heat to moderate. Reduce the heat to low and simmer for 30 minutes. Remove and discard the spices, add the bourbon as you wish, stir well, and serve the wassail warm from a punch bowl in punch cups.

ABOUT 2 ½ QUARTS

Toasted Orange Pecans

I don't think anything excites Mother more than the arrival every fall of the 25-pound case of fresh pecans she orders from Atwell Pecan Company in Wrens, Georgia, some of which she holds back from all her holiday baking to be simply toasted and served with cocktails. Regular salted pecans toasted till just golden brown are a real treat in themselves, but this variation she came up with a few years ago for our Christmas Eve feast is truly exceptional.

⅔ cup butter
3 tablespoons orange-flavored liqueur (like Cointreau or Grand Marnier)
1 tablespoon finely grated orange rind
4 cups (about 1½ pounds) pecan halves
1 tablespoon salt

Preheat the oven to 300°F.

In a large saucepan, melt the butter over moderate heat, add the liqueur and orange rind, and stir till well blended. Remove the pan from the heat, add the pecans, and toss to coat well. Spread the nuts evenly on a large baking sheet and toast in the oven, uncovered, till golden brown, about 30 minutes, tossing the nuts from time to time. Drain on paper towels, sprinkle the salt on top, let cool completely, and serve with cocktails. (The pecans keep in a tightly covered container up to 2 weeks.)

4 CUPS PECANS

Jezebel

Named after the evil biblical temptress, Jezebel is a fiery, unique sauce spooned over cream cheese that has as many variations in Southern households as does pimento cheese. This particular version Mother got from my sister, Hootie, and be warned that it can make your hair stand on end—which is the way Southerners like it. Jezebel is always served with crackers and eaten with cocktails or punch.

One 18-ounce jar pineapple preserves (or, if necessary, peach preserves)
One 10-ounce jar apple jelly
¼ cup cider vinegar
2 tablespoons prepared horseradish
1 tablespoon cracked black peppercorns
1 teaspoon dry mustard
⅛ teaspoon salt
Two 8-ounce packages cream cheese

In a large mixing bowl, combine the preserves, jelly, and vinegar and stir till well blended. Add the horseradish, peppercorns, mustard, and salt and stir till well blended. Chill the spread at least 2 hours, then spoon it over the cream cheese on two crystal serving plates or trays and serve with assorted crackers.

ABOUT 3 ½ CUPS

Country Ham Braised in Cider and Molasses

For as long as I can remember, we've driven up to Glendale Springs in the mountains of North Carolina twice a year just to procure one or two of Clayton Long's cured, well-aged, inimitable country hams, one of which is usually reserved for Mother's special Christmas Eve buffet. This is the one and only time she would ever dream of soaking a ham, a concession she makes to those few guests who might object to the saltiness. Good home-cured country hams are available in most areas of the nation if you only ask around and keep your eyes and ears open, but if you have no luck, a Smithfield is an acceptable substitute for this preparation. To fully dramatize the joint, be sure to trim off enough meat to expose the bone and wrap it with paper frills.

One 12- to 13-pound cured country ham (or Smithfield ham)
1 cup molasses
1 cup firmly packed light brown sugar
1 gallon apple cider
3 medium-size onions, chopped
3 medium-size carrots, scraped and chopped
2 cups dry bread crumbs mixed with 2 cups firmly packed light brown sugar

Scrub the ham well with a stiff kitchen brush under running water, then position it in a large, deep, oval pan. Add cool water to cover and let the ham soak for 12 hours at room temperature, changing the water twice.

Remove the ham from the pan, rinse the pan well, return the ham to the pan, and add enough water to come halfway up the sides. Add the molasses and brown sugar to the water, stir as well as possible, then add enough cider to just cover the ham. Add the onions and carrots and bring the liquid to a very low simmer. Cover partially and simmer slowly for 3 hours. Let the ham cool completely in the liquid.

Preheat the oven to 425°F.

Place the ham on a work surface, remove the skin and all but ¼ inch of the fat, and score the fat in diamonds with a sharp paring knife. Rinse the roasting pan well after discarding the contents, then place the ham in the pan on a rack fat side up and coat with the bread crumb and brown sugar mixture, pressing down with your fingers. Bake, uncovered, till the crumbs are browned, about 20 minutes.

To serve, position the ham on a large, heavy, wooden or ceramic platter and carve into thin slices with an electric or serrated knife.

AT LEAST 8 SERVINGS,
WITH PLENTY OF LEFTOVERS

Party Potatoes Beverly

One Christmas Eve, Mother's neighbor Beverly Dellinger showed up with a casserole of these unusual potatoes, the recipe for which Mother jotted down the second dinner was over, with the exclamation that "they're one of the best things I ever put in my mouth." Ever since, the potatoes have become a staple on the menu, and while they do require a little effort to make, guests always finish every last morsel. (In my house, I personally like to make potato pancakes with any leftovers. Delicious!)

8 large russet potatoes
One 8-ounce package cream cheese, at room temperature
One 16-ounce carton sour cream
¼ cup (½ stick) plus 2 tablespoons butter, softened and cut into pieces
⅓ cup chopped fresh chives
1 large garlic clove, minced
Salt and black pepper to taste
Mild paprika to taste

continued

Grease a large casserole or baking dish and set aside.

Peel the potatoes, then cut them into cubes and place in a large pot with enough water to cover them. Bring to a boil, reduce the heat to moderate, cover, and cook till the potatoes are very tender, about 20 minutes. Drain in a large colander.

Preheat the oven to 350°F.

In a large mixing bowl, beat together the cream cheese and sour cream with an electric mixer till well blended, then add the drained potatoes and beat till the mixture is smooth. Add ¼ cup of the butter, the chives, and the garlic. Season with salt and pepper and beat till well blended and smooth. Scrape the mixture into the prepared casserole, dot the top with the remaining 2 tablespoons butter, sprinkle paprika over the top, and bake till crusty, about 25 minutes.

8 SERVINGS

Winter Squash Casserole

This squash casserole is a delectable takeoff on Mother's signature yellow crookneck squash soufflé, the main difference being the spices and brown sugar used instead of Parmesan to counteract the blandness of the winter squash. Since the unbaked casserole freezes beautifully, Mother often makes two and freezes one for future use.

2 large acorn or butternut squashes
½ cup (1 stick) butter, cut into pieces
2 large eggs, beaten
½ teaspoon ground cinnamon
½ teaspoon ground nutmeg
¼ cup half-and-half
1 cup firmly packed light brown sugar
Salt and black pepper to taste
¾ cup chopped brazil nuts

Preheat the oven to 350°F. Grease a large casserole or baking dish and set aside.

Bake the whole squashes on a large heavy baking sheet till they are tender when stuck with a fork, 1½ to 2 hours. When cool enough to handle, out the squashes into quarters, remove the seeds and skins, place the flesh in a large mixing bowl, and mash well with a potato masher or heavy fork. Add the butter, eggs, cinnamon, and nutmeg, beat the mixture with an electric mixer till well blended and smooth, and scrape into the prepared casserole.

Increase the oven temperature to 375°F.

In a small mixing bowl, combine the half-and-half, brown sugar, salt and pepper, and nuts, stir till well blended, pour over the squash mixture, and bake till golden brown, about 45 minutes.

8 SERVINGS

Martha Pearl Advises

I use ceramic electric heating trays on buffets to keep casseroles hot. They're a good investment and actually not that expensive.

Holiday Seven-Layer Salad

"Martha Pearl," announced her friend Gerry Pizzo, a Chicago transplant, a few years ago, "if you don't let me bring something for the buffet, we're just not coming." Gerry then showed up with a dramatic glass punch bowl *full of this complex salad that everybody ended up raving about. Curiously, Gerry mixes her salad to meld in the refrigerator at least 8 hours before serving, whereas Mother feels the salad doesn't suffer in the least by not being mixed till guests have had the chance to see the colorful layers. Mother also often includes a drained 8-ounce can of water chestnuts to give the salad even more dimension. Both ladies use only Hellmann's mayonnaise for this salad.*

1 large head romaine lettuce, leaves torn into bite-size pieces
3 celery ribs, coarsely chopped
1 red onion, finely chopped
1 1/2 cups frozen peas, thawed
8 ounces sharp cheddar cheese, shredded
6 slices lean bacon, fried crisp and crumbled
5 large hard-boiled eggs, peeled and coarsely chopped
3 tablespoons sugar
Salt and black pepper to taste
1 1/2 cups mayonnaise (Mother prefers Hellmann's)

In a medium-size glass punch bowl, layer separately the first seven ingredients, cover with plastic wrap, and chill overnight. When ready to serve, place the bowl on the table to show the colorful layers, then add the sugar, salt and pepper, and mayonnaise and toss till the ingredients are well blended and coated with mayonnaise.

8 SERVINGS

Glazed Cranberry and Apple Tart

This is one of Mother's classic Christmas tarts, but for more textural contrast, she sometimes tops the apple puree with about ½ cup of slivered almonds before adding the cranberries.

5 medium-size Rome or other tart apples
¼ cup (½ stick) butter
Ground cinnamon to taste
¼ cup half-and-half
1 cup plus 1 tablespoon water
1½ cups sugar
One 12-ounce package fresh cranberries, picked over and rinsed
2 drops red food coloring (see Martha Pearl Advises, page 128)
1 chilled 10-inch Basic Tart Shell (page 23)
½ cup currant jelly

Peel and core the apples and chop them coarsely. In a medium-size skillet, heat 3 tablespoons of the butter over low heat, then add the apples and cinnamon, stir well, cover, and cook for 5 minutes. Uncover, add the half-and-half, increase the heat to moderate, and continue cooking the apples for 10 minutes, mashing with a fork to a rough puree. Remove from the heat and let cool.

In a medium-size saucepan, combine 1 cup of the water and 1 cup of the sugar and stir over moderate heat till the sugar has dissolved completely. Add the cranberries and food coloring, stir, and cook for 1 minute. Remove the pan from the heat and let cool. Drain the cranberries in a colander.

Preheat the oven to 375°F.

Spoon the apple puree evenly over the bottom of the chilled tart shell, then pour the cranberries over the puree and carefully spread them out into a single layer. Sprinkle the remaining ½ cup sugar over the cranberries, dot the top with the remaining 1 tablespoon butter, and bake till the crust is golden brown, about 40 minutes.

continued

In a small saucepan, combine the jelly and the remaining 1 tablespoon water, stir well over low heat till blended and smooth, and brush the glaze over the top of the tart. Let the tart cool to room temperature before serving.

ONE 10-INCH TART; 8 SERVINGS

Missy's Buttermilk Biscuits

"Missy" is what all of Mother's grandchildren and great-grandchildren call her, and when they come to visit, the first thing the older relatives ask her to make is a batch of these legendary biscuits. Just a reminder: for the lightest, fluffiest biscuits, do not handle the dough too much, and never knead it as with other breads. Also, watch the biscuits very carefully after 10 minutes to make sure the tops don't overbrown. These are the ultimate Southern biscuits.

2 cups all-purpose flour
4 teaspoons baking powder
$\frac{1}{2}$ teaspoon baking soda
$\frac{1}{2}$ teaspoon salt
$\frac{1}{4}$ cup Crisco vegetable shortening
1 cup buttermilk

Preheat the oven to 450°F.

Sift together the flour, baking powder, baking soda, and salt into a large mixing bowl. Add the shortening and cut it in with a pastry cutter or two knives till the mixture is well blended and mealy. Add the buttermilk and mix with a wooden spoon till the dough is soft, adding a little more buttermilk if necessary.

Turn the dough out onto a lightly floured work surface and, using a light touch, turn the edges of the dough toward the middle, pressing with your hands. Press the dough out to a $\frac{1}{4}$-inch thickness, then cut straight down into even rounds with a biscuit cutter or small juice glass and place the rounds ½-inch apart on a large, ungreased baking sheet. Gather up the scraps of dough and repeat the procedure until all the dough is used. Bake the biscuits just till lightly browned on top, about 12 minutes. Serve hot.

ABOUT 16 BISCUITS

Martha Pearl Advises

I'm not as Southern as a friend who literally makes biscuits three times a day for her family, but it's rare there's not a batch of fresh biscuits in my kitchen. The uses for biscuits are countless: split and toasted for breakfast, packed into lunch boxes and picnic baskets, turned into shortcakes and toppings for savory pies and sweet cobblers, served under hash or sausage gravy, and stuffed with ham for small cocktail appetizers. I don't understand how anybody could live without biscuits.

A Classic Southern
Christmas Breakfast

IF YOU THINK THAT AFTER HER CHRISTMAS EVE buffet extravaganza Mother wouldn't dream of entertaining again for at least twenty-four hours, you don't know the importance of Christmas breakfast or brunch in her holiday routine. When my father was alive and there was still a big family at home, the tradition was always to attend early eight o'clock church, after which Daddy would come home and go through the ritual of making milk punches in a special large glass shaker while Mother began the makings of a hearty Southern breakfast interrupted by the opening of presents around the Christmas tree (before the dog wreaked devastation). In those days, it was strictly a family affair—casual, intimate, low-key.

Now the breakfast has evolved mostly into a much more social sit-down brunch for new neighbors at which Mother pulls out all the stops with a white cutwork linen cloth, handmade Christmas runner, and elaborate poinsettia centerpiece on the large mahogany table. A silver coffee service is arranged on her highly ornate tea cart and, depending on the menu, out come the silver chafing dish and platters and baskets and finest flatware. Guests come dressed in their church best, a special table for children is set up in the living room, and to keep the little ones entertained, Mother initiates a "second Santa Claus" by refilling the stockings on the mantel with toys and other goodies.

Although every year the Christmas brunch menu changes, guests can always count on the staple that has almost become Mother's signature preparation, namely her homemade fruit preserves to be spread over some form of biscuit, and they can also look forward to receiving one of her small gift coffeecakes wrapped lovingly in red and green plastic and tied with a big bow.

Martha Pearl Advises

Since I've learned that children really prefer to eat just with one another, I usually set a separate table for them—especially for a major holiday meal. The kids are happier, and it's easier on the adults.

Menu

Milk Punches

Sausage-Apple Ring with Scrambled Eggs

Crusted Grits Soufflé

Citrus, Raisin, and Almond Compote

Biscuit Muffins

Peach and Strawberry Preserves

Chicory Coffee

Milk Punches

This is the exact formula my father always followed when he went through the ritual of making milk punches on Christmas morning, and it is the one we follow to this day. To prevent excess dilution, shake the punch just as quickly as possible, and don't overdo the nutmeg.

12 ounces bourbon
3 cups milk
5 teaspoons confectioners' sugar
5 drops pure vanilla extract
Cracked ice
Ground nutmeg to taste

In a tall cocktail shaker, combine all the ingredients except the nutmeg and shake till icy cold and frothy. Pour the punch into Old-Fashioned glasses and sprinkle each drink lightly with nutmeg.

8 S E R V I N G S

Sausage-Apple Ring with Scrambled Eggs

Having known for years the affinity between pork and apples, Mother came up not long ago with this clever, attractive, and delicious new way to serve eggs and our traditional country sausage on her Christmas brunch buffet. It can be a bit tricky transferring the sausage-and-apple mixture from the mold to the baking pan, so to assure that the ring holds its form, she suggests chilling it in the mold an hour or so before unmolding, if time permits.

2 pounds bulk sausage

1½ cups cracker crumbs

1 cup cored and finely chopped apples

½ cup milk

¼ cup minced onions

1 dozen large eggs

2 teaspoons ground sage

1 teaspoon red pepper flakes

2 tablespoons butter

¼ cup heavy cream

1 cup freshly grated Parmesan cheese

½ cup finely chopped fresh parsley leaves

Salt and black pepper to taste

Mild paprika to taste

Preheat the oven to 350°F. Grease a large ring mold and set aside.

In a large mixing bowl, combine the sausage meat, cracker crumbs, apples, milk, onions, 2 of the eggs, the sage, and the red pepper flakes and, using your hands, mix till very well blended. Press the mixture evenly into the prepared mold, then carefully invert the molded mixture into a shallow baking pan and bake for 1 hour. Tilt the pan and suck off any excess grease with a baster, then, using a spatula, transfer the mold to a large silver serving platter.

In a large skillet, heat the butter over low heat. In a large mixing bowl, whisk together the remaining 10 eggs and the heavy cream, add the cheese and parsley, season with salt and pepper, and pour the mixture into the skillet. Stirring with a fork, slowly scramble the eggs till set but still soft. Fill the sausage ring with the scrambled eggs and sprinkle paprika over the top.

AT LEAST 8 SERVINGS

Crusted Grits Soufflé

If there's a way to cook grits, my mother knows it—boiled and served with butter, fried in patties, baked with cheese and garlic in a casserole, incorporated into breads, sautéed in cakes topped with shrimp or oysters—but this crusty soufflé demonstrates the peak of her art. Do not try to use quick grits for this recipe.

3 cups water

1½ teaspoons salt

¾ cup regular hominy grits

¾ cup (1½ sticks) butter, softened and cut into pieces

1 tablespoon bacon grease

2 teaspoons Worcestershire sauce

Black pepper to taste

6 large eggs, beaten

½ cup dry bread crumbs

¼ cup (½ stick) butter, melted

Grease a medium-size casserole or baking dish and set aside.

In a large, heavy saucepan, combine the water and salt, bring to a rapid boil, and add the grits gradually enough so that the boiling continues at a brisk rate, stirring constantly. Cover the pan, reduce the heat to low, and simmer for 15 minutes, stirring occasionally.

Preheat the oven to 350°F.

Remove the saucepan from the heat, add the softened butter, bacon grease, and Worcestershire, season with pepper, and stir till well blended and the butter has melted. Add the beaten eggs, stir till well blended and smooth, and scrape the mixture into the prepared casserole. Sprinkle the bread crumbs over the top, drizzle the melted butter evenly over the bread crumbs, and bake till the soufflé is puffy and the top golden brown, about 45 minutes. Serve hot.

8 SERVINGS

Citrus, Raisin, and Almond Compote

4 large grapefruits (preferably pink)

1 cup seedless golden raisins

1 cup sliced almonds, toasted (see Martha Pearl Advises, page 119)

2 tablespoons sugar

2 tablespoons orange-flavored liqueur (like Cointreau or Grand Marnier)

8 small fresh parsley sprigs

Cut the grapefruits in half, carefully loosen each section with a citrus or serrated paring knife, and place the sections in a large serving bowl. Pull the membranes and any white pith off the sections and discard.

Add the raisins, almonds, sugar, and liqueur to the grapefruit sections and mix till well blended. Cover the compote with plastic wrap and chill about 2 hours before serving, garnished with the parsley.

8 SERVINGS

Biscuit Muffins

Once a staple in many Southern households, biscuit muffins have, for some reason (perhaps because of the lengthy baking required), become as rare as authentic rice bread. Which is sad, since these slightly sweet muffins are so ideal for special events like Mother's Christmas brunch—especially when spread with homemade or top-quality commercial fruit preserves. "My mama used to bake these 'biscuit' in cast-iron muffin molds," Mother remembers, "and Lord, were they out of this world." Given the improbability of finding such molds today, Mother does urge you to use as heavy-gauge muffin tins as possible.

2$\frac{1}{2}$ cups bleached all-purpose flour
1 teaspoon salt
3 tablespoons sugar
1$\frac{1}{2}$ teaspoons baking powder
$\frac{1}{4}$ teaspoon baking soda
10 tablespoons (1$\frac{1}{4}$ sticks) butter, cut into small pieces
1 cup buttermilk

Preheat the oven to 350°F.

Sift together the flour, salt, sugar, baking powder, and baking soda into a large mixing bowl. Add the butter and work it into the dry ingredients with your fingers till the mixture resembles coarse meal. Add the buttermilk and stir with a large wooden spoon till just blended (do not overstir). Spoon the mixture into a muffin tin with 12 cups (each about $\frac{1}{3}$-cup capacity) and bake till golden brown and crusty, 40 to 45 minutes. Serve hot.

12 BISCUIT MUFFINS

A Yuletide Sandwich Tea

OF ALL THE ENTERTAINING THAT MOTHER DOES
throughout the year, I don't think she enjoys any occasion more than the elegant
afternoon sandwich tea she sponsors for ten to twelve lady friends during the
week before Christmas. "Lord, what fun we have," she exclaims. "It's just a short
break from all the busy shopping and gift wrapping and decorating, but in a
couple of hours we catch up on which in-laws are coming for the holidays,
what's happening at the church and in the Charity League, and, to be sure, who's
cooking what and for whom."

Technically, everything is set up both on the enclosed sunporch and in
the dining room: a tea table decorated with tiny Christmas trees and sleighs
and reindeer; a tea cart laden with delicate holiday cups and saucers; and a
dining room table covered with a green net cloth and boasting a stunning
floral arrangement with candles, small china plates with a holly design, and
at least six different finger sandwiches and other special treats Mother might
come up with.

Over the years, I've had the opportunity to glimpse a couple of these
teas and, with all the ladies in their tailored suits and gloves and furs and high-
heel shoes, I can only describe what I've witnessed as a scene straight out of
Eudora Welty or William Faulkner. It's the Old South in all its dignity and

refined glory, to be sure, the only modern touch being Mother's innovative sandwiches and delicacies and her continuous cajoling that the food "has no calories."

Menu

Sugar and Spice Tea

Shrimp and Watercress Paste Rolled Sandwiches

Minced Country Ham Biscuits

Fruity Cream Cheese Sandwiches

Ground Chicken and Almond Sandwiches

Bacon-Stuffed Mushrooms

Grasshopper Squares

Sugar and Spice Tea

"When I was a young lady," Mother relates, "everybody in the South called this 'Russian Tea,' for what reason I have no idea except that it's pretty exotic." The name may have changed over the decades, but sugar and spice tea is still an almost obligatory beverage at bridge parties, social drop-ins, and this sort of sandwich tea that Mother loves to serve "the girls" at Christmastime—always, of course, from a silver teapot and in delicate, small, porcelain cups.

5 tablespoons tea leaves
8 cups boiling water
2 cups sugar
8 cups cold water
2 teaspoons whole cloves
2 sticks cinnamon
Juice of 1 lemon
Juice of 6 oranges

Place the tea leaves in a large bowl, pour the boiling water over the top, let steep for 5 minutes, and strain the tea through a fine-mesh strainer into a large saucepan. In another saucepan, combine the sugar, cold water, cloves, and cinnamon, bring to a boil over moderate heat, reduce the heat to low, and simmer for 5 minutes. Strain the spiced water into the tea, add the lemon and orange juices, stir well, and pour the tea into a silver teapot.

Serve in small teacups.

18 TO 20 CUPS TEA

Martha Pearl Advises

The easiest way to make iced (and hot) tea is in an ordinary drip coffeemaker. Place the tea bags in the bottom of the empty pot, let the hot water drip over the bags, and allow to stand till the desired strength is attained.

Shrimp and Watercress Paste Rolled Sandwiches

Rolled sandwiches have always been a Southern specialty at fancy teas, and Mother learned the art during her twenties from a famous caterer in Charlotte by the name of Mrs. Pressley ("the sandwich queen," as she was called by those who used her services and tried to collect her recipes). The trick here is to become so adept at rolling the sandwiches that the toothpicks can be removed before serving. Mother also makes the sandwiches with pimento cheese, curried ground ham and herbs, and smooth olive and anchovy spreads.

1½ pounds fresh shrimp
1 small bunch watercress, stems removed and leaves rinsed well
2 tablespoons fresh lemon juice
1 tablespoon dry sherry
¼ teaspoon dry mustard
⅛ teaspoon ground mace
½ cup (1 stick) butter, softened
Salt and black pepper to taste
10 to 12 slices soft, white loaf bread, crusts trimmed

Place the shrimp in a large saucepan with enough water to cover, bring to a boil, remove from the heat, and let stand for 1 minute. Drain the shrimp and, when cool enough to handle, peel, devein, and cut in half.

In a blender or food processor, combine the cooked shrimp, the watercress, lemon juice, sherry, mustard, and mace and process till the shrimp are finely chopped. Transfer the mixture to a large mixing bowl, add the butter, season with salt and pepper, and stir till the paste is well blended and smooth.

Using a rolling pin, slightly flatten the bread slices, spread each slice with a thin layer of shrimp paste, roll up each slice as tightly as possible, and secure the sandwiches with toothpicks. Store the sandwiches in an airtight container till ready to serve. (If the sandwiches hold together by themselves, remove the toothpicks before serving.)

10 TO 12 ROLLED SANDWICHES

Martha Pearl Advises

To facilitate making rolled sandwiches, the ingredients should be ground or finely chopped. Another trick is to roll the bread with a rolling pin just enough to flatten it slightly.

Minced Country Ham Biscuits

Others might toss out the scraps of a country ham, but not Mother, who saves and freezes hers, not only to be used as cooking meat for vegetables, but also to be ground and seasoned for these delightful ham biscuits. "So much more delicate for a tea than just pieces of meat stuck between biscuit halves," she comments. If you don't have any cured country ham, regular smoked ham is acceptable.

FOR THE BISCUITS

2 cups all-purpose flour

4 teaspoons baking powder

$\frac{1}{2}$ teaspoon salt

$\frac{1}{4}$ cup Crisco vegetable shortening

1 cup milk

FOR THE SPREAD

$1\frac{1}{2}$ cups finely chopped cured country ham

3 tablespoons bourbon

2 teaspoons dry mustard

Cayenne pepper to taste

$\frac{1}{2}$ cup (1 stick) butter, softened

Preheat the oven to 450°F.

To make the biscuits, sift together the flour, baking powder, and salt into a large mixing bowl. Add the shortening and cut it with a pastry cutter or two knives till the mixture resembles coarse meal. Add the milk gradually and mix with a wooden spoon just till the dough is soft, adding a little more milk if necessary. Transfer the dough to a lightly floured work surface and, using a light touch, turn the edges toward the middle, pressing with your hands. Press the dough out to a $\frac{1}{4}$-inch thickness, then cut straight down into even small rounds with a $1\frac{1}{4}$-inch biscuit cutter and place the rounds no more than $\frac{1}{2}$ inch apart on a large, ungreased baking sheet. Bake the biscuits till lightly browned on top, about 12 minutes, and let cool.

To make the spread, combine the ham, bourbon, mustard, and cayenne in a blender or food processor, process till the ham is finely chopped, and scrape into a small mixing bowl. Combine the butter and half the ham mixture in the blender or processor, blend till smooth, scrape the butter mixture back into the ham mixture, and stir till well blended.

Break the biscuits in half and fill each with spread.

AT LEAST 30 SMALL BISCUITS

Fruity Cream Cheese Sandwiches

Without question, these are some of Mother's most unusual finger sandwiches, especially when made with her homemade date-nut bread. "In the old days, we could buy pretty good date-nut bread in cans," she informs, "but now I make my own since I'm not crazy about what you find in bakeries—if they bake the bread at all." This spread is delicious, but you can also combine whole cranberry sauce or chopped dried apricots with the cream cheese, with tasty results.

One and a half 8-ounce packages cream cheese, softened
1 large ripe banana, peeled
One 8-ounce can crushed pineapple, drained
¾ cup seedless golden raisins, finely chopped
¾ cup chopped toasted nuts (pecans, almonds, or walnuts) (see Martha Pearl Advises, page 119)
16 thin slices date-nut bread (recipe follows) or raisin bread, crusts trimmed

In a large mixing bowl, combine all the ingredients but the bread and mix till well blended and smooth. Spread the mixture over 8 of the bread slices, top with the remaining slices, and cut into small finger sandwiches. To keep the sandwiches soft, store in an airtight plastic container till ready to serve.

24 FINGER SANDWICHES

Date-Nut Bread

1 cup coarsely chopped pitted dates (see Martha Pearl Advises, page 45)
1 cup boiling water
½ cup sugar
1 teaspoon baking soda
1 tablespoon butter, melted
1 large egg, beaten
1½ cups all-purpose flour, sifted

½ cup coarsely chopped pecans

½ teaspoon pure vanilla extract

Place the dates in a bowl, pour the boiling water over them, cover, and let stand at least 6 hours.

Preheat the oven to 325°F. Grease and flour a large loaf pan, tapping out any excess, and set aside.

Transfer the dates and soaking water to a large mixing bowl, add the sugar, baking soda, butter, and egg, and stir till well blended. Gradually add the flour, stirring with a wooden spoon till the mixture is smooth. Add the pecans and vanilla and stir till well blended, then scrape the batter into the prepared pan and bake till the loaf pulls away from the sides of the pan, about 1 hour. Let the loaf cool on a wire rack for 10 minutes, then turn out to cool completely. Wrap the loaf tightly in plastic wrap and store overnight before slicing.

1 LOAF

Martha Pearl Advises

I use lots of cream cheese for sandwiches, salad bases, cakes, and icings since it has a firmer consistency than mayonnaise, butter, or whipping cream.

Ground Chicken and Almond Sandwiches

So fastidious is Mother about these delicate tea sandwiches that she not only insists on cooking the chicken from scratch but runs it through a meat grinder to attain just the right spreading consistency. At first I thought it was all a lot of wasted effort, but after I tasted one of the sandwiches (which are utterly addictive), I got the point.

One 3½-pound chicken, cut up
Small bunch celery leaves
Salt to taste
1 cup minced celery
½ cup finely chopped toasted almonds (see Martha Pearl Advises, page 119)
2 tablespoons minced fresh parsley leaves
2 large hard-boiled eggs, shelled and finely chopped
Black pepper to taste
¾ cup mayonnaise (Mother prefers Hellmann's)
1 teaspoon fresh lemon juice
20 to 24 slices white loaf bread
Fresh parsley sprigs for garnish

Place the chicken and celery leaves in a large pot with enough salted water to cover, bring to a boil, reduce the heat to moderate, cover, and simmer about 1 hour. With a slotted spoon, transfer the chicken to a plate and, when cool enough to handle, remove and discard the skin, clean the meat from the bones, and cut into chunks. Chill the chicken for 1 hour, covered.

Pass the chicken through the medium blade of a meat grinder into a large mixing bowl, add all the remaining ingredients but the bread and parsley sprigs, and mix till the salad is well blended and smooth.

Using a pastry cutter, cut a 2½- to 3-inch round out of each slice of bread (save leftover bread to make bread crumbs). Spread salad over half the rounds, top with the remaining rounds, and stick a parsley sprig into the top of each sandwich when ready to serve. (To keep the sandwiches soft, store in an airtight plastic container till ready to serve.)

20 TO 24 MINIATURE SANDWICHES

To toast most nuts like pecans, almonds, and hazelnuts, preheat the oven to 300°F, spread the nuts across a baking sheet, and bake till slightly browned, about 10 minutes, stirring several times and watching them closely. To toast walnuts, bake about 12 minutes. To toast benne (sesame) seeds, stir them in a dry, cast-iron skillet over moderate heat for about 3 minutes.

⟨⬤Bacon-Stuffed Mushrooms

Mother calls these her "winter" stuffed mushrooms; in the warmer months, she might stuff them with well-picked-over fresh lump crabmeat or chopped cooked shrimp mixed with a little mayonnaise and serve them hot or cold.

30 medium-size fresh mushrooms
8 strips lean bacon
1 tablespoon butter
3 green onions (whites and part of green tops included), minced
1 cup sour cream
¼ teaspoon Worcestershire sauce
¼ teaspoon salt
Black pepper to taste

Rinse and dry the mushrooms, remove the stems and chop them finely, and arrange the caps in a shallow baking dish.

In a large skillet, fry the bacon over moderate heat till crisp, drain on paper towels, and crumble finely. Pour all but 1 tablespoon of grease from the skillet, add the butter, and let melt. Add the chopped mushroom stems and onions, cook over low heat for 5 minutes, stirring, and transfer to a small mixing bowl. Add the sour cream, Worcestershire, salt, and pepper and mix till well blended.

Preheat the oven to 350°F.

Spoon equal amounts of the mixture into the mushroom caps and bake till the tops are golden, about 20 minutes. Serve the mushrooms with heavy toothpicks.

30 STUFFED MUSHROOMS; 10 TO 12 SERVINGS

Grasshopper Squares

Mother originally got this basic recipe from a friend who made her "Cointreau Squares" with orange liqueur. "Then I began thinking," she says, "since chocolate has as much affinity with mint as with orange, why not substitute crème de menthe for a nice change?"

1¼ cups (2½ sticks) butter
½ cup unsweetened cocoa powder
3½ cups sifted confectioners' sugar
1 large egg, beaten
1 teaspoon pure vanilla extract
2 cups fine graham cracker crumbs
⅓ cup green crème de menthe liqueur
1½ cups semisweet chocolate chips

For the first layer, combine ½ cup (1 stick) of the butter and the cocoa in a small saucepan and stir over low heat till the butter is melted. Remove the pan from the heat, add ½ cup of the confectioners' sugar, the egg, vanilla, and cracker crumbs, and stir till well blended. Press the mixture onto the bottom of a large baking pan and set aside. Wipe out the saucepan.

For the second layer, heat another ½ cup (1 stick) of the butter in the saucepan till melted, pour into a small mixing bowl, add the crème de menthe, and, using an electric mixer, gradually beat in the remaining 3 cups confectioners' sugar till the mixture is smooth. Spread the mixture evenly over the bottom layer in the baking pan, fit a piece of waxed paper over the top, and chill for 1 hour. Wipe out the saucepan.

For the top layer, combine the remaining ¼ cup (½ stick) butter and the chocolate chips in the saucepan and stir over low heat till melted and well blended. Remove the waxed paper and spread the chocolate mixture over the second layer. Chill the confection for 2 hours, then cut into small squares. (Store unused squares in a tightly covered container in the refrigerator.)

ABOUT 8 DOZEN SQUARES

A Tots' Jingle Bell Party

I CAN STILL SEE THE SCENE AS IF IT WERE yesterday: red and green crepe paper streamers hanging from light fixtures; a big, wooden, red-nosed reindeer filled with small gifts on the fireplace; Mother's handmade snow families, miniature Christmas tree with gift ornaments, and stuffed Santa Claus; all sorts of hidden toys that had to be searched for around the house; and, to be sure, more sinfully sweet goodies than any child has the right to eat. I and my childhood friends couldn't have been more than six or eight years old, but the memory of Mother's jingle bell parties remains indelible.

I've always said that my mother has somehow retained basically the soul of a child, explanation enough of why, even at her advanced age, she continues to be so youthful and is able to communicate so easily with tots. And nothing illustrates this trait more than the one-hour party she sponsors every Christmas for the kids of relatives and neighbors. "It's really my favorite Christmas party," she confesses. "I guess I just still like to pretend that I'm one of Santa's helpers—and I do think this type of entertaining helps to teach children how to interact and behave in social circumstances."

Foodwise, Mother makes no pretense about her fancies being necessarily healthy and nutritious, the main idea being that the kids simply be served a few treats they really love to eat and have lots of fun. They come dressed in nice suits and Christmas dresses. They eat off colorful paper plates and drink from paper cups. They play games and use coloring books. And they receive special gift bags filled with food goodies. "I don't fix a morsel for the mothers," declares Martha Pearl. "This Christmas party is strictly for the children—their own holiday moment. And who knows: perhaps all the fanciful food will get them into the kitchen with their mothers to eventually learn to cook more serious dishes."

And how do these capricious edibles taste to an adult? Not bad. Not bad at all.

Menu

Chicken Sour Cream Muffin Sandwiches

Ham-and-Cheese Pizza

"Champagne" Fruities

Santa Claus Popcorn Balls

Surprise Candy Kisses

M&M's Holiday Wreaths

Chicken Sour Cream Muffin Sandwiches

Mother's idea behind these muffins was to produce a small sandwich that is softer than a traditional biscuit and has no sugar. "Of course, the kids love all my sweet treats most, but I also want them to see how good savory foods can be at this sort of party."

¼ cup (½ stick) butter, softened
¾ cup sour cream
1¼ cups all-purpose flour, sifted
2 teaspoons baking powder
1 teaspoon salt
Mayonnaise (Mother prefers Hellmann's) or softened butter
24 thin slices cooked chicken breast

Preheat the oven to 350°F.

In a large mixing bowl, beat together the butter and sour cream with an electric mixer till smooth. In a small mixing bowl, combine the flour, baking powder, and salt, stir well, add the dry ingredients to the butter mixture, and stir till well blended and smooth. Spoon equal amounts of the batter into two 12-cup miniature, ungreased muffin tins till half full and bake till golden brown, about 20 minutes. Let the muffins cool.

Slice the muffins in half, spread each half with mayonnaise or softened butter, sandwich the chicken slices between the halves, and serve.

24 MINIATURE MUFFIN SANDWICHES

Ham-and-Cheese Pizza

We know that this pizza is better with a good homemade tomato sauce, but, as Mother has discovered, "much as children love pizza, some just will not eat it when there's sauce." She also does a ground beef and cheese topping, and if it's a small party, she might make individual pizzas by placing a large coffee mug over the rolled-out dough and cutting around it.

1 envelope active dry yeast

1 cup warm water

1 tablespoon olive oil

1 teaspoon salt

2½ cups all-purpose flour

Cornmeal

3 to 3½ cups grated mozzarella cheese, to your taste

½ pound baked ham, chopped

In a large mixing bowl, sprinkle the yeast over the warm water and let proof for 10 minutes. Add the olive oil and salt and stir. Gradually add the flour, stirring with a wooden spoon till the dough is firm. Transfer the dough to a lightly floured work surface and knead till elastic, about 5 minutes, adding a little more flour if the dough becomes too sticky. Gather the dough into a ball, place in a lightly oiled bowl, cover with plastic wrap, and let rise in a warm area till doubled in bulk, about 1 hour. Divide the dough into equal parts, form each into a ball, and cover with a clean kitchen towel till ready to use.

Preheat the oven to 500°F. Oil two 12-inch pizza pans, sprinkle each lightly with cornmeal, and set aside.

Place a ball of dough on a lightly floured work surface, roll it out with a floured rolling pin to form a 12-inch circle, and press the dough onto one of the prepared pans, not quite up to the edges. Repeat with the second ball of dough and second prepared pan. Distribute the cheese and ham evenly over the tops and bake separately till the crusts are browned, about 20 minutes.

To serve, cut the pizzas into small enough slices to be eaten with small fingers.

TWO 12-INCH PIZZAS; AT LEAST
16 SMALL SLICES

"Champagne" Fruities

3 cups fresh orange juice, chilled

3 cups grape juice, chilled

3 cups ginger ale

2 oranges, peeled clean, thinly sliced, seeded, and cut into quarters

In a large pitcher, combine the two juices and ginger ale and stir. Position a solid chunk of ice in a medium-size crystal punch bowl, pour the punch over the ice, and float the orange pieces on the top. Serve the fruities in punch cups and garnish each with an orange quarter slice.

9 CUPS

Santa Claus Popcorn Balls

Always interested in even the most childish forms of cooking, Mother was fascinated by a big bowl of red and green balls she noticed at a Sunday school party she once attended at the church, only to be told by the kitchen manager that they were just colored popcorn. Perceiving such a notion as ideal for her Jingle Bell Party, she learned about the technique of using dry Jell-O instead of liquid food coloring to keep the balls as firm as possible. And do the kids love this stuff!

¾ cup (1½ sticks) butter

3 cups miniature marshmallows

2 tablespoons dry cherry-flavored Jell-O

2 tablespoons dry lime-flavored Jell-O

12 cups popped popcorn, unsalted

In a medium-size saucepan, melt the butter over low heat, gradually add the marshmallows, and stir steadily till all have melted. Remove from the heat and pour half the mixture into a small saucepan. Stir the cherry Jell-O into one mixture and the lime Jell-O into the other till well blended.

In a large mixing bowl, combine 6 cups of the popcorn with the red mixture and stir to coat; in another large bowl, repeat with the remaining 6 cups popcorn and the green mixture. Divide each colored popcorn into 6 portions and, with well-buttered hands, form each portion into a ball. Allow the balls to dry for several hours, then wrap each in red and green plastic wrap.

12 POPCORN BALLS

Surprise Candy Kisses

Ingenuity is the only word I can come up with to describe the way Mother created these chocolate goodies that children (and yes, some adults) eat with abandon. Notice that you do not brown these kisses, just bake them till the pastry is firm and dry.

1 cup (2 sticks) butter, softened
½ cup sugar
1 teaspoon pure vanilla extract
2 cups all-purpose flour
One 9-ounce package Hershey Chocolate Kisses

In a large mixing bowl, cream together the butter, sugar, and vanilla with an electric mixer, then gradually add the flour, beating steadily. Form the dough into a ball, cover tightly in plastic wrap, and chill overnight.

Preheat the oven to 375°F.

Peel and discard the foil from the kisses and place them in a bowl. Flatten about 1 tablespoon of the chilled dough in the palm of your hand, place a kiss in the center, wrap the dough completely around the kiss, and place on a large, ungreased baking sheet. Repeat with the remaining dough and kisses. Bake till the pastry is just dry and set, not browned, 10 to 15 minutes. Let cool, then store in airtight containers till ready to serve.

3 ½ DOZEN KISSES

M&M's Holiday Wreaths

With children, the eyes must be entertained as much as the mouths, so one of Mother's methods is to tie ribbons through these clever wreaths and hang them on a miniature, artificial Christmas tree she sets up for the youngsters. Be sure to wear rubber gloves when forming the wreaths, and be sure to let the wreaths dry thoroughly overnight before handling them.

1 cup (2 sticks) butter
60 large marshmallows
One 1-ounce bottle green food coloring
6 cups Rice Krispies cereal
1 small package plain M&M's candies

In a large saucepan, melt the butter over low heat, then gradually add the marshmallows, stir steadily till all have melted, and remove from the heat. Gradually stir in the food coloring till well blended and gradually add the Rice Krispies, stirring well.

Butter your hands well, then shape small pieces of the mixture into wreaths, place the wreaths on waxed paper, and decorate each with M&M's. Let the wreaths sit for 24 hours to dry thoroughly, then store between layers of waxed paper in airtight containers till ready to serve.

5 TO 6 DOZEN WREATHS

Martha Pearl Advises

When dealing with food coloring, always wear rubber gloves and spread a large piece of waxed paper across the working surface.

A New Year's Good Luck Supper

MOTHER IS AND ALWAYS HAS BEEN ONE OF THE most patently superstitious Southerners I know (she would *never*, for example, bow out of an undesirable invitation with the excuse of being sick), and for her just the idea of allowing New Year's to come and go without eating some form of good-luck pork, black-eyed peas, and cornbread with close friends is utterly unthinkable. "My supper is almost identical to the ones my mother and grandmother fixed on New Year's when I was growing up," she tells, "and I wouldn't dream of ever changing a single dish except the dessert." Bad luck, you know.

Although the sit-down supper is pretty informal, Mother decorates the table with an attractive red cotton tablecloth, leaf-shaped green plates, and, nestled in a low flower arrangement, her antique china cupid doll with "Happy New Year" painted across the front. At each place is a small nameplate wooden pig with a yarn tie around the neck, as well as a little plastic bag of dried black-eyed peas to promote even more good luck. As for the sacred ritual of serving stewed tomatoes over the hoppin' John, her only explanation is, "That's the way Mama did it, and that's the way I do it." Ditto the open bar, set up in the den and stocked with every type of booze imaginable plus various wines—just as Daddy used to handle it. "It's certainly no secret that Southerners love to drink," Mother quips, "and especially on New Year's, people want to really live it up." That, I should add, is an understatement.

Martha Pearl Advises

Since Southerners still love to drink cocktails in the old-fashioned manner, I always set up a proper bar on a large, covered desk or an outside table with all the necessities: major types of booze and mixers, red and chilled white wine, an ice bucket, seasonal cocktail napkins, a variety of glassware, olives, maraschino cherries, lemon peels, and lime wedges—the works.

Menu

Open Bar

Cracklin' Roast Fresh Ham with Cider Mustard Gravy

Turnip and Mustard Greens Combo with Ham Hock

Smoky Hoppin' John

Maw Maw's Stewed Tomatoes

Ann's Skillet Cornbread

Hot Ginger Cake with Lemon Raisin Sauce

Cracklin' Roast Fresh Ham with Cider Mustard Gravy

My Georgia great-grandmother did a "cracklin' ham" on New Year's, my grandmother and Aunt Toots did one, and Mother has carried on the tradition for as long as I can remember. ("Mama used to get all over Aunt Toots for eating all the cracklin' and not passing it around," Mother laughs.) The good-luck superstition aside, I choose to bake a fresh ham any day over a pork roast (the flavor is so much better, and the waste is minimal) and I never understand why others don't. And for heaven's sake don't be shy about eating the cracklin': most of the fat is rendered during baking and the skin is utterly sumptuous.

One 5- to 6-pound fresh ham
$3\frac{1}{2}$ cups apple cider
2 teaspoons salt
$\frac{1}{4}$ cup all-purpose flour
$\frac{1}{2}$ cup water
2 tablespoons Dijon mustard
Black pepper to taste

Preheat the oven to 325°F.

With a sharp paring knife, puncture and score the skin on the ham and position the ham on a rack in a large, shallow roasting pan. Pour $\frac{1}{4}$ cup of the cider over the ham, sprinkle with the salt, and roast for $1\frac{1}{2}$ hours. Pour another cup of cider over the ham and continue to bake till the skin is fully crisp, about $2\frac{1}{2}$ hours, basting from time to time. Transfer the ham to a large serving platter, keep warm, remove the rack from the pan, and pour off as much fat as possible.

In a small mixing bowl, whisk together the flour and water to make a paste, add the mustard, and whisk till well blended.

continued

Place the roasting pan over moderate heat and add the remaining 2¼ cups cider, scraping the bottom of the pan for bits and pieces. Add the mustard paste, season with pepper, and stir constantly till the gravy is thickened. Strain through a fine-mesh strainer into a saucepan and keep the gravy hot till ready to serve.

Remove the cracklin' skin from the ham and cut into small pieces. Carve the ham into slices and serve with the cracklin's and gravy.

8 TO 10 SERVINGS

Martha Pearl Advises

I never throw away the crisp skin of any baked ham. Chopped finely, it's great for cracklin' cornbread and biscuits, salads, and added to any number of cooked vegetables.

Turnip and Mustard Greens Combo with Ham Hock

Since my maternal grandmother, Maw Maw, found collards too strong for her taste, Mother grew up eating a combination of turnip and mustard greens cooked with ham hock on New Year's. If you really want to see the fur fly, put before my mother a mess of greens that haven't been stemmed and ribbed. "The stems and ribs are tough as whiteleather," she huffs, "and anybody who can't take the time to remove them is just plain down lazy." Remember also that one of the secrets to great Southern greens is long, slow simmering. As for the cooked ham hock, Mother doesn't trim, then chop the meat, and serve it over the greens. I do.

2 pounds turnip greens
2 pounds mustard greens
1 medium-size ham hock, skin removed
1 tablespoon sugar
2 teaspoons salt
2 medium-size onions, coarsely chopped
1 cup cider vinegar
Black pepper to taste

Remove and discard the stems and ribs of the greens, place the leaves in a sink or large pot of cold water, and swish around to remove all the dirt and grit, repeating the procedure with more fresh water if necessary. Tear the leaves into several pieces each and set aside.

Place the ham hock in a large pot and add enough water to cover. Bring to a boil, reduce the heat to low, simmer for 15 minutes, and add the sugar and salt. Return to a boil and gradually add the torn leaves. Reduce the heat to low, cover, and simmer the greens till soft and tender, 1 to 1½ hours.

In a medium-size mixing bowl, combine the onions, vinegar, and pepper and stir till well blended.

continued

Drain the greens well in a colander, transfer to a large serving bowl, top with the onions and vinegar, and toss well.

8 SERVINGS

Smoky Hoppin' John

Hoppin' John is the ultimate New Year's good-luck dish, and while most Southerners serve the peas by themselves, Mother can't imagine eating them without stewed tomatoes spooned over the top the way her whole family used to do in Georgia. In a bind, Mother will use frozen black-eyes, but she finds the canned ones too mushy and the dried peas require too much lengthy soaking and cooking. The peas should be cooked till tender—and never al dente.

¼ **pound slab bacon, cut into** ¼**-inch cubes**
1 **small onion, finely chopped**
1 **celery rib, finely chopped**
1 **garlic clove, minced**
2 **pounds black-eyed peas (fresh or frozen)**
Salt and black pepper to taste
Red pepper flakes to taste
3 **cups water**

In a large saucepan, fry the bacon over moderate heat till crisp, then pour off all but about 1 tablespoon of the grease. Add the onion, celery, and garlic and stir for 2 minutes. Add the remaining ingredients, bring to a boil, reduce the heat to low, cover, and simmer till the peas are tender but not mushy, about 1½ hours, adding a little more water if necessary. Serve the peas topped with a big spoonful of stewed tomatoes (page 135) on each serving.

8 SERVINGS

Fresh black-eyed peas intended for salads and other cold dishes should be cooked no longer than about 1 hour, but when they're served as a vegetable, I (like most Southerners) cook mine 2 hours, till very tender but not mushy.

Maw Maw's Stewed Tomatoes

Mother remembers her mother not only putting up tomatoes in summertime so she'd have them for New Year's but also using leftover breakfast toast to thicken her stewed tomatoes. Mother herself began canning summer tomatoes when Daddy had his first tomato patch, a tradition she continues to this day either with tomatoes from farmers' markets or in my East Hampton garden. She couldn't imagine eating black-eyed peas without these stewed tomatoes served over the top.

8 ripe tomatoes (or two 28-ounce cans tomatoes), cut up coarsely
2 teaspoons cider vinegar
1 teaspoon salt
1 teaspoon sugar
Black pepper to taste
½ cup crushed croutons (fresh or packaged)

In a medium-size saucepan, combine all the ingredients but the croutons and stir well. Bring to a slow boil over moderate heat and cook, uncovered, for 10 minutes, stirring once or twice. Add the croutons, mix well, and serve spoonfuls of the tomatoes over portions of Smoky Hoppin' John (page 134).

8 SERVINGS

Ann's Skillet Cornbread

Mother always thought the skillet cornbread she'd been making for decades was the best in creation till her neighbor and close friend, Ann Scarborough, baked up this version from her home state of Mississippi one evening. "Ann uses water-ground cornmeal, not an ounce of flour, and a little bacon grease for flavor, and I have to admit there's simply no cornbread like it." Finding water-ground cornmeal these days, of course, is a challenge, but I will say that the batch of this cornbread I made using regular yellow cornmeal was delicious.

2 cups yellow cornmeal (preferably water-ground)
1 teaspoon baking soda
1 teaspoon salt
2 large eggs, beaten
1 cup buttermilk
¼ cup bacon grease

Preheat the oven to 450°F.

In a large mixing bowl, combine the cornmeal, baking soda, and salt and stir till well blended. Add the eggs and buttermilk and stir with a wooden spoon till well blended and smooth. In a 9- to 10-inch cast-iron skillet, heat the bacon grease, add it to the cornmeal mixture, and stir till well blended. Scrape the batter into the hot skillet, place the skillet in the oven, and bake till the cornbread is golden brown, 20 to 25 minutes. Turn the cornbread out onto a serving plate and cut into small wedges.

8 SERVINGS

Hot Ginger Cake with Lemon Raisin Sauce

Mother's plain ginger cake is delectable by itself (and ideal for a warm-weather picnic or cookout), but go to the trouble of serving it with this sauce as she does on New Year's and you have a truly special dessert.

FOR THE GINGER CAKE

¹/₂ cup Crisco vegetable shortening

¹/₂ cup firmly packed light brown sugar

1 large egg

¹/₂ cup molasses

1 cup milk

2 cups all-purpose flour

2 teaspoons baking powder

¹/₂ teaspoon salt

2 teaspoons ground ginger

1 teaspoon ground cinnamon

FOR THE SAUCE

1¹/₂ cups granulated sugar

3 tablespoons cornstarch

1¹/₂ cups water

³/₄ cup fresh lemon juice

Grated rind of 1 lemon

2 large egg yolks, beaten

3 tablespoons butter

¹/₂ cup seedless golden raisins

Preheat the oven to 350°F. Grease and flour a medium-size baking pan, tapping out any excess, and set aside.

In a large mixing bowl, cream together the shortening and brown sugar with an electric mixer till smooth and fluffy, then add the egg and beat till well blended. In a small mixing bowl, combine the molasses and milk, stir till well blended, add to the creamed mixture, and beat till well blended. In another small mixing bowl, combine the flour, baking powder, salt, ginger, and cinnamon and mix well, then add to the batter and stir till well blended. Scrape the batter into the prepared pan and bake till a knife inserted into the center comes out clean, 40 to 45 minutes.

To make the sauce, combine the sugar and cornstarch in a medium-size heavy saucepan and stir till well blended. Add the water, lemon juice, and lemon rind and stir constantly over moderate heat till the mixture comes to a boil. Reduce the heat to low and simmer for 2 minutes. Add 1 tablespoon of the hot lemon sauce to the egg yolks, whisking constantly, then whisk in 3 or 4 more tablespoons of sauce one at a time (see Martha Pearl Advises, below). Pour the egg mixture into the hot sauce and stir for about 2 minutes, never allowing the sauce to boil. Remove the pan from the heat, add the butter and raisins, and stir till the butter melts.

To serve, cut the hot ginger cake into squares and spoon the hot sauce over the tops.

8 SERVINGS

Martha Pearl Advises

To temper egg yolks with a hot liquid (meaning to keep them from scrambling), gradually add a few tablespoons of the liquid to the eggs, whisking briskly and constantly till you have about ½ cup of mixture. Then pour the tempered mixture back into the hot liquid, whisking constantly.

A Super Bowl Sports Buffet

"SHORTLY AFTER MARRYING A MAN WHO WAS AS nuts about sports as most Southerners," Mother relates, "it didn't take long to realize that I either had to learn to enjoy certain games and entertain Harold's jock friends or spend a lot of time by myself." Suffice it that she met the challenge, and ever since it's become a tradition toward the end of January for Mother to celebrate all the hoopla by inviting up to a dozen football enthusiasts to don their college jerseys and caps with respective colors and insignias, bring banners of their alma maters, and guzzle gallons of lethal Goalpost Punch while partaking of a bountiful Southern buffet and watching the professional games.

By four in the afternoon, colorful balloons bob on the ceilings, a huge punch bowl flanked with magnolia leaves is filled, and the buffet table is set with a brown, rough-textured cloth, a large arrangement of rust, yellow, and white chrysanthemums in a bronze urn, heavy pottery plates, and tiny mascots of favorite North Carolina teams (Duke Blue Devils, Carolina Rams, Wake Forest Deacons, etc.). There are TVs in several rooms, big throw pillows on the carpets for those who like to circulate, and, of course, canisters to hold cash bets. Lots of food is consumed at this affair (Mother usually doubles all recipes), the atmosphere is gleeful if not downright boisterous, and, as Mother says, "I'm just glad the children can't see and hear us." Just about the only refined touch is the plump yellow chrysanthemums with team-color bows that she passes out to the ladies to be pinned on their shoulders.

Martha Pearl Advises

Only on rare occasions do I force my guests to eat on their laps at a buffet. If the gathering is large, I set up card tables in various rooms; for more intimate get-togethers, I scatter small nest tables around the house.

Menu

Goalpost Punch

Holy Fried Creole Oysters

Baked Country Sausage and Leeks Supreme

Congealed Football Broccoli Mold

Corn Light Bread

Gingered Pear, Raisin, and Walnut Conserve

Cranberry Upside-Down Cake

Goalpost Punch

The longer this powerful brew is left to mull, the better its flavor, but to do it justice, the punch must stand at least overnight—and at room temperature. For this shindig, Mother usually doubles the recipe.

6 tablespoons green tea leaves

8 cups boiling water

2 cups orange juice

1 cup fresh lemon juice

1½ quarts dry white wine

2 cups dark rum

2 cups bourbon

2 cups gin

1 cup firmly packed light brown sugar

1 cup maraschino cherries

1 liter soda water

Place the tea leaves in a large saucepan, pour the boiling water over the leaves, and let steep for about 10 minutes. Strain the tea through a fine-mesh strainer into a large stainless steel or enameled pot or bowl, add the orange juice, lemon juice, wine, rum, bourbon, gin, brown sugar, and cherries, and stir till the sugar dissolves. Cover with plastic wrap and let stand overnight at room temperature.

Place a block of ice in a large punch bowl, pour the punch and the soda water over the ice, and serve in punch cups.

ABOUT 1½ GALLONS PUNCH

Martha Pearl Advises

If you're unable to buy a block of ice for punch bowls, freeze your own in one or two plastic containers, depending on what your freezer can accommodate.

Holy Fried Creole Oysters

Mother calls these oysters "holy" for the simple (and typically Southern) reason that she first had them when she and Daddy visited the retired rector of her Episcopal church in Charlotte after he and his wife moved to Louisiana. "I'd been eating fried oysters my whole life," she explains, "but when she served these made with Creole mustard, I just had to have that recipe." Do serve these oysters as soon as possible after frying.

2 cups dry bread crumbs
Salt and black pepper to taste
1 cup (2 sticks) butter, warmed slightly
1 cup Creole mustard, warmed slightly
30 to 35 fresh shucked oysters, drained
Vegetable oil for frying

On a plate, combine the bread crumbs and salt and pepper, mix well, and set aside. In a large mixing bowl, combine the butter and mustard and stir till blended thoroughly.

Dip the oysters into the butter mixture, dredge lightly in the seasoned bread crumbs, and place on a large plate. In a large, heavy skillet, heat about 1 inch of vegetable oil to 375°F on a thermometer or till a morsel of bread tossed into the pan sizzles quickly, then fry the oysters in the oil, without crowding them, for 2 minutes total, turning them once, and drain on paper towels. Serve the oysters piping hot in a cloth-lined straw basket.

AT LEAST 8 SERVINGS

Martha Pearl Advises

For any fried oysters, I buy the largest grade available, am careful not to overcoat them with cracker or bread crumbs, and, to prevent sogginess, always wait between batches for the fat to heat back up to the right temperature.

Baked Country Sausage and Leeks Supreme

While this is the ultimate buffet casserole that never fails to impress a large gathering (actually, Mother usually makes two of them for this get-together, to play it safe), it's also great for a simple winter dinner with just a salad, good bread, and a sturdy red wine. And the unbaked casserole minus the bread crumbs and melted butter freezes well for future use.

¾ pound bulk sausage

10 large leeks (3 to 3½ pounds)

3 tablespoons butter

2 garlic cloves, minced

2 cups heavy cream

Large pinch of ground nutmeg

Salt and black pepper to taste

⅓ cup dry bread crumbs

¼ cup (½ stick) butter, melted

In a large, heavy skillet, break up the sausage meat and fry over moderate heat till nicely browned all over. Drain on paper towels and set aside.

While the sausage is frying, trim the leeks of all but about 2 inches of the green tops, slice the whites down the middle almost to the root end, and rinse the layers thoroughly under cold running water to remove all grit. Slice the leeks crosswise at 2-inch intervals.

Preheat the oven to 425°F.

In a large, heavy saucepan, heat the 3 tablespoons of butter over moderate heat, then add the garlic and stir for 1 minute. Add the leeks and cook, stirring, till they have wilted, about 3 minutes. Add the heavy cream and nutmeg, season with salt and pepper, and cook till the leeks are tender, 10 to 15 minutes.

continued

Pour the mixture into a large, shallow baking dish and spoon the drained sausage over the top. Sprinkle the bread crumbs on top, drizzle the melted butter over the crumbs, and bake till golden brown, about 20 minutes. Serve hot.

8 SERVINGS

Congealed Football Broccoli Mold

Here is Mother at her cleverest at entertaining with food: using an oval mold the shape of a football and pimento strips to simulate the laces. The presentation is not only fanciful but quite handsome.

One 10-ounce package frozen broccoli, thawed

1 envelope unflavored gelatin

½ cup water

1 cup chicken stock or broth

⅔ cup mayonnaise (Mother prefers Hellmann's)

⅓ cup sour cream

1 tablespoon fresh lemon juice

1 tablespoon minced onion

2 teaspoons Worcestershire sauce

3 large hard-boiled eggs, peeled and chopped

One 4-ounce jar whole pimentos (see **Martha Pearl Advises**, page 205),
    cut into thin strips

Grease a medium-size oval mold and set aside.

Cook the broccoli according to the package directions, drain, chop finely, and set aside.

In a small saucepan, soften the gelatin in the water for about 5 minutes, then add the broth and stir over low heat till the gelatin has dissolved completely. Pour the mixture into a large mixing bowl, add the mayonnaise, sour cream, lemon juice, onion, and Worcestershire, and beat with an electric mixer till smooth. Chill the mixture till partially set, about 30 minutes, then fold in the broccoli and eggs. Scrape the mixture into the prepared mold, cover with plastic wrap, and chill till firm, at least 2 hours.

Unmold the oval onto a serving platter and use the pimento strips to simulate football laces. Keep chilled till ready to serve.

8 SERVINGS

Corn Light Bread

A specialty of the Appalachians and western part of the South since the early nineteenth century, corn light bread is a cross between ordinary cornbread and white bread and is traditionally made with water-ground cornmeal. Mother had never tasted this bread (nor had I) till we visited friends in Nashville and were told it simply wouldn't work without the special cornmeal (increasingly difficult to find even in the South). The minute she returned home with a recipe in her purse, however, Mother made a couple of loaves of the sweet-and-sour bread using her regular yellow cornmeal and proclaimed the bread "just as good as what I had in Tennessee."

3 cups yellow cornmeal (preferably water-ground)
1 cup all-purpose flour
1 cup sugar
1½ teaspoons salt
½ teaspoon baking soda
3 cups buttermilk
¼ cup Crisco vegetable shortening, melted

Preheat the oven to 350°F. Grease two medium-size loaf pans and set aside.

Into a large mixing bowl, sift together the cornmeal, flour, sugar, salt, and baking soda. Gradually add the buttermilk and melted shortening and stir till the batter is well blended and smooth. Scrape equal amounts of batter into the prepared pans and bake till the bread pulls away from the sides of the pans, about 45 minutes. Turn out the loaves onto a wire rack and let cool before slicing.

2 LOAVES

Gingered Pear, Raisin, and Walnut Conserve

Mother loves to make any number of seasonal conserves to accompany various hearty casseroles and roasted meats. This is one of her winter combinations, but, using the same basic technique, she might well substitute fresh ripe peaches or apricots for the pears, chopped dates for the raisins, and experiment with other spices. Whatever ingredients you choose, remember to cook the conserve just till it is neither too thin nor too thick—and never add any liquid.

2 pounds ripe Bosc or Anjou pears, peeled, cored, and diced
2 pounds sugar
½ pound seedless golden raisins
½ pound walnuts, coarsely chopped
1 teaspoon ground ginger

In a large mixing bowl, combine the pears and sugar, stir well, cover with plastic wrap, and let stand overnight in the refrigerator.

Transfer the mixture to a large, heavy saucepan, bring to a low boil, cover, and simmer over moderately low heat till the pears are tender, about 30 minutes. Add the raisins, walnuts, and ginger, return to a simmer, and cook till the conserve is thickened, 15 to 20 minutes, stirring once or twice. Transfer the conserve to a ceramic bowl and either seal in hot, sterilized jars or cover with plastic wrap and refrigerate till ready to serve.

ABOUT 2 ½ PINTS

The Resurrection Breakfast Pecan Waffles with Orange Syrup *(page 175)*,
Shrimp and Grits *(page 173)*, Orange Blossoms *(page 173)*

Gumbo Night

CLOCKWISE FROM BOTTOM LEFT:

Jefferson Davis Pie *(page 22)*,

Big Mary's Pineapple Slaw

(page 20),

Savannah Red Rice *(page 18)*,

Creole Shrimp and Oyster Gumbo

(page 17)

The Golden Gobbler Feast

CLOCKWISE FROM BOTTOM LEFT:

Roast Turkey with Oyster and
Almond Stuffing *(page 53)*,
Streak-O'-Lean Snappies with
Pecan Butter *(page 56)*,
Holiday Bourbon Cake *(page 60)*,
Southern Comfort Ambrosia
(page 59),
Congealed Cranberry, Orange, and
Pineapple Salad *(page 57)*

A Christmas Eve Country Ham Buffet

CLOCKWISE FROM BOTTOM LEFT:

Missy's Buttermilk Biscuits
(page 98),

Country Ham Braised in Cider
and Molasses *(page 92)*,

Holiday Seven-Layer Salad
(page 96),

Glazed Cranberry and Apple
Tart *(page 97)*,

Winter Squash Casserole
(page 94)

A Super Bowl Sports Buffet

CLOCKWISE FROM TOP RIGHT:

Goalpost Punch *(page 141)*,

Congealed Football Broccoli

Mold *(page 144)*,

Holy Fried Creole Oysters

(page 142),

Baked Country Sausage and

Leeks Supreme *(page 143)*,

Corn Light Bread

(page 145)

A Low-Country Perloo Party

St. Cecilia's Punch
(page 183),
Chicken and Ham Perloo
(page 186),
Joseph's Hoecakes
(page 189)

A Tassel Celebration
Barbecued Country-Style Pork
Ribs *(page 227)*,
Crab and Shrimp Chowder
(page 225),
Gingered Rhubarb-Strawberry
Fool *(page 232)*

A Beach Supper

CLOCKWISE FROM BOTTOM LEFT:

Beach Shrimp Peel

(page 248),

Waccamaw Stuffed Tomatoes

(page 252),

Corn on the Cob

(page 253),

Peach Flips *(page 247)*,

Mixed Berry Cobbler

(page 254)

A Guild Finale Luncheon CLOCKWISE FROM BOTTOM LEFT: Cold Dilled Asparagus *(page 237)*, Gewürztraminer Wine, Butterscotch Delights *(page 242)*, Ribbon Loaf Sandwiches *(page 240)*

Cranberry Upside-Down Cake

So how did Mother come up with a cranberry upside-down cake for her Super Bowl buffet a few years ago? Simple. "I found a bag of fresh cranberries from Christmas in the freezer and, quite frankly, wanted to get rid of them," she confesses. If you think upside-down cake must be made only with pineapple or peaches, just wait till you try this sapid version.

½ cup (1 stick) butter
1½ cups sugar
½ teaspoon ground cinnamon
2½ cups fresh cranberries, picked over, washed, and patted dry
2 large eggs
1 teaspoon pure vanilla extract
1½ cups sifted all-purpose flour
1 teaspoon baking powder
1 teaspoon baking soda
1 teaspoon salt
½ cup buttermilk
Whipped cream

Preheat the oven to 350°F. Grease a large, square baking pan and set aside.

In a small saucepan, melt ¼ cup (½ stick) of the butter over moderate heat, then add 1 cup of the sugar and the cinnamon and cook till the sugar dissolves, stirring constantly. Pour the mixture evenly into the prepared pan, add the cranberries in an even layer, and set aside.

In a large mixing bowl, cream together the remaining ¼ cup (½ stick) butter and ½ cup sugar with an electric mixer till smooth, then add the eggs and vanilla and beat till well blended. In a small mixing bowl, combine the flour, baking powder, baking soda, and salt and add alternately with the buttermilk to the egg mixture, beating till the batter is smooth. Scrape the batter evenly over the cranberries and bake till a knife inserted into the center comes out clean, 35 to 40 minutes. Remove from the oven, let the cake cool for 10 minutes, run a knife around the sides to loosen it, and invert onto a serving plate. Cut the warm cake into squares and top each with a dollop of whipped cream.

8 SERVINGS

A Southern Greek Dinner

WHAT EXPLAINS A SOUTHERN LADY FROM MACON, Georgia, preparing a gala Greek dinner on the second Saturday of every March? Easy. First of all, Charlotte, North Carolina, boasts the largest Greek community between New York City and Tarpon Springs, Florida. Second, my father was half Greek, meaning that after he and Mother married, she began cooking many of the dishes that appealed to Daddy, his family, and their many Greek friends. "Let's just say that the dear Greek ladies of Charlotte were always so happy to share their recipes with me," Mother recalls wistfully, "and, of course, I was exposed to so many dishes while attending Greek bazaars, weddings, anniversary celebrations, and 'name day' (birthday) events."

While Daddy was still alive, this annual feast could easily involve many Greek and American guests; he always hired an accordionist to play lively Greek folk songs; and the house was decorated with lots of Greek flags, small evzones (little Greek soldiers) in traditional military dress, and a blue-and-white tablecloth with matching napkins on the large dining room table. Mother's food seemed to be everywhere: bowls of briny olives, oil-soaked feta cheese, pistachio nuts, and sapid dips; platters of spinach-and-cheese triangles, tangy salads, meat tarts; and sweet and sour breads. And the ouzo and dry red and white Greek wines flowed before, during, and after dinner. That the language spoken was an interchangeable blend of Greek and Southern drawl only enhanced the exotic entertainment for my sister, Hootie, and me.

Today, Mother doesn't have as many Greek friends as in the past, and it's next to impossible to find a good accordion player, but otherwise her Greek dinner with a Southern accent (e.g., her "Greek" cornbread) is as big a hit as ever with the lucky ones she invites. "I don't see why anyone with strong ethnic connections—Irish, German, French, Jewish—wouldn't entertain this way from time to time," she encourages. "And what's really interesting to me is how something like Greek beans or okra and tomatoes, or roast lamb and potatoes, or cornbread has lots in common with plain old Southern food."

Martha Pearl Advises

I love a tasteful fresh flower arrangement on any dinner table so long as it's low and doesn't interfere with guests' eye contact and conversation. On large buffet tables, by contrast, the more elaborate the arrangement, the better.

Menu

Spinach-Cheese Triangles

Greek-Style Roast Leg of Lamb with Potatoes

Greek Beans and Tomatoes

Dilled Beet, Feta, and Onion Salad

Greek Cornbread

Almond-Yogurt Cake

Spinach-Cheese Triangles

Mother learned to make these small spanakopitas nearly fifty years ago from a Greek waitress who worked at a small restaurant in Charlotte. "I've forgotten the sweet lady's name, but I'd literally buy all the ingredients, take them to her house, and she'd teach me exactly what to do." She also sometimes stuffs the triangles with seasoned cooked ground beef, lamb, or pork. Remember that the secret to working with phyllo is to keep it covered at all times with a damp towel, never allowing it to dry out in the least. Mother is never without a dozen or so triangles in the freezer, ready to pop into the oven at a moment's notice.

One 10-ounce package frozen chopped spinach, thawed
2 tablespoons olive oil
½ cup minced green onions
½ pound feta cheese, finely crumbled
¼ pound ricotta cheese
2 large eggs, well beaten
2 tablespoons chopped fresh parsley leaves
1 tablespoon dry bread crumbs
½ pound phyllo pastry (available frozen in supermarkets), thawed
1 cup (2 sticks) butter, melted

Wrap the thawed spinach in paper towels, squeeze to remove all the moisture, and set aside.

In a small skillet, heat the olive oil over moderate heat, then add the onions and cook for 3 minutes, stirring. Add the spinach, stir till all the moisture has evaporated, and transfer the mixture to a large mixing bowl. Add the two cheeses, eggs, parsley, and bread crumbs and stir the mixture till well blended.

Preheat the oven to 350°F.

Lay the phyllo out on a counter and keep covered at all times with a damp tea towel. Place one sheet of pastry on your work surface and cut widthwise into 2½- to 3-inch-wide strips.

continued

Brush a strip with melted butter and spoon 1 teaspoon of the cheese mixture into the center, about 1 inch away from the edges. Fold one corner over into a triangle, then continue folding like a flag to the end of the strip, brushing each finished triangle with melted butter. Repeat with the remaining strips, placing each triangle on an ungreased baking sheet. Bake till golden brown, 20 to 25 minutes, turning once, and serve piping hot with cocktails or as a first course. (Unbaked triangles may be stacked between sheets of waxed paper and frozen in airtight containers for up to 3 months. When ready to serve, separate the triangles while still frozen and bake an extra 10 minutes.)

ABOUT 50 TRIANGLES

Martha Pearl Advises

To keep phyllo pastry from drying out, I keep mine covered with both a damp tea towel and plastic wrap. If you can't work fast enough with phyllo, brush the entire sheet of pastry with melted butter before cutting out pieces.

Greek-Style Roast Leg of Lamb with Potatoes

Complex as it might sound, Mother learned many years ago how to cook Greek food from my Swedish grandmother when she and her Greek husband (my paternal grandfather) followed the immigrant tradition in the South of housing newly arrived relatives till they could find work, get married, and fare on their own. And since Charlotte was (and still is) a major Greek-American community, the first thing anybody remotely connected to these households was taught to cook was lamb roasted with everything from orzo to tomatoes to green beans to potatoes to Southern okra. My grandfather and father loved roast lamb (well-cooked, in the Greek style, of course), and to this day Mother still prepares it just as she did on Sunday nights for them, us kids, and any number of other Greek and Southern friends.

One 5- to 6-pound leg of lamb
3 garlic cloves, thinly slivered
Salt and black pepper to taste
2 tablespoons dried oregano, crumbled
¼ cup Greek olive oil
Juice of 2 large lemons
20 small red potatoes
3 tablespoons tomato paste
¼ cup cool water
2 cups hot water
1 teaspoon crumbled dried rosemary
1 teaspoon dried thyme
Fresh rosemary sprigs for garnish

Preheat the oven to 450°F.

With a sharp knife, make small slits on both sides of the lamb and insert the garlic slivers into the slits. Season the lamb all over with salt and pepper and 1 tablespoon of the oregano, then brush lightly with the olive oil. Place the lamb fat side up on a rack in a large roasting pan, pour the lemon juice over the top, and roast for 30 minutes, uncovered.

Meanwhile, peel the potatoes and place in a large mixing bowl. In a small mixing bowl, combine the tomato paste and cool water, mix till well blended, pour over the potatoes, and toss to coat evenly. Add the hot water to the roasting pan, arrange the potatoes around the lamb, and sprinkle them with the remaining 1 tablespoon oregano, the rosemary, and the thyme. Reduce the oven temperature to 325°F and continue roasting, uncovered, till the lamb reaches an internal temperature of 160°F on a meat thermometer and is fork-tender, about 1½ hours, basting the meat and potatoes from time to time with the pan juices and adding a little more water if necessary.

Transfer the lamb and potatoes to a large platter and keep hot. Remove the rack from the roasting pan and bring the juices to a boil on top of the stove, scraping any bits and pieces from the bottom of the pan and adding enough water to make about 2 cups of light gravy. Keep the gravy hot.

To serve, carve the lamb, arrange the slices in the middle of a large, heated serving platter, arrange the potatoes around the edges, and garnish with rosemary sprigs. Pour the gravy into a sauceboat and pass.

8 SERVINGS

Greek Beans and Tomatoes

My father hated the green beans cooked with side meat that most Southerners so relish, which is why Mother turned to their close friend, a Mrs. Dross, to learn how to prepare them Greek-style with tomatoes. We still call them simply "Greek beans," the irony being that they're simmered just as long as traditional Southern ones are—"for plenty of flavor," Mother reminds.

2 pounds fresh green beans, ends trimmed and each broken into thirds
2 medium-size onions, diced
3 garlic cloves, minced
One 15-ounce can whole tomatoes (juice included), diced
2 teaspoons salt
½ teaspoon crumbled dried oregano
Black pepper to taste
¼ cup Greek olive oil

In a large, heavy pot, combine the beans, onions, and garlic and toss. Add the tomatoes plus their juice, the salt, oregano, pepper, and olive oil and stir till everything is well blended. Bring to a gentle boil, reduce the heat to low, cover, and simmer the beans for 1½ hours. (Do not add any water.)

8 SERVINGS

Martha Pearl Advises

Perfect green beans are fully green (not pale), almost crisp, and they snap easily in half and never bend. I don't hesitate a moment in the market to snap a few beans to test their freshness.

Dilled Beet, Feta, and Onion Salad

This is Mother's updated take on traditional Greek feta salad—minus the tomatoes, cucumbers, and pickled hot peppers—and I must say the combination works beautifully as an accompaniment to the lamb and potatoes.

Two 1-pound cans sliced beets, drained
½ pound feta cheese, crumbled
1 Spanish onion, thinly sliced
2 tablespoons chopped fresh dill
½ cup Greek olive oil
½ cup red wine vinegar
2 tablespoons sugar
Salt and black pepper to taste

In an attractive serving bowl, combine the beets, feta, onion, and dill and toss. In a small mixing bowl, whisk together the olive oil, vinegar, sugar, and salt and pepper, pour over the beets, and toss well. Cover the bowl with plastic wrap and chill for 2 hours, tossing again before serving.

8 SERVINGS

Greek Cornbread

Over the years, Mother, like other Charlottean ladies in the Greek-American community, has adapted any number of Greek dishes to the Southern style of cooking, this slightly sweet cornbread (derived from Greek bobota) being a prime example. To my taste, it's one of the best and most unusual breads in her repertory.

1½ cups yellow cornmeal

1 cup all-purpose flour

1 teaspoon baking powder

¼ teaspoon baking soda

½ teaspoon salt

1 cup warm water

¼ cup Greek olive oil

¼ cup honey

2 teaspoons grated orange rind

Preheat the oven to 375°F. Grease a 9-inch square baking pan and set aside.

Into a large mixing bowl, sift together the cornmeal, flour, baking powder, baking soda, and salt. In a small mixing bowl, combine the water, olive oil, and honey, whisk rapidly till well blended, add to the dry mixture, and beat with a wooden spoon till the batter is smooth. Stir in the orange rind, scrape the batter into the prepared pan, and bake till golden brown, about 25 minutes. Serve the hot cornbread in squares.

8 SERVINGS

Almond-Yogurt Cake

Whereas so many Southern cakes have rich icings or glazes, most Greek ones are enhanced with various hot syrups that are allowed to cool to a sugary gloss before traditionally being cut into squares. To give this cake a more Southern accent, Mother has often substituted sour cream for the yogurt and pecans for the almonds, a variation that works beautifully without compromising the dessert's basic integrity.

continued

3 cups cake flour

2 teaspoons baking powder

1 teaspoon baking soda

2 cups plain yogurt

1/2 cup orange juice

2 cups sugar

1/2 cup honey

1 cup chopped blanched almonds

2 tablespoons grated orange rind

1 teaspoon ground cinnamon

FOR THE SYRUP

3 cups water

3 cups sugar

1 tablespoon grated orange rind

Preheat the oven to 350°F. Grease a 9-inch square baking pan and set aside.

To make the cake, sift together the flour, baking powder, and baking soda into a large mixing bowl, then add the yogurt, orange juice, sugar, honey, almonds, orange rind, and cinnamon and stir with a wooden spoon till very well blended and smooth. Scrape the batter into the prepared pan and bake till a knife inserted into the center comes out clean, about 35 minutes.

Meanwhile, to make the syrup, combine the water, sugar, and orange rind in a medium-size, heavy saucepan, bring to a simmer, stirring, and cook over moderate heat till the syrup is thickened, 10 to 15 minutes.

Pour the hot syrup directly over the hot cake, let cool completely, and cut into squares.

8 SERVINGS

Spring

An Easter Egg Picnic

The Resurrection Breakfast

A Low-Country Perloo Party

The Yellow Bell Bridge Luncheon

A Bereavement Buffet

A Formal Cocktail Supper

A Tassel Celebration

For Mother, spring is a time to clean off the porch and patio, scrub the big wooden picnic table, uncover the grill, and fill the sunroom full of flowers, but even more strategic to her entertaining is the appearance in the markets of the first fresh asparagus, cherries, mangoes, rhubarb, strawberries, and watermelon. By April, there's an abundance of fat Carolina shrimp and succulent crabmeat, hunter friends begin dropping off bagged quail from the field, tiny okra and baby new potatoes are already being harvested, and, by the first of May, she's even making the first of many treks down to Cottle's Strawberry Farm in Weddington, North Carolina, in hopes of finding a few ripe berries.

Spring is the season to sponsor an Easter egg picnic for both children and adults, to host a formal cocktail supper, and, in the old plantation tradition of the Carolina and Georgia Low Country, to throw an authentic "perloo" party. Why so many Southerners seem to die in April and May is a strange phenomenon that baffles Mother; all she knows is that she's called upon to organize more bereavements during these months than at any other time of year.

In the South, ladies' bridge luncheons are almost synonymous with the warm, flowery days of spring, and, like her mother and grandmother, my mother cherishes these gracious, cordial, almost formal get-togethers as much as any social event of the year. In sharp contrast, the way she celebrates a high school or college graduation in late May couldn't be more casual and carefree. "The great thing about entertaining during the springtime—indoors and out," she exclaims, "is the flexibility of setting, mode of dress, decorating, and style of food. And as for the weather, well, it couldn't be more perfect—give or take a few rainy days that I just don't let worry me one iota."

An Easter Egg Picnic

AFTER ATTENDING GOOD FRIDAY SERVICE AT THE church every year, Mother's major project is the dyeing of two dozen hard-boiled Easter eggs (complete with an animal or religious decal affixed to each egg) intended for a children's Easter egg hunt at her picnic the following day for friends and neighbors. Although the picnic itself—served outside on a long wooden table decorated with a colorful paper cloth, a large ceramic white bunny rabbit holding a profusion of tulips, and small biddy nests in front of each plate—is basically an adult affair, no doubt the highlight of the event is the children scurrying about the shrubs and flowers and grass searching for the bright eggs—and especially the prized golden one (which is actually a plastic egg that Mother has gilded). Mother even makes colored baskets stuffed with green Easter "grass" and tied with a big bow, each with a child's name marked on the side.

Since, after all, she's cooking for both adults and children, Mother's picnic fare is a sensible balance of serious and fanciful food, though, as she relates, "The parents and grandparents usually eat as many peanut butter sticks and biddy nests as the youngsters." For this affair, she does try to prepare as many dishes as possible in advance since she also has her Resurrection breakfast the following morning to think about, an explanation of why all the food is served chilled or at room temperature.

Menu

Peanut Butter Sticks

Shrimp, Avocado, and Potato Salad with Horseradish Dressing

Cheesy Chicken Drumettes

Herbed Eggplant and Red Onions

Deviled Tarragon Eggs

Fudgy Coconut Biddy Nests

Iced Tea and Lemonade

Peanut Butter Sticks

Mother created these yummy sticks specially for the children at her Easter egg picnic, the only problem being that the adults eat them as fast as the kids. If the sticks are stored in a really airtight container, they will maintain their crisp texture for up to two weeks.

....

One 1-pound loaf thin white sandwich bread
One 9-ounce jar creamy peanut butter
$\frac{1}{2}$ cup vegetable oil
7 ounces (half a 14-ounce box) cornflakes, crushed

Preheat the oven to 200°F.

Trim off the edges of the bread slices and cut each slice across into 5 sticks. Place the sticks on one or two ungreased baking sheets, place in the oven for 2 hours to dry, then let cool.

In the top of a double boiler set over simmering water, combine the peanut butter and oil and stir till well blended and smooth. Remove the double boiler from the heat but keep the mixture over the hot water.

Using tongs, dip the bread sticks into the peanut butter mixture till well coated, then drain momentarily on paper towels. On a plate, toss the sticks in the cornflake crumbs and place on sheets of waxed paper to dry, about 1 hour. Store the sticks in a large, airtight container.

ABOUT 100 STICKS

Shrimp, Avocado, and Potato Salad with Horseradish Dressing

Such is Mother's passion for tiny, new, red potatoes that she literally makes special trips to the country market in early spring in hopes of finding the spuds. The combination of these potatoes, sweet shrimp, and sensuous avocado produces a remarkable salad, but what really gives it Mother's special touch is the tangy horseradish in the dressing. To prevent sogginess (with this or any dressed potato salad), never make this dish more than a day in advance, and don't keep any leftover salad more than a day.

3 pounds new potatoes, left unpeeled

1½ pounds medium-size fresh shrimp

3 ripe avocados

2 small onions, finely chopped

¼ cup chopped fresh dill

1½ cups mayonnaise (Mother prefers Hellmann's)

½ cup sour cream

2 tablespoons red wine vinegar

2 tablespoons prepared horseradish

Black pepper to taste

1 large bunch watercress, rinsed, patted dry, and stems removed

Scrub the potatoes lightly and place in a large pot with enough salted water to cover. Bring to a boil, reduce the heat to moderate, cover, and cook till the potatoes are just pierceable with a fork, 10 to 15 minutes. Drain, cut into quarters, place in a large mixing bowl, and let cool.

Meanwhile, place the shrimp in a large saucepan with enough water to cover, bring to a boil, and drain. When cool enough to handle, shell and devein the shrimp and add to the potatoes. Peel and pit the avocados, cut the flesh into small dice, and add to the potatoes and shrimp. Add the onions and dill and toss the salad lightly.

In a small bowl, combine the mayonnaise, sour cream, vinegar, and horseradish, season with pepper, stir till well blended, and scrape the dressing over the salad. Toss together gently but thoroughly, cover with plastic wrap, and chill at least 1 hour.

To serve, line a large serving platter with watercress and mound the salad in the center.

8 TO 10 SERVINGS

ᨓ Cheesy Chicken Drumettes

Here's another of Mother's creations that appeals as much to adults as to children and is perfect for any picnic. Not only is the size of the drumstick just right, but in Mother's opinion, "No part of the chicken is as tender and sweet as the wings." Just be sure not to overbake these drumettes, which dries out and toughens them.

1 cup freshly grated Parmesan cheese

2 tablespoons finely chopped fresh parsley leaves

1 tablespoon dried oregano

2 teaspoons mild paprika

2 teaspoons salt

$\frac{1}{2}$ teaspoon black pepper

4 pounds chicken wing drumsticks (drumettes)

$\frac{1}{2}$ cup (1 stick) butter, melted

Preheat the oven to 350°F. Line a large, heavy baking sheet with aluminum foil, fold up the sides to form a rim, and set aside.

On a large, flat dish, combine the cheese, parsley, oregano, paprika, salt, and pepper and mix well. Dip each drumette in the melted butter, roll in the cheese mixture to coat well, place on the prepared baking sheet, and bake till cooked through and lightly browned, about 1 hour, turning once. Serve at room temperature.

8 TO 10 SERVINGS

Herbed Eggplant and Red Onions

Mother certainly has nothing against the large, glossy, deep purple Black Beauty egg-plants found year-round in supermarkets, but what she really prefers are the smaller, firmer, more tender purple or white varieties that show up in spring—often called "fry-ing" eggplants. While these are drier than the larger types, she still salts them to leach out as much bitterness and water as possible. For added depth of flavor, she also sometimes sprinkles a little—but not too much—grated Parmesan over the top before baking.

4 small eggplants, rinsed and cut into 1-inch-thick rounds
Salt
1 cup chopped fresh parsley leaves
3 large onions, thinly sliced
2 cups drained chopped canned tomatoes
2 garlic cloves, minced
$\frac{1}{2}$ teaspoon dried thyme, crumbled
$\frac{1}{4}$ teaspoon dried oregano, crumbled
$\frac{1}{4}$ teaspoon dried rosemary, crumbled
Salt and black pepper to taste
$\frac{3}{4}$ cup olive oil

Sprinkle the eggplant rounds generously on both sides with salt, place in a colander in the sink, and let stand for 1 hour. Rinse the eggplant thoroughly under cold running water and pat the rounds dry with paper towels.

Preheat the oven to 275°F.

Arrange half the eggplant rounds in a large baking dish and sprinkle on half the parsley. Arrange the onion slices and tomatoes on top of the parsley, distribute the garlic, thyme, oregano, rosemary, and salt and pepper evenly over that, and sprinkle on the remaining pars-ley. Arrange the remaining eggplant rounds on top, pour the olive oil evenly over the eggplant, cover the dish tightly with aluminum foil, and bake for 2 hours. Stir the mixture with a fork, cover again, and bake for 1 hour longer. Let cool completely and serve at room temperature.

8 SERVINGS

Deviled Tarragon Eggs

Years ago, when Tupperware parties were the rage and agents would come to homes to demonstrate products, Mother latched onto one of her most treasured possessions: a plastic Tupperware deviled-egg container with a lid that is perfect for storing exactly 18 egg halves. Recently, she's been trying to find such a container for a friend, complaining that "They're now as hard to locate as hen's teeth." In any case, feel free to experiment with the stuffing for these eggs. Fresh tarragon adds unique flavor, but also good are minced anchovies, capers, sweet pickles, and other herbs.

9 large eggs

$\frac{1}{3}$ cup mayonnaise (Mother prefers Hellmann's)

$1\frac{1}{2}$ tablespoons Dijon mustard

2 teaspoons cider vinegar

Salt and black pepper to taste

2 teaspoons minced green onions (white part only)

2 teaspoons minced fresh tarragon leaves

Mild paprika to taste

Tiny fresh tarragon leaves for garnish

Place the eggs in a large saucepan with enough water to cover, bring to a rolling boil, turn off the heat, and let stand for 18 minutes. Drain the water from the pan, add cold water to cover the eggs, and when cool enough to handle, crack and remove the shells.

Cut the eggs in half lengthwise, place the yolks in a small mixing bowl, and arrange the whites cavity side up on a large serving plate. Mash the yolks well with a fork, then add the mayonnaise, mustard, and vinegar, season with salt and pepper, stir till the mixture is smooth, and transfer to a pastry bag fitted with a ¼-inch tip. Sprinkle equal amounts of the minced onions into the cavity of each egg white, sprinkle equal amounts of the minced tarragon over the onions, then pipe equal mounds of the yolk mixture into the cavities. Sprinkle each stuffed egg half with paprika and garnish the tops with tarragon leaves. Cover with plastic wrap and chill till ready to serve.

18 STUFFED EGGS

continued

Martha Pearl Advises

If you're worried about hard-boiled eggs used for an Easter egg hunt spoiling, today you can buy plastic eggs that look exactly like the real McCoy—and they won't crack. Remember, however, that sound Easter eggs can later be turned into egg salad and deviled eggs and used to make numerous dishes.

Fudgy Coconut Biddy Nests

When Mother first began working on this clever dessert for children, she simply made a big white Easter cake and decorated the top with a nest filled with jelly beans (or "chicken biddies"). She then decided that individual cupcakes were an even better idea, arranged them on a large tray, and decorated the edges with marshmallow Easter chickens. Here she uses chocolate cupcakes, but she does remind that any flavor works well. She also warns to use rubber gloves when working with the green coconut since the food coloring stains fingers.

FOR THE CUPCAKES

2 squares unsweetened chocolate

½ cup milk

½ cup firmly packed light brown sugar

⅓ cup Crisco vegetable shortening

½ cup granulated sugar

2 large eggs

1 teaspoon pure vanilla extract

1¼ cups all-purpose flour

½ teaspoon baking soda

¼ teaspoon salt

FOR THE NESTS

7 ounces (2 packages) frozen unsweetened grated coconut

One 1-ounce bottle green food coloring (see Martha Pearl Advises, page 128)

½ cup Karo white corn syrup

One 5-ounce package small colored jelly beans

Preheat the oven to 350°F. Line one dozen 2½-inch muffin tins with paper liners and set aside.

In the top of a double boiler over simmering water, combine the chocolate and milk and stir till the chocolate melts. Add the brown sugar, stir till well blended and smooth, and set aside to cool.

continued

In a large mixing bowl, cream together the Crisco and granulated sugar with an electric mixer at medium speed till fluffy. Add the eggs one at a time, beating well after each addition, then add the vanilla and stir till well blended. In a small mixing bowl, combine the flour, baking soda, and salt and stir to blend well. Add the chocolate mixture and flour mixture alternately to the shortening mixture, stirring till well blended. Scrape the batter into the prepared muffin tins, filling each three-quarters full, and bake till a straw or cake tester inserted into the centers comes out clean, 25 to 30 minutes. Transfer the cupcakes to a wire rack to cool completely. With a sharp knife, level the tops of the cakes and set them aside.

To make the nests, place the coconut in a large mixing bowl and stir with a fork to separate the flakes. Gradually add the food coloring by drops, stirring and lifting the coconut constantly till it is dark green. Spread the coconut out on sheets of waxed paper to dry, about 1 hour.

Brush the top of each cupcake with the Karo syrup, spoon about 2 teaspoons of coconut in the center of each, and, using the spoon and your fingertips, form a small nest. Fill each nest with jelly beans and serve the nests on a large tray.

1 DOZEN BIDDY NESTS

The Resurrection Breakfast

ONE OF MY MOST NOSTALGIC CHILDHOOD MEMORIES is attending the outdoor Easter sunrise service in Charlotte's Freedom Park with my parents and sister, after which we and a few family friends would return home, Daddy would mix Orange Blossoms for the adults, and Mother would serve her ritualistic Southern Resurrection breakfast of shrimp and grits, pecan waffles, some type of fruit compote, and wonderful hot cross buns.

Mother is the first to admit that she's a creature of habit and tradition, and never is this trait more manifest than when it comes to this same special breakfast she prepares after early church every Easter morning for a few close friends. Hanging on the front door is the same stained-glass red cross I remember as a child, ladies still arrive wearing gloves and colorful hats, and, if I'm home, I'm now the one who mixes the Orange Blossoms served in the living room decked out with the largest and most exquisite Easter lilies imaginable, plus a huge white stuffed rabbit perched in a chair next to the hearth. While not everyone is of the same religious denomination, somehow the conversation always revolves around the same subjects: how the church was decorated, who wore what, which children behaved and which didn't, the quality of the music and sermon, and so on.

For this rather formal sit-down meal, Mother covers the dining room table with a pink linen cloth, uses fine flowered napkins, and, for an appropriate centerpiece, fills a flat basket of green straw with china bunnies and chickens and different-size eggs—all surrounded by delicate spring flowers. The shrimp and grits are served in her age-old chafing dish, the waffles on a silver tray, and the hot cross buns in a mesh basket with a linen bun cover. It's not a terribly elaborate breakfast (by Southern standards), but a highly gracious one in old-fashioned Southern style that befits the joyous occasion.

Menu

Orange Blossoms

Shrimp and Grits

Pecan Waffles with Orange Syrup

Mango, Grapefruit, and Grape Compote

Hot Cross Buns

Chicory Coffee

Orange Blossoms

Vodka or light rum can be substituted for the gin, but whichever spirit you use, be sure not to water down the cocktails by shaking them too long.

12 ounces orange juice
6 ounces gin
6 teaspoons sugar
3 cups cracked ice

In a large cocktail shaker, combine all the ingredients, shake rapidly till well chilled, strain into 6 cocktail glasses, and serve immediately.

6 DRINKS

Shrimp and Grits

Mother first tasted shrimp and grits (or, as they're often called in the Carolina Low Country, "breakfast grits") when we were staying at the old Francis Marion hotel in Charleston, South Carolina, many years ago, and she was so taken with the luscious dish that it soon became the highlight of our Resurrection breakfast. Although she's since been impressed with versions at both the Pinckney Cafe in Charleston and Atherton Mill in Charlotte that have tomatoes in the sauce, she still thinks there's nothing like this age-old classic made with the smallest shrimp possible and a little bacon grease. As far as I'm concerned, shrimp and grits is one of the most distinctive hallmarks of authentic Southern cookery—and not just for breakfast.

continued

5 cups water

1 teaspoon salt

1 cup regular hominy grits

2 tablespoons butter

2 pounds small shrimp, peeled and deveined

2 tablespoons butter

2 tablespoons bacon grease

2 small onions, finely chopped

$\frac{1}{2}$ small green bell pepper, seeded and finely chopped

$\frac{1}{4}$ cup all-purpose flour

Salt and black pepper to taste

To cook the grits, combine the water and salt in a large, heavy saucepan, bring to a brisk boil, and slowly sift the grits through the fingers of one hand into the water while stirring with the other. Reduce the heat to a gentle simmer and continue cooking till the grits are thick, about 30 minutes, stirring frequently to prevent sticking. Add the butter, stir till well blended, cover, and keep warm in a bowl till ready to serve.

To prepare the shrimp, place them in a large saucepan with enough water to just cover. Bring to a boil, remove the pan from the heat, let stand for 1 minute, and drain, reserving the cooking liquid in a bowl.

In a large, heavy skillet, heat the butter and bacon grease together over moderate heat, then add the onions and green pepper and stir for 8 minutes. Sprinkle the flour on top and continue to stir till the mixture begins to brown, about 2 minutes. Gradually add about 2 cups of the reserved shrimp cooking liquid and whisk briskly till the gravy is smooth. Add the shrimp, season with salt and pepper, and stir for 2 minutes, adding a little more cooking liquid if the gravy seems too thick.

Serve the shrimp and gravy over large spoonfuls of grits.

6   S E R V I N G S

Pecan Waffles with Orange Syrup

Succinctly, if you love waffles, you haven't lived till you've tasted them made with pecans (or walnuts) and served with this simple orange syrup of Mother's—such a welcome change from ordinary maple syrup! To keep the waffles from getting soggy, never cover them while keeping them warm in the oven, and if you're as serious as Mother about great waffles, you'll invest in an electric heating tray like the one she places on the table.

FOR THE BATTER

2 large eggs

1½ cups half-and-half

¼ cup (½ stick) butter, melted

1½ cups all-purpose flour

2 teaspoons baking powder

1 teaspoon salt

½ cup finely chopped pecans

FOR THE ORANGE SYRUP

2 cups sugar

1 cup fresh orange juice

¼ cup Karo light corn syrup

Grated rind of 1 orange

To make the batter, combine the eggs, half-and-half, and melted butter in a large mixing bowl and beat with an electric mixer till smooth. Into a small mixing bowl, sift together the flour, baking powder, and salt, then add this to the egg mixture and beat at medium speed till well blended. Add the pecans, beat till well blended and smooth, and set aside.

To make the orange syrup, combine the sugar, orange juice, and corn syrup in a medium-size saucepan, bring to a boil over moderate heat, and stir till the sugar is completely dissolved and the mixture syrupy. Remove the pan from the heat, add the orange rind, stir till well blended, and keep warm.

continued

To make each waffle, ladle a small mound of batter onto the middle of an electric waffle iron set at high heat (the amount of batter depends on the size of the iron) and cook according to manufacturer's instructions till golden brown. Stack the waffles on a plate and keep warm till ready to serve with the warm orange syrup.

12 TO 14 WAFFLES; ABOUT 6 SERVINGS

Martha Pearl Advises

Nothing is more fun than a large waffle breakfast or brunch where two or three waffle irons are utilized and guests can eat at approximately the same time. I myself have two irons, and if I need a third, I simply borrow one from a neighbor.

Mango, Grapefruit, and Grape Compote

Contrary to what many think, Florida grapefruits are just as sweet and juicy in April as in January, while in the South it's becoming increasingly possible to find fresh mangoes in the markets as early as Eastertime. Rarely, however, do you find softly ripe mangoes in even the fanciest specialty shops, so if you don't care to wait up to a week for the fruit to ripen on the windowsill, use Mother's trick of placing the mangoes in a paper bag with a very ripe banana. Almost miraculously, they ripen in a day or so.

2 cups water

1 cup sugar

1 stick cinnamon, 2 cloves, and 1 strip lemon rind, wrapped together in cheesecloth

4 ripe, soft mangoes (see headnote)

2 pink grapefruits

3 cups (1 pound) seedless red grapes

In a small saucepan, combine the water, sugar, and spice package, bring to a boil, reduce the heat to low, and simmer for 5 minutes. Remove the spice package and let the syrup cool completely.

Peel the mangoes, cut the flesh from the seeds as evenly as possible, and place the chunks in a serving bowl. Peel the grapefruits, cut out the sections (removing as much white pith as possible), and add to the mangoes. Cut the grapes in half and add to the mangoes and grapefruit. Pour the syrup over the fruits, toss gently, cover with plastic wrap, and chill till ready to serve in glass compote dishes or colored tulip cups.

6 SERVINGS

Hot Cross Buns

Since Mother loathes commercial hot cross buns ("They're heavy, made with few raisins, and have absolutely no flavor"), she's always made her own for Easter. This is a yeast bread that requires two rises and is thus time-consuming to deal with, so Mother usually bakes off the buns at her leisure and freezes them till ready to thaw and ice.

FOR THE BUNS

1 cup milk

⅓ cup butter, cut into pieces

½ cup granulated sugar

1 teaspoon salt

1 envelope active dry yeast

¼ cup warm water

2 large eggs

5 cups all-purpose flour

1 cup seedless golden raisins

1 teaspoon ground allspice

3 tablespoons butter, melted

FOR THE ICING

2 cups confectioners' sugar, sifted

2 tablespoons milk

To make the buns, scald the milk in a saucepan, remove from the heat, add the butter, sugar, and salt, and stir till the butter is melted. Let cool to lukewarm.

In a large mixing bowl, sprinkle the yeast over the warm water, stir till dissolved, add the milk mixture and eggs, and stir till well blended. Gradually add the flour, beating with an electric mixer at medium speed till the dough is smooth. Add the raisins and allspice and stir with a wooden spoon till well blended. Place the dough in a greased bowl, cover with a clean kitchen towel, and let rise in a warm, draft-free area till doubled in bulk, about 1½ hours.

Grease a large, heavy baking sheet and set aside.

Turn the dough out onto a floured work surface and, using your hands, form it into a roll 16 inches long. Cut the roll crosswise into 16 pieces and shape each piece into a ball. Flatten each ball slightly with the palm of your hand, place the balls on the prepared baking sheet, cover with the towel, and let rise another 1½ hours.

Preheat the oven to 400°F.

Carefully cut a cross about ¼ inch deep on the top of each bun, brush each with the melted butter, bake till golden brown, about 25 minutes, and transfer to a wire rack to cool.

To make the icing, combine the confectioners' sugar and milk in a medium-size mixing bowl and beat till thickened, then carefully spoon the icing along the indented cross on each bun. Allow the icing to set a bit before serving.

16 BUNS

A Low-Country
Perloo Party

SOME OF THE MOST GRACIOUS STYLES OF ENTER-
taining on earth have been conducted for centuries in Charleston, Savannah, and
other areas of the Carolina and Georgia Low Country, many of which Mother
was exposed to as a young lady and which have always had tremendous influence
on our entire family and the way we cook. Perloo (or pilau, or perlo, or purloo,
or peelau), a close cousin to Creole jambalaya, has evolved in its
various guises as virtually a Low Country signature dish, a sumptuous rice
concoction so beloved by my mother that she began throwing an informal party
in its honor years ago. Each dish on her menu has a long, fascinating history in
the Low Country, and I hazard to say that an invitation to this party is one of the
most sought-after in Charlotte—though Mother would consider me "indiscreet"
for saying so.

Appropriately, guests are greeted by a basket of spring flowers nestled in
Spanish moss (when it can be found in Charlotte) on the front door, a huge bowl
of St. Cecilia's punch in the sunroom or on the patio, and a crock of shrimp paste
with crackers. Whether Mother serves dinner inside or out, the table is set with
a brightly colored cotton cloth and dishcloth napkins, a pottery container of
mixed tulips, buttercups, yellow bells, and baby's breath, and rustic ceramic
plates like those she once admired at a home down on Edisto Island. There's

nothing fancy about this party, and while Mother offers beer and iced tea, most folks opt simply for another cup of punch.

Though the menu for this party is highly regional, all the delectable dishes can be easily prepared anywhere. The only thing missing would be Mother's spirited stories about every item.

Martha Pearl Advises

At informal occasions, mixing old and new china is fun and interesting to guests. At more formal affairs, on the other hand, I never hesitate to use my finest heirloom silver, serving pieces, and linens. Why store away beautiful cutwork cloths and napkins when, actually, the more they're used and laundered, the lovelier they are?

Menu

St. Cecilia's Punch

Curried Shrimp Paste

Easy She-Crab Soup

Chicken and Ham Perloo

Plantation Baked Tomatoes

Joseph's Hoecakes

Benne Cookies

Beer and Iced Tea

St. Cecilia's Punch

Years ago over lunch at a home in Mt. Pleasant outside Charleston, South Carolina, Mother not only tasted her first St. Cecilia's punch but was told how the lethal concoction was introduced at the St. Cecilia musical society there in the early eighteenth century and how it reflects the English (tea), French (champagne and cognac), and West Indian (rum) influences on the local culture. Since the punch deals such a wallop, she later adopted it for her Low Country perloo party, and she insists that it absolutely must be made with only green tea, fresh pineapple, dark Myers's rum, and preferably French champagne. As for the block of ice, "I once could get it at the good old icehouse, but now I have to clear out half the freezer of the refrigerator and freeze my blocks in big plastic tubs." The problem is solved if you have a deepfreeze, but Mother does warn that simply using ice cubes will only dilute the punch's flavor and strength.

4 lemons, thinly sliced and seeded
1 pint brandy
2 cups water
2 cups sugar
¼ cup green tea leaves
½ fresh pineapple, peeled, cored, and thinly sliced
1 pint dark rum
Three 750ml bottles dry champagne
2 liters soda water

Place the lemon slices in a large glass bowl, pour the brandy over them, cover with plastic wrap, and let marinate overnight.

In a large saucepan, combine the water and sugar and bring to a boil over moderate heat, stirring. Place the tea leaves in a large bowl, pour the sugar water over them, and let cool. Add the pineapple to the lemon and brandy mixture and strain the cooled tea into the mixture.

continued

Pour the fruit-and-brandy mixture into a large crystal or silver punch bowl, add the rum, and mix well. When ready to serve, place a large block of ice in the mixture. Add the champagne and soda water, stir to blend well, and ladle the punch into crystal or silver punch cups (or, as Mother does, into silver julep cups).

30 TO 40 PUNCH CUPS

Curried Shrimp Paste

Shrimp paste is one of the Low Country's most original contributions to fine Southern cooking, a subtle spread that lends itself to endless interpretation and one that Mother's convinced has much better texture when made with a meat grinder instead of a blender or food processor (as so many people now do). Traditionally, shrimp paste contains no curry powder, but when Mother decided to try this variation, guests at her perloo party exclaimed so that she now usually adds it. If she doesn't curry the paste, she might enhance it with a tablespoon of semisweet sherry.

1½ pounds medium-size shrimp
½ cup (1 stick) butter, softened
2 green onions (whites and part of green leaves included), minced
1 teaspoon medium-hot curry powder
1 teaspoon Worcestershire sauce
½ teaspoon fresh lemon juice
¼ teaspoon dry mustard
Ground mace to taste
Salt and black pepper to taste
Toast points (see Martha Pearl Advises, page 38) or crackers

Place the shrimp in a large saucepan with enough water to cover, bring to a boil, remove from the heat, let stand for 1 minute, and drain in a colander. When cool enough to handle, peel and devein the shrimp and run them through the fine blade of a meat grinder into a large mixing bowl. Add all the remaining ingredients except the toast points and stir till the mixture forms a paste. Scrape into a crock and chill for 1 hour before spreading on toast points or crackers.

ABOUT 2 CUPS PASTE; AT LEAST 8 SERVINGS

Easy She-Crab Soup

Mother has two basic recipes for this distinctive, suave, inimitable Low Country soup, one made in a double boiler with traditional crab roe, the other, easier version prepared simply in a saucepan with a bit of lemon rind and chopped hard-boiled eggs substituted for the expensive roe—the way the black cooks at old Henry's restaurant in Charleston used to do. Quite frankly, I can't tell the difference between the two, the only imperative being that you must whisk constantly while adding the milk and cream to the butter-and-flour roux. We like lots of sherry in our she-crab soup, but feel free to adjust according to your own taste.

1 cup (2 sticks) butter

¼ cup all-purpose flour

4 cups milk

4 cups heavy cream

2 small onions, minced

1½ pounds fresh lump crabmeat (see **Martha Pearl Advises, page 52**), picked over for shells
    and cartilage

3 large hard-boiled egg yolks, finely chopped

2 teaspoons grated lemon rind

1 teaspoon ground mace

2 tablespoons Worcestershire sauce

2 teaspoons salt

1 teaspoon ground white pepper

¼ cup dry sherry

Mild paprika to taste

continued

In a large, heavy pot, melt the butter over moderate heat, then add the flour and whisk till well blended. Increase the heat slightly and, whisking constantly, gradually add the milk, then the cream, whisking till the mixture thickens slightly and is smooth. Stir in the remaining ingredients, except the sherry and paprika, reduce the heat to low, cover, and simmer for 20 minutes. Stir in the sherry, pour the soup into a tureen, sprinkle paprika over the top, and serve.

AT LEAST 8 SERVINGS

Martha Pearl Advises

When cooking with sherry, add it as close to the end and near serving time as possible, since it loses its flavor quickly when heated.

Chicken and Ham Perloo

Low Country perloo (like Creole gumbo and jambalaya) is an indigenous rice dish made with everything from tiny river shrimp, mixed seafood, various types of poultry and meats, even game, and who knows today what is authentic historically. Mother does make a delicious bacony shrimp perloo and a spicy chicken one, but guests (and I) find this chicken and ham version truly extraordinary. Be sure to fluff the perloo quickly but well before serving.

One 3- to 3½-pound chicken (giblets included), cut up
½ cup (1 stick) butter
2 medium-size onions, chopped
2 celery ribs, chopped
1 medium-size green bell pepper, seeded and chopped
2 large ripe tomatoes, chopped (juices included)
¾ pound cooked ham, cut into cubes

1 teaspoon dried sage, crumbled

1 teaspoon dried thyme

1 small fresh red chili pepper, seeded and minced

Salt and black pepper to taste

2 cups uncooked long-grain rice

Place the chicken plus the giblets in a large pot and add enough water to cover. Bring to a boil, reduce the heat to moderate, cover, and cook till the chicken is tender, about 30 minutes. With a slotted spoon, transfer the chicken and giblets to a plate and reserve the stock. When cool enough to handle, skin and bone the chicken, cut the meat into cubes, and set aside. Coarsely chop the giblets and set aside.

In another large pot, melt the butter over moderate heat, then add the onions, celery, and bell pepper and cook, stirring, till the onions are golden, about 10 minutes. Add the tomatoes plus their juices, the chicken and giblets, ham, sage, thyme, and chili pepper, season with salt and pepper, and stir well. Add the rice and 1 quart of the reserved chicken stock, stir, and bring to a low boil. Reduce the heat to low, cover, and simmer till the broth is absorbed and the rice is tender, about 30 minutes. Fluff the perloo with a fork before serving in a large pottery casserole.

8 SERVINGS

Plantation Baked Tomatoes

In the glory days of the Carolina Low Country, cooked rice might well have been used instead of bread crumbs to bind the stuffing for these tomatoes, but every time Mother has tried the old technique, she's found the texture just too heavy. No doubt the early rice planters hadn't so much as heard of Parmesan cheese, but it does made a big difference.

2 medium-size onions, finely chopped

3 cups fresh bread crumbs

$\frac{1}{2}$ cup freshly grated Parmesan cheese

1 teaspoon dried thyme

1 teaspoon dried oregano, crumbled

4 pounds (about 5) firm, ripe tomatoes, sliced $\frac{1}{4}$ inch thick

$\frac{1}{2}$ cup (1 stick) butter, cut into pieces

Preheat the oven to 350°F. Butter a medium-size casserole and set aside.

In a large mixing bowl, combine the onions, bread crumbs, cheese, thyme, and oregano and mix till well blended. Arrange a layer of tomatoes across the bottom of the prepared casserole and sprinkle part of the bread crumb mixture over the top. Continue to make layers, ending with the bread crumb mixture on top. Dot the top with the butter and bake till the top is golden brown, about 30 minutes. Serve piping hot.

8 SERVINGS

Joseph's Hoecakes

Hoecakes go back to the days when Indians and slaves in the South cooked breads on the metal ends of hoes over open fires, no doubt the origins of Southern cornbread. For years, our family used to vacation at the legendary Patricia Inn at Myrtle Beach, South Carolina, where in the gracious dining room our loyal black waiter, Joseph, was forever discussing cooking and recipes with Mother. He told her the right way to fry breakfast spots, how to prepare "philpy" (rice bread), and what constitutes a genuine Huguenot torte, but one of the liveliest discussions I remember pertained to how the addictive hoecakes served at lunch were made. You'd just as soon not eat these cakes unless they're slathered with plenty of butter.

2 cups white cornmeal
1 teaspoon salt
1 cup boiling water
2 to 3 tablespoons Crisco vegetable shortening or bacon grease

In a large mixing bowl, combine the cornmeal and salt, then pour on the boiling water in a slow, steady stream, beating constantly with a wooden spoon till the batter is smooth. For each hoecake, in your hands, pat about 2 tablespoons of batter into a flat round 3 to 4 inches in diameter, and continue patting till all the batter is used up.

Heat about 1 tablespoon of the shortening or bacon grease in a large, cast-iron skillet over high heat, reduce the heat to low, add a few of the hoecakes, and fry till golden brown and crisp, about 2 minutes on each side. Repeat with the remaining fat and hoecakes, transferring them to a platter and keeping them as hot as possible until served.

16 TO 18 HOECAKES

Benne Cookies

Although we've been eating benne (or sesame seed) cookies for decades, it was not till we had lunch on the screened porch at Middleton Plantation near Charleston, South Carolina, a few years ago that Mother proclaimed the ones made by an old black cook there the best she'd ever tasted—and, of course, proceeded to get the exact recipe. Baking "bennes" is very risky business, so stay alert from beginning to end. The seeds themselves must be watched constantly to avoid burning, the cookies won't peel off the foil if they're baked too long, and the texture is simply not right if the cookies are pale and puffed (they must be just slightly browned). Never are timing and careful watching more important than when making bennes.

1 cup benne (sesame) seeds
¾ cup (1½ sticks) butter, melted
1½ cups firmly packed light brown sugar
1¼ cups all-purpose flour
¼ teaspoon baking powder
¼ teaspoon salt
1 teaspoon pure vanilla extract
1 large egg, beaten

Preheat the oven to 300°F, then toast the benne seeds on an ungreased large baking sheet till golden, 10 to 15 minutes. Transfer to a plate to cool and increase the oven temperature to 325°F. Line the baking sheet, plus another large one, with sheets of greased aluminum foil and set aside.

In a large mixing bowl, combine the toasted benne seeds with all the remaining ingredients and stir with a wooden spoon till well blended and smooth. Drop the batter by ½ teaspoons onto the prepared baking sheets about 1½ inches apart and bake till evenly browned, 15 to 20 minutes (if pale in the centers and puffed, the cookies are not ready), watching constantly to avoid burning. Remove from the oven, then immediately and carefully peel the cookies from the foil and let cool on paper towels. Store the cookies in a tightly covered container.

ABOUT 85 COOKIES

The Yellow Bell
Bridge Luncheon

IF ANYTHING SYMBOLIZES FOR MOTHER THE
arrival of spring more than the blooming of the yellow bell (forsythia), it is the
kickoff bridge luncheon she hosts for eight ladies during the last week of April.
Catching up on gossip is important at this informal luncheon, but even more
paramount at the get-together is the exchange of recipes collected and tested
over the winter. "All the gals are pretty good cooks," Mother admits, "but some
are jealous of others and guard certain recipes like hawks." She hesitates, laughing
naughtily. "Of course, I share all of mine."

The timed routine never changes. Guests arrive at exactly eleven A.M. and
are served glasses of chilled rosé wine in the sunroom. At eleven-thirty, everybody moves to the living room decorated with yellow bells in profusion, takes a
seat at one of two card tables draped with handsome needlepoint covers and set
with decks of cards, score pads, and flowered tallies, and gets down to serious
playing—and more sipping. When Mother is dummy, she retreats to the kitchen
to ladle chilled soup into cups and arrange the food on Williamsburg china
plates. At one o'clock, special protective bridge cloths with matching napkins are
placed over the valuable needlepoint covers and lunch is served. At two o'clock,
playing resumes till the rubbers are finished, and needless to say, more wine is
poured. For every trick a lady goes down, she puts a penny in an ornamental dish

on the edge of each table, then they play "bingo" with the cards and whoever gets rid of her cards first wins the kitty.

The quaint, charming tenor of the whole occasion couldn't be more Southern, and if the card-playing and chatter and eating and drinking must come to an end promptly by three-thirty, it's only so that everybody can get home before the four o'clock traffic begins.

Martha Pearl Advises

For fairly fancy and intimate occasions like my Yellow Bell Bridge Luncheon or Resurrection Breakfast, I like to buy small, ceramic, hand-painted frames to use as place cards and take-home favors.

Menu

Rosé Wine

Chilled Carrot and Almond Soup

Celery Hearts Stuffed with Olive Pimento Cheese

Grand Slam Creamed Chicken on Toast Points

Frozen Fruit Salad

Raspberry Meringue Nests

Orange Iced Tea (page 310)

Chilled Carrot and Almond Soup

Mother has always found the combination of carrots and almonds to be exotic, whether for a salad, for a sandwich spread, or for this spicy soup that she likes to serve in small teacups. "Personally, I prefer to drink a fine Alsatian wine with this soup," she almost whispers, "but since the gals at my bridge luncheon love rosé wine with just about anything, I'd never make a fuss."

3 tablespoons butter
2 medium-size onions, chopped
3 cups chicken stock or broth
6 medium-size carrots, scraped and cut into rounds
3 whole cloves
$\frac{1}{2}$ stick cinnamon
$\frac{1}{2}$ cup chopped blanched almonds
3 cups milk
Black pepper to taste

In a large saucepan, melt the butter over moderate heat, then add the onions and cook, stirring till soft, about 3 minutes. Add the broth, carrots, cloves, and cinnamon, bring to a boil, reduce the heat to low, cover, and simmer till the carrots are very soft, about 40 minutes.

Remove and discard the cloves and cinnamon, pour the mixture into a large blender or food processor, add the almonds, and process to a puree. Pour the mixture into a bowl, stir in the milk, season with pepper, let cool, then chill at least 3 hours before serving.

8 SERVINGS

Celery Hearts Stuffed with Olive Pimento Cheese

So beloved and popular in the South are celery hearts stuffed with pimento cheese (for cocktail parties, picnics, ladies' luncheons, school lunch boxes, and just snacks) that some people actually make a meal of them. (Mother remembers her own mother going down the line of the old S & W cafeteria in Charlotte and passing by all the elaborate composed salads in favor of a plate of stuffed celery). For years, Mother made her pimento cheese exclusively with extra-sharp aged cheddar; then she learned how the spread could be enhanced by a little grated Parmesan—plus some chopped olives. And why make a whole pound of pimento cheese for this one recipe? "For the simple reason that no Southerner ever makes less than a pound of anything," she huffs indignantly. "I'm never without a crock of pimento cheese in the refrigerator—for stuffing celery, to make sandwiches, or spread on crackers, just everything."

1 pound extra-sharp aged cheddar cheese

3 tablespoon freshly grated genuine Parmesan cheese

One 7-ounce jar pimentos (see Martha Pearl Advises, page 205), drained, liquid reserved, and diced

½ cup finely chopped green olives

1 teaspoon fresh lemon juice

1 teaspoon Worcestershire sauce

Cayenne pepper to taste

⅔ cup mayonnaise (Mother prefers Hellmann's)

8 celery heart ribs, rinsed, dried, and cut in half

Grate the cheddar finely into a large mixing bowl, add the Parmesan, pimentos, and olives, and mix well with a fork. Add the lemon juice, Worcestershire, cayenne, and mayonnaise and mash the mixture with a fork till well blended and like a paste. (If the mixture is too thick, add a little of the reserved pimento liquid.)

Stuff each celery half with pimento cheese, arrange the halves on a glass relish plate, and keep chilled, covered with plastic wrap, till ready to serve. (Scrape the remaining pimento cheese into a crock, cover, and keep chilled for up to 1 week for snacks and sandwiches.)

8 S E R V I N G S

Grand Slam Creamed Chicken on Toast Points

Who knows the origins of this quintessential Southern dish that has graced bridge luncheon tables so long that it's almost become a joke? Mother recalls that creamed chicken (in fancy pastry cups, on toast points, and over rice) was served at any and all social events when she was growing up during the Depression—due, most likely, to the low cost of chicken. ("My mama used to talk about getting a whole chicken for twenty-five cents," she relates.) The irony is that there's still no dish that Southern ladies love more, and the hard-core truth is that a carefully prepared creamed chicken spiked with pimentos, nuts, and sherry is, yes, utterly delicious.

continued

8 slices white loaf bread

2 tablespoons plus $\frac{1}{2}$ cup (1 stick) butter

$\frac{1}{2}$ cup thinly sliced fresh mushrooms

$\frac{1}{2}$ cup all-purpose flour

1 teaspoon salt

$\frac{1}{2}$ teaspoon black pepper

1 cup chicken stock or broth

2 cups half-and-half

3 cups diced cooked chicken breast

$\frac{1}{4}$ cup finely chopped pimentos (see Martha Pearl Advises, page 205)

$\frac{1}{2}$ cup slivered blanched almonds

$\frac{1}{4}$ cup semidry sherry

Trim the edges of the bread, cut each slice in half diagonally, toast the pieces lightly, and set aside.

In a small skillet, melt the 2 tablespoons butter over moderate heat, then add the mushrooms, cook, stirring till they absorb the butter, about 8 minutes, and set aside.

In a large saucepan, melt the remaining $\frac{1}{2}$ cup (1 stick) butter over moderate heat, then add the flour, salt, and pepper and stir till well blended and smooth. Remove the pan from the heat and gradually add the broth and half-and-half, stirring constantly till well blended and smooth. Return the pan to the heat, reduce the heat to low, and cook till thick, about 10 minutes, stirring constantly. Fold in the reserved mushrooms, the chicken, pimentos, almonds, and sherry and cook till the mixture is heated thoroughly.

Arrange two pieces of toast with the points aimed outward on each serving plate and spoon equal amounts of creamed chicken over the top of each.

8   SERVINGS

Frozen Fruit Salad

Mother has been preparing frozen fruit salads ever since, as a teenager, she hosted her first bridge club. "We always served one of these salads, and, Lord, did we think they were something." Today, some of her other salads might be considerably more sophisticated, but for one of her spring bridge luncheons, she still loves nothing more than to concoct a frozen salad using the season's very first fresh cherries, peaches, and blueberries. "And let me tell you one thing," she adds, "the gals at my kickoff luncheon still think a good frozen salad is the height of elegance." If you care to go to the trouble of using fresh pineapple (as Mother often does), substitute 2 cups of chopped fresh for the canned.

One 3-ounce package cream cheese, softened
¼ cup mayonnaise (Mother prefers Hellmann's)
2 tablespoons sugar
2 tablespoons fresh lemon juice
2 cups rinsed, pitted, and halved ripe cherries
1 cup peeled, pitted, and sliced ripe peaches
½ cup stemmed and rinsed fresh blueberries
2 ripe bananas, peeled and sliced
One 8-ounce can pineapple bits, drained
1 cup heavy cream, whipped to stiff peaks
8 Bibb lettuce leaves
8 rinsed and pitted ripe cherries for garnish

In a large mixing bowl, beat the cream cheese, mayonnaise, sugar, and lemon juice with a wooden spoon till well blended and smooth. Add the cherries, peaches, blueberries, bananas, and pineapple and stir gently till well blended. Fold in the whipped cream till well blended, scrape the mixture into a large loaf pan, cover with plastic wrap, and place in the freezer overnight.

continued

When ready to serve, slice the loaf with a sharp knife into 8 sections, place each section on a lettuce leaf on a salad plate, let stand for about 10 minutes to soften slightly, and garnish each salad with a whole cherry.

8 SERVINGS

Martha Pearl Advises

*During the cold months, I have no qualms about making frozen fruit salads with frozen or canned fruits. If using frozen fruits, just be sure **not** to thaw them, to minimize sogginess in the salad.*

Raspberry Meringue Nests

This dessert was inspired by some meringue shells with chocolate syrup that Mother was served at a bridesmaids' luncheon, the only problem being that she simply didn't like what she ate. Seeing potential in the concept, however, she improved the meringue nests and came up with another sauce, the results being one of her most delectable and popular confections.

FOR THE MERINGUE NESTS

4 large egg whites, at room temperature

½ teaspoon cream of tartar

1 teaspoon pure vanilla extract

1 cup sugar

FOR THE SAUCE

⅔ cup sugar

2 tablespoons cornstarch

**2 pints fresh raspberries, gently rinsed, or two 10-ounce packages frozen raspberries,
   thawed**

2 tablespoons fresh lemon juice

T O S E R V E

Vanilla ice cream

To make the nests, line a large baking sheet with a sheet of parchment or brown paper, trace eight 3½-inch circles on the surface, and set aside.

In a large mixing bowl, beat the egg whites with an electric mixer at high speed till frothy, add the cream of tartar and vanilla, and beat till soft peaks form. Gradually add the sugar by tablespoons, beating till stiff, glossy peaks form.

Preheat the oven to 250°F.

Form nests by placing about 2 tablespoons of the egg whites in each traced circle on the prepared baking sheet and, with the back of a spoon, hollowing out the centers to form nests. Bake for 50 minutes, turn off the heat, and leave the nests in the oven for 15 minutes to dry completely. Remove and let cool.

To make the sauce, combine the sugar and cornstarch in the top of a double boiler over simmering water and mix till well blended. Add the raspberries and stir till thickened and glossy. Add the lemon juice, stir, and let cool.

To serve, place the nests on 8 dessert plates, spoon a scoop of vanilla ice cream in the center of each, and top with raspberry sauce.

8 S E R V I N G S

A Bereavement Buffet

"IN ALL MY YEARS, I CAN'T REMEMBER A FUNERAL of a family member or close friend that wasn't followed by a large bereavement buffet," Mother declares with utter seriousness. No doubt people all over the country gather solemnly to observe the death of loved ones, but often much to the consternation of non-Southerners, nowhere does a formal bereavement assume the atmosphere of a social event—a veritable celebration—like in the South. Even I was a bit shocked, for instance, when Mother told me about a recent bereavement held at a Charlotte country club where, while the guests partook of a heroic buffet luncheon, listened to a Dixieland combo, and clapped, the ashes of the deceased gentleman, an obsessed golfer, were scattered over the golf course from a twin-engine plane!

Of course, at ordinary Southern bereavements people simply bring various dishes to the home of the deceased, but since, over the years, Mother has earned something of a reputation for the bereavement buffets she volunteers to sponsor ("to make it a little easier on the mourners in the immediate family"), it's not rare for her to organize three or four of these get-togethers at her place per year—and to prepare most of the food herself. The menus are discussed with family and friends, directions are given for flowers (acres of flowers!) to be sent to her address, friends pitch in to keep plenty of food on the table throughout the afternoon as mourners come and go, and never once is there an empty coffeepot, or iced-tea pitcher, or, indeed, wine cooler.

Mother's bereavement luncheon buffets can be true gastronomic feats, her only comment being, "Well, honey, we have to remember that lots of these poor out-of-town guests haven't put a morsel of food in their mouths since breakfast."

Martha Pearl Advises

Since, at bereavements, people are coming and going all afternoon, dishes have to be replenished, and cleanup can be a real job, I usually hire some help. Ditto large cocktail parties and suppers where a good bartender can both pour drinks and pass appetizers.

Menu

Asparagus Stand-Ups

Chicken, Brown Rice, and Pimento Casserole

Chilled Salmon Loaf

Congealed Beet Salad

Prayer Bread

Chocolate, Walnut, and Raspberry Torte

Coffee, Iced Tea, and White Wine

Asparagus Stand-Ups

*Mother wishes she could take credit for this clever asparagus preparation, but the truth
is that she attended a bereavement buffet held at a clubhouse near her, was utterly taken
by the coated asparagus standing upright in wide glasses, and right then and there got
the recipe from the chef. Do make sure that the asparagus are as uniform in size as possible, and don't roll them too heavily in the cheese—a mistake Mother once made and
still regrets. These asparagus do not keep once they've been coated with cheese.*

3 dozen medium-size stalks fresh asparagus
1½ cups olive oil
¾ cup red wine vinegar
½ teaspoon dry mustard
3 garlic cloves, crushed
½ teaspoon dried oregano, crumbled
½ teaspoon dried thyme
1 teaspoon salt
½ teaspoon black pepper
1½ cups freshly grated Parmesan cheese

Cut off and discard any woody bases of the asparagus, cut the asparagus into uniform lengths,
and trim off the scales. Place the asparagus in a large, shallow pan, add enough water to barely
cover, bring to a boil, and blanch till the stalks are just tender but still firm, 3 to 4 minutes.
Drain off the boiling water, add enough cold water to cover and refresh, then drain the
asparagus on paper towels till almost dry.

In a bowl, whisk together the olive oil, vinegar, and mustard till well blended, then add the
garlic, oregano, thyme, salt, and pepper, whisk well, and pour into a long, shallow ceramic
dish. Add the asparagus to the marinade, turn briefly, cover with plastic wrap, and leave to
marinate in the refrigerator for at least 2 hours.

When ready to serve, sprinkle the cheese on a flat surface, take the asparagus from the marinade, roll each stalk lightly in the cheese, and, using wide-mouth glasses shorter than the
asparagus, stand them upright in the glasses. Serve immediately.

3 DOZEN ASPARAGUS

Chicken, Brown Rice, and Pimento Casserole

The South is known for its elaborate casseroles, and I know of none that illustrates the art better than this succulent beauty that Mother has served at Lord knows how many bereavements. Regular long-grain rice, of course, could be used, but once you've tasted full-flavored brown rice (which is unpolished, with only the husks removed), the ordinary white variety seems feeble by comparison. Whereas most people simply place a casserole such as this directly on the table, Mother once went to the trouble of finding a silver chafing dish into which her casserole fits perfectly—and which can be covered with a handsome lid.

5 cups water
2 teaspoons salt
2 cups uncooked brown rice
½ cup (1 stick) butter
1 large onion, chopped
2 celery ribs, chopped
1 pound fresh mushrooms, chopped
½ cup all-purpose flour
2 cups chicken stock or broth
2 cups half-and-half
6 cups cubed cooked chicken
1 cup slivered toasted almonds (see Martha Pearl Advises, page 119)
One 4-ounce jar pimentos (see Martha Pearl Advises, page 205), drained and chopped
½ teaspoon dried tarragon
Salt and black pepper to taste
2 tablespoons dry sherry

In a large saucepan, bring the water and salt to a brisk boil, add the rice, and stir. Cover the pan, reduce the heat to a simmer, and cook till all the water has been absorbed and the rice is tender, 40 to 45 minutes. Fluff the rice with a fork and keep warm.

Preheat the oven to 350°F. Grease a large, attractive casserole and set aside.

In a large, heavy skillet, melt the butter over moderate heat, then add the onion, celery, and mushrooms and stir for 5 minutes. Sprinkle the flour over the top and stir 3 minutes longer. Add the broth and half-and-half and stir steadily till the mixture thickens, about 10 minutes. Pour the mixture into the prepared casserole, add the rice, chicken, almonds, pimentos, tarragon, salt and pepper, and sherry, stir till well blended, and bake, covered, till bubbly, about 30 minutes. Serve directly from the casserole.

1 0   T O   1 2   S E R V I N G S

Martha Pearl Advises

Pimentos can have tough skins, so when buying jars, try to find the whole or half pimentos, which are so much easier to peel (when necessary) than the small pieces.

Chilled Salmon Loaf

This simple but colorful loaf is strictly Southern by virtue of the rice, not bread crumbs, used to bind the mixture. If the loaf is served hot, it is usually accompanied by a tomato sauce in the South and, for a more sophisticated occasion, Mother whisks the egg whites separately, folds them into the combined mixture, and turns the loaf into more of a "soufflé."

Mild paprika
3 cups canned salmon, drained, picked over for skin and bones, and flaked
3 cups cooked rice of your choice
⅔ cup milk
4 large eggs, beaten
2 tablespoons butter, melted
1 small onion, finely chopped
¼ cup finely chopped green olives
¼ cup finely chopped fresh parsley leaves
2 tablespoons finely chopped fresh dill
Juice of 1 lemon
Salt and black pepper to taste
Thinly sliced cucumbers, for garnish

Preheat the oven to 475°F. Grease a large fish mold, sprinkle the bottom and sides with paprika, and set aside.

In a large mixing bowl, combine the remaining ingredients except the cucumbers, and, using your hands, mix till well blended. Scrape the mixture into the prepared mold and bake the loaf till firm, about 45 minutes. Transfer the loaf to a wire rack, drain off any liquid, let cool completely, cover with plastic wrap, and chill for at least 2 hours.

To serve, unmold the loaf onto a large serving platter, sweep the paprika to make fin designs, garnish the edges with cucumber slices, and serve.

10 TO 12 SERVINGS

Canned red salmon is fine for molded salads, loaves, and croquettes so long as you carefully remove any skin and bones. The red salmon is a lot more expensive than the pink, but it's worth it.

Congealed Beet Salad

Mother is convinced that, contrary to public opinion, people do love beets when they're prepared in an imaginative, attractive manner, and each time she's served this beautiful salad at one of her bereavements, mourners have never failed to finish every last morsel. "One reason," she supposes, "is that it's not so cloyingly sweet like so many congealed salads." So popular has the salad always been, in fact, that she advises making two or even three of them at a time.

Two 1-pound cans whole beets
2 envelopes unflavored gelatin
3 tablespoons sugar
$\frac{1}{3}$ cup orange juice
3 celery ribs, chopped
$\frac{1}{4}$ cup chopped fresh dill
Salt to taste
Romaine lettuce leaves

Grease a large mold and set aside.

Drain the juice from the beets into a small saucepan and, if necessary, add enough water to measure $1\frac{1}{2}$ cups of liquid. Sprinkle the gelatin over the liquid and let soak for 5 minutes. Heat the mixture till just warm, stir till the gelatin is completely dissolved, and pour into a large mixing bowl to cool. Meanwhile, shred the beets into another bowl and set aside.

continued

Add the sugar and orange juice to the gelatin mixture and stir till well blended. Add the shredded beets, celery, and dill, season with salt, and stir well. Pour the mixture into the prepared mold, cover with plastic wrap, and chill till firm, at least 3 hours.

Arrange lettuce leaves around the sides of a large serving platter, unmold the salad in the center, and serve.

10 TO 12 SERVINGS

Martha Pearl Advises

Although I love cooking with beets, their potential to stain everything in sight drives me crazy. Never allow a beet stain on a counter, chopping-block, finger—anything—to stand so long as a minute. An equal mixture of lemon juice and vinegar will remove a beet stain immediately, so I always keep a tiny glass of the solution within arm's reach.

Prayer Bread

Since this unusually light whole wheat bread requires three risings, Mother has always called it her "prayer" bread for one quaint reason: "The bread takes so long to rise that you could actually pray between risings." Be sure to slather this bread with plenty of butter.

2 envelopes active dry yeast

2 cups warm water

1 cup hot water

1 cup sugar

3 teaspoons salt

1 cup Crisco vegetable shortening

3 large eggs, beaten

4 cups all-purpose flour

4 cups whole wheat flour

In a small mixing bowl, sprinkle the yeast over the warm water and let proof for 5 to 10 minutes. In a large mixing bowl, pour the hot water over the sugar, salt, and shortening, stir with a wooden spoon till the shortening has melted, and let cool.

Add the yeast mixture and the eggs to the shortening mixture and stir with a wooden spoon till well blended. Gradually add the two flours, stirring till the dough is smooth and not sticky, adding a little more flour if necessary. Transfer the dough to a lightly floured work surface and knead for 8 to 10 minutes. Rinse, dry, and grease the mixing bowl, place the dough in the bowl, cover with a clean kitchen towel, and let rise in a warm draft-free area till doubled in bulk, about 1 hour. Punch the dough down, cover, and let rise again till almost doubled in bulk, 30 to 40 minutes. Meanwhile, grease two medium-size loaf pans and set aside.

Divide the dough in half, pat each half firmly into the prepared pans, cover with kitchen towels, and let rise again till the dough almost reaches over the sides of the pans, about 30 minutes.

Meanwhile, preheat the oven to 375°F. Bake the loaves for 20 minutes, then reduce the oven temperature to 350°F and bake till the loaves are nicely browned and hollow-sounding when tapped, about 45 minutes. Turn the loaves out on a wire rack to cool before slicing.

2 MEDIUM-SIZE LOAVES

Chocolate, Walnut, and Raspberry Torte

"Honey, I'll tell you the basic ingredients for the torte, but that's all I'll tell," I remember Pearl saying to Mother in polite but serious fashion. A staunch Virginian who eventually opened a small restaurant in New York City, Pearl Byrd Foster was a legendary character and remarkable cook, a true innovator who guarded her recipes like gold, and an old-fashioned Southern lady whom Mother loved and respected. Since this torte has no flour and depends on bread crumbs and nuts for texture, trying to duplicate Pearl's original was a real challenge for Mother. Suffice it that what she finally came up with is one of the most sumptuous desserts in her repertoire—and one which dear Pearl just might have admitted is as good as her own.

FOR THE TORTE

½ cup (1 stick) butter, softened

1 cup sugar

4 large eggs

¼ cup dry bread crumbs

1 tablespoon pure vanilla extract

¼ teaspoon salt

6 ounces bittersweet chocolate, melted and cooled a bit

1 cup finely chopped walnuts

1 cup raspberry preserves

FOR THE GLAZE

3 ounces semisweet chocolate

⅓ cup butter, softened and cut into pieces

TO GARNISH

Walnut halves

Preheat the oven to 375°F. Butter the bottom and sides of two 9-inch round cake pans, line the bottoms with waxed paper, butter the paper, and set the pans aside.

In a medium-size mixing bowl, cream together the butter and sugar with an electric mixer at medium speed till fluffy, then beat in the eggs one at a time. Add the bread crumbs, vanilla, salt, melted chocolate, and chopped walnuts and stir till well blended and smooth. Divide the batter equally between the two prepared pans, "spank" the bottoms of the pans with a hand to distribute the batter evenly, and bake till a cake tester inserted in the center comes out dry, about 25 minutes. Let the pans cool on a wire rack, then run a knife around the edges to loosen the cakes. Turn the cakes out onto the rack, peel off the waxed paper, and place the waxed paper under the rack to catch excess glaze. Spread the raspberry preserves over the top of one cake, then position the other cake on top of the preserves.

To make the glaze, combine the chocolate and butter in the top of a double boiler over simmering water and stir till melted and well blended. Remove the pan from the heat and beat the mixture till it just begins to thicken.

Slowly pour the glaze over the top of the torte and smooth the top and sides with a rubber spatula. Arrange walnut halves around the edges of the torte and let stand for at least 1 hour before serving.

ONE 9-INCH TORTE; 10 TO 12 SERVINGS

A Formal Cocktail Supper

I HAVE NO IDEA WHEN, WHY, OR HOW THE FORMAL "cocktail supper" originated in the South, but it's a gracious tradition that Mother has been observing every May since she was a bride. "Most of my year-round affairs are pretty informal," she explains, "but come the warm days of spring with all the wonderful fresh food and flowers, I just love to take out my finest china and silver, do a few fancy dishes, hire a good bartender, see people all dressed up, and generally put on the dog."

And "put on the dog" she does. On the large cocktail table are a silver wine cooler holding French champagne, uncorked bottles of fine vintage red and white wines, every spirit and mixer imaginable, proper wineglasses and cut-glass tumblers, and linen cocktail napkins. Since it's unheard of in the South to serve wine and cocktails without a few appetizers, Mother distributes at least two at various locations in the living room and sunroom.

For the sit-down supper, the extended mahogany table is covered with her finest cutwork tablecloth and decorated in the center with three delicate stemmed bowl vases set over a mirror with a red carnation floating in each goblet. The china is her mother's antique gold-and-white Bavarian, the glassware Waterford crystal, and the serving vessels either silver, bone china, or elegant porcelain casseroles. And this is one time when Mother has help (the bartender) to clear dishes from the table and keep glasses replenished.

Menu

Champagne, Wine, and Open Bar

Fancy Parmesan-Cheddar Straws

Spicy Clam Spread

Smothered Quail

Pecan Wild Rice and Mushrooms

Company Spinach Casserole

Top-Hat Walnut Shortbreads

Fancy Parmesan-Cheddar Straws

Mother used to make her spicy cheese straws exclusively with sharp cheddar in Old Southern fashion, then she discovered that the addition of Parmesan not only provided deeper flavor but made the straws brown better. Beware, however, not to overbrown the straws, which toughens and dries them out. For variation, she sometimes adds a finely chopped fresh herb to the dough—so long as it doesn't overwhelm the flavors of the cheeses. Stored between layers of waxed paper in a tightly sealed container, these straws freeze beautifully for weeks.

3 cups all-purpose flour

1 teaspoon salt

$\frac{1}{2}$ teaspoon cayenne pepper

1 cup (2 sticks) butter, cut into small pieces

$\frac{1}{2}$ pound freshly grated Parmesan cheese

$\frac{1}{2}$ pound grated sharp cheddar cheese

Into a large mixing bowl, sift together the flour, salt, and cayenne, then add the butter and work the mixture with your fingertips till it resembles coarse meal. Add the two cheeses and continue working the dough till it is no longer crumbly.

Preheat the oven to 350°F.

On a lightly floured work surface, roll out half the dough into a rectangle about $\frac{1}{4}$ inch thick and cut it into strips about $\frac{1}{4}$ inch wide and 4 to 5 inches long. Place the strips on a large, ungreased baking sheet and bake till just lightly browned, about 20 minutes. Let the straws cool, transfer them to a large plate, and repeat the procedure with the remaining dough. Store the straws in a tightly sealed container.

ABOUT 120 STRAWS

Spicy Clam Spread

Southerners expect and almost demand a savory spread at any event involving cocktails (which means virtually all social get-togethers), so Mother certainly would never disappoint her guests at a formal cocktail supper, even when one or two other appetizers are served. (We won't even get into how Rebels also relish sweet appetizers with their drinks.) She uses this basic formula also to make crabmeat, spinach, and ham spreads, so feel free to experiment.

Two 6½-ounce cans minced clams, liquid included
½ cup (1 stick) butter, melted
1 medium-size onion, minced
2 tablespoons finely chopped fresh parsley leaves
1 teaspoon dried oregano, crumbled
Tabasco Sauce to taste
¾ cup dry bread crumbs
1½ cups grated sharp cheddar cheese
Freshly grated Parmesan cheese to taste
Mild paprika to taste

Preheat the oven to 350°F. Grease a medium-size gratin dish and set aside.

In a medium-size mixing bowl, combine the clams plus their liquid, the butter, onion, parsley, oregano, Tabasco, and bread crumbs and mix till well blended. Scrape the mixture into the prepared dish, sprinkle the top with the two cheeses and paprika, and bake till golden, about 20 minutes. Serve the spread with crackers or small Melba toast rounds.

ABOUT 4 CUPS SPREAD

Smothered Quail

How well I remember Mother's brother-in-law, my Uncle Robert, showing up at the house with a dozen or so quail he'd shot in the field, plucked, cleaned, and ready for Maw Maw and Mother to fry, braise, roast, barbecue, or "smother" in this classic Southern style. Marinating not only tenderizes the birds but really enhances their subtle savor, and while they are delicious by themselves, you can make a simple gravy by sprinkling 3 tablespoon of flour over about 3 tablespoons of fat in the skillet, stirring the mixture for 1 minute, adding 2 cups chicken broth, and stirring over moderate heat to thicken.

12 cleaned quail (about $\frac{1}{3}$ pound each)
Salt and black pepper to taste
$\frac{1}{2}$ cup gin
$\frac{1}{2}$ cup vegetable oil
1 large onion, chopped
1 cup chopped celery leaves
1 teaspoon dried tarragon, crumbled
Tabasco Sauce to taste
$\frac{1}{2}$ cup (1 stick) butter
12 strips lean bacon
12 toast triangles (see Martha Pearl Advises, page 38)

Season each quail inside and out with salt and pepper and arrange them in a single layer in a large baking dish. In a medium-size mixing bowl, whisk together the gin and oil till well blended, then add the onion, celery leaves, and tarragon, season with Tabasco, and stir. Pour the marinade over the quail, cover with plastic wrap, and refrigerate for at least 6 hours, turning the quail twice.

Preheat the oven to 350°F.

Remove the quail from the marinade and wipe dry with paper towels. Melt half the butter in a large cast-iron skillet over moderately high heat, add half the quail, lightly brown them on all sides, and transfer to a large, shallow casserole. Repeat with the remaining butter and quail. Wrap each quail snugly with a strip of bacon, strain the marinade over the birds, cover with a sheet of aluminum foil, and bake till the quail are very tender about 45 minutes.

On a large silver serving platter, arrange each quail on a toast triangle and serve.

6 TO 12 SERVINGS

Pecan Wild Rice and Mushrooms

Although wild rice is expensive, a little goes a long way and is utterly delicious (and elegant) when combined with mushrooms, pecans, and herbs. Be sure to wash the rice thoroughly under cold running water and to cook it only till the grains open. Wild rice becomes limp if kept warm too long (if necessary, Mother keeps hers in a double boiler), so plan the cooking accordingly. For her formal cocktail supper, Mother serves her smothered quail on toast points, but for a small family dinner, she might well position the birds over mounds of this delectable rice.

2 cups wild rice
5 cups chicken stock or broth
Salt to taste
⅓ cup butter
1 large onion, minced
½ pound fresh mushrooms, finely chopped
½ cup finely chopped pecans
¼ teaspoon dried sage, crumbled
¼ teaspoon dried marjoram, crumbled
Black pepper to taste

In a strainer, wash the rice well under cold running water, then place in a large, heavy saucepan. Add the broth, bring to a boil, reduce the heat to moderate, and cook till all the rice has opened, about 35 minutes, stirring once or twice. Reduce the heat to the lowest possible temperature, fluff the rice with a fork, cover, and let stand.

In a medium-size, heavy skillet, melt the butter over moderate heat, then add the onion, mushrooms, pecans, sage, and marjoram, season with pepper, and stir till the vegetables are soft, 5 to 7 minutes. Scrape the contents of the skillet into the rice, fluff well, transfer to a large serving bowl, and serve.

8 TO 10 SERVINGS

Martha Pearl Advises

When cooking with wild rice, remember that 1 cup of raw rice yields about 4 cups of cooked. Cooked wild rice freezes well and can be reheated with a little hot water.

Company Spinach Casserole

Mother calls this her spinach casserole for people who don't like spinach—and she's convinced that most Southern men loathe plain boiled or steamed spinach even when butter-saturated. "I know fellows at my cocktail supper who won't touch the spinach their wives cook but who wolf down my casserole," she whispers proudly. "The secret is the seasoning, which should be checked carefully before the dish is baked. And don't be timid when judging the cheese, garlic, and nutmeg." For this casserole, she actually prefers frozen spinach for ideal texture.

Four 10-ounce packages frozen chopped spinach
2 cups sour cream
1 cup freshly grated Parmesan cheese
1 garlic clove, minced
Ground nutmeg to taste
Salt and black pepper to taste
1 cup dry bread crumbs
¼ cup (½ stick) butter, cut into pieces

Place the spinach in a large pot, add enough water to just cover, and bring to a boil. Reduce the heat to moderate, cover, cook till the spinach is tender, about 8 minutes, and drain in a colander, pressing down with the back of a spoon.

Preheat the oven to 350°F. Grease a large casserole and set aside.

In a large mixing bowl, combine the drained spinach, sour cream, Parmesan, and garlic, season with nutmeg, salt, and pepper, and stir till well blended. Scrape the mixture into the prepared casserole, sprinkle the bread crumbs over the top, dot the crumbs with the butter, and bake till bubbly and golden brown on top, 20 to 30 minutes. Serve piping hot.

AT LEAST 10 SERVINGS

Top-Hat Walnut Shortbreads

Perhaps it's her Scottish heritage, but for Mother shortbread is one of the greatest cookies ever conceived. "It's rich but not too sweet, it has the texture of a good pound cake, and it goes well with almost anything—ice cream, fruits, syrups, custards, etc." She created this chocolate "top-hat" shortbread years ago for a cocktail supper, and guests raved about it so that she made it a staple for the spring event. If you have time, the dessert is even better when the chocolate is allowed to harden slightly in the refrigerator.

2 cups all-purpose flour

1 cup cornstarch

1 teaspoon salt

1 cup (2 sticks) butter, softened

1 cup sugar

1½ teaspoons pure vanilla extract

1 cup finely chopped walnuts

One 6-ounce bag (1 cup) semisweet chocolate chips

Preheat the oven to 350°F.

Into a medium-size mixing bowl, sift together the flour, cornstarch, and salt. In a large mixing bowl, cream together the butter and sugar with an electric mixer at medium speed till fluffy, then add the vanilla and walnuts and beat with a wooden spoon till well blended. Gradually add the dry ingredients, beating just till they are well blended.

Divide the dough in half, place the halves on a large, heavy, ungreased baking sheet, and, using the palms of your hands, press the halves out into smooth 8-inch circles. Prick the dough all over with a fork and bake just till golden and firm to the touch, about 30 minutes. Transfer the hot shortbreads to two plates and immediately sprinkle equal amounts of chocolate chips over the tops. When the chocolate melts, spread it over the tops in a smooth layer, let cool completely, and cut the shortbreads into small wedges.

ABOUT 20 WEDGES

continued

Martha Pearl Advises

All shortbread must be made with pure butter—for both flavor and texture. With many dishes, you can cheat by substituting margarine or vegetable shortening for butter, but never with shortbread.

A Tassel Celebration

MOTHER'S QUITE EXPLICIT AS TO WHY SHE STILL celebrates high school and college graduations the way she did years ago for my sister and me. "People forget that this is one of the most important moments in youngsters' lives—I know because, during the Depression, I never had the chance to attend any college—and I believe in doing something special that they'll remember. After all, it's not every day that one has a child or grandchild who reaches this milestone."

And celebrate she does, first with a large ribbon stretched across the front door with CONGRATULATIONS stenciled in bold colors. Balloons bob on the ceiling, school-color streamers flutter from a chandelier down to a bouquet of flowers in the middle of the dining table, and place cards are small, gold-tasseled, black mortarboards with names written in white ink. Even the napkins are rolled up like diplomas and tied with ribbons.

For this event, the Southern fare is always hearty, and at one such dinner I attended, I couldn't help but overhear Mother telling her graduated nephew who was moving away, "Now, honey, don't you forget where your roots are and what kind of food you were raised on."

For any tassel celebration, I always ask the older guests to bring along a personal, handwritten recipe that the graduate can take away as a memento of the occasion and reminder of the Southern food on which he or she was raised. I wrap them all in a colorful ribbon and present the packet at the end of the dinner.

Menu

Bourbon Collins

Crab and Shrimp Chowder

Barbecued Country-Style Pork Ribs

Cheesy Scalloped Potatoes with Chives

Avocado, Banana, and Pecan Salad

Pocketbook Refrigerator Rolls

Gingered Rhubarb-Strawberry Fool

Iced Tea or Beer

Bourbon Collins

FOR EACH DRINK

2 ounces bourbon

½ ounce fresh lime juice

1 teaspoon sugar

Club soda

Lime peel

In a cocktail shaker, combine the bourbon, lime juice, and sugar with cracked ice and shake quickly till well chilled. Pour into a tall, chilled 12-ounce collins glass and fill to the top with club soda. Twist the lime peel and drop into the drink.

1 DRINK

Crab and Shrimp Chowder

It could be said that nothing ushers in Mother's late spring entertaining more than all the beautiful fresh Carolina crabmeat and fat shrimp that fill the markets, this sublime chowder being but one example of how she utilizes the two regional products. Crab claw meat might be the devil to pick for shell and cartilage, but it's not only sweeter than lump backfin meat but considerably cheaper. And what about substituting canned or frozen crabmeat for fresh in this chowder (or any other crab dish)? I strongly suggest you not so much as bring up the topic with Martha Pearl Villas, who succinctly condemns such muck as "stringy, dried out, disgusting." If, for some reason, you can't find good crabmeat or impeccably fresh shrimp, forget about making this chowder.

continued

4 strips lean bacon, cut into small pieces

2 medium-size onions, diced

4 medium-size potatoes, peeled and diced

1 cup water

7 cups milk

Salt and black pepper to taste

**¾ pound fresh claw crabmeat (see Martha Pearl Advises, page 52), carefully picked for
     shells and cartilage**

¾ pound small fresh shrimp, shelled and deveined

Mild paprika for sprinkling

In a large, heavy saucepan, fry the bacon over moderate heat till crisp, then drain on paper towels and set aside. Add the onions, potatoes, and water to the fat in the pan, bring to a simmer, cover, and cook till the water has evaporated and the potatoes are tender, 15 to 20 minutes. Add the milk, season with salt and pepper, and return the mixture to a simmer. Add the crabmeat, shrimp, and reserved bacon, return to simmer, and cook for 5 minutes, stirring.

Serve the chowder sprinkled with paprika.

8   S E R V I N G S

Barbecued Country-Style Pork Ribs

Cut from the shoulder end of the loin, country-style pork ribs have not only the highest meat-to-bone ratio but the least fat of all ribs. While most people just plop the ribs on a grill and brush them with a commercial barbecue sauce (a method that almost guarantees toughness), Mother first simmers hers slowly till fork-tender, then finishes them off in the oven with a tangy homemade sauce. And trust me, never will you taste better ribs. Just be careful not to burn the sauce by baking the ribs too long.

8 meaty country-style pork ribs
¼ cup vegetable oil
1 medium-size onion, finely chopped
1 celery rib, finely chopped
1 garlic clove, minced
1½ cups water
1 cup catsup
½ cup cider vinegar
3 tablespoons Worcestershire sauce
1 tablespoon chili powder
1 tablespoon firmly packed dark brown sugar
1 teaspoon dry mustard
1 teaspoon salt
1 teaspoon black pepper

Arrange the ribs in a large pot, add enough water to cover, and bring to a boil, skimming the top if there's any froth. Reduce the heat to low, cover, and simmer the ribs till fork-tender, about 2 hours.

Meanwhile, heat the oil in a large, heavy, stainless steel or enameled saucepan over moderate heat, then add the onion, celery, and garlic and stir for about 5 minutes. Add the remaining ingredients and stir till well blended. Bring the sauce to a simmer and cook, uncovered, for 20 minutes, stirring from time to time to prevent sticking.

Preheat the oven to 350°F.

continued

With a slotted spoon, transfer the ribs from the water to a large, shallow baking dish, pour the sauce over the ribs, and bake till slightly browned, about 20 minutes. Turn the ribs over and bake till the other sides are slightly browned, 15 to 20 minutes, basting several times with the sauce.

Serve the ribs and sauce on a large, deep platter.

8 SERVINGS

Martha Pearl Advises

Whenever preboiling beef shortribs, pork ribs, or chicken before baking with other ingredients, I always save the flavorful simmering liquid in case a little is needed to keep the baked dish from drying out and burning. The liquid is also essential to pour over leftovers I plan to store in the refrigerator.

Cheesy Scalloped Potatoes with Chives

Mother is usually obsessed with using her favorite red potatoes for salads, stews, hashes, and the like, but when it comes to any form of scalloped potatoes that need plenty of starch for ideal texture, she settles for nothing less than genuine Idahos. And since fresh chives are growing in profusion by graduation time, she livens up the classic dish with at least a quarter cup. Do check these potatoes after about 40 minutes to make sure they don't dry out; the top should be crispy golden but the inside buttery soft.

¾ cup grated Swiss cheese
¾ cup freshly grated Parmesan cheese
¼ cup chopped fresh chives
3 pounds (about 6) large Idaho potatoes
¾ cup (1½ sticks) butter, cut into pieces
Salt and freshly ground black pepper to taste
1½ to 1¾ cups half-and-half, as needed

Preheat the oven to 400°F. Butter the bottom and sides of a large, attractive baking or gratin dish and set aside. In a bowl, combine the cheeses and chives and set aside.

Peel the potatoes and slice them widthwise in very thin slices. Arrange an overlapping layer of potatoes in the prepared dish, sprinkle the layer with part of the cheese mixture, dot with a few butter pieces, and season with salt and pepper. Continue making layers with the potatoes, cheese mixture, butter, and salt and pepper until all used up, then pour enough half-and-half around the sides to almost but not quite cover the potatoes. Bake till the top is golden brown, about 45 minutes, basting the potatoes once or twice.

8 SERVINGS

Avocado, Banana, and Pecan Salad

When shopping for avocados and bananas for a salad such as this, make sure that each is soft and just ready to turn fully ripe. The avocados should be dark green with a few faint spots, the bananas a deep yellow.

3 medium-size ripe but soft-firm avocados
4 bananas
½ cup crushed pecans
Juice of 1 lime
¼ cup vegetable oil
Freshly ground black pepper to taste

Peel the avocados, remove and discard the pits, cut the flesh into ¼-inch wedges, and place in a glass or ceramic serving bowl. Peel and string the bananas, cut into ¼-inch-thick rounds, and add to the avocados. Add the pecans and toss together very lightly.

In a small bowl, whisk together the lime juice and oil till well blended, pour the dressing over the fruit and nuts, season with pepper, and toss gently but thoroughly, squeezing on a little more lime juice if the avocados seem to be darkening. Transfer to a large serving dish or bowl and cover with plastic wrap till ready to serve, chilling if preferred.

8 SERVINGS

Pocketbook Refrigerator Rolls

Since these delicious all-purpose rolls are time-consuming to produce, Mother always makes at least three to three and a half dozen so she'll have plenty left over for another occasion. The fresh dough will keep well for about a week in the refrigerator, covered, but what she generally does is bake the rolls in advance for 5 minutes or till just firm, let them cool, place in a tightly sealed plastic bag, and freeze till ready to

pop into the oven to brown. "The frozen are just as good as the freshly baked,"
she assures.

2 envelopes active dry yeast
1 cup warm water
1 cup Crisco vegetable shortening
1 cup sugar
1 cup boiling water
2 large eggs, beaten
6 cups all-purpose flour
1 tablespoon salt
$\frac{1}{2}$ cup (1 stick) butter, cut into pieces
Melted butter

In a small mixing bowl, sprinkle the yeast over the warm water and let proof for 5 to 10 minutes.

In a large mixing bowl, cream together the shortening and sugar with an electric mixer at medium speed till fluffy, add the boiling water, beat till well blended, and let cool. Stir in the eggs and yeast mixture, then sift the flour and salt into the mixture and beat till well blended and the dough is smooth. Cover the bowl tightly with plastic wrap and refrigerate overnight.

Grease a large baking sheet and set aside.

On a lightly floured work surface, roll the dough out $\frac{1}{2}$ inch thick and cut out rounds with a 3-inch biscuit cutter, gathering up the scraps, rerolling, and cutting out more rounds. Place a small bit of butter in the center of each round and fold one side of the round over the other, pinching the two sides together. Place the rolls on the prepared baking sheet, cover with a clean kitchen towel, and let rise in a warm draft-free area for 2 hours.

Meanwhile, preheat the oven to 400°F.

Bake the rolls just till lightly browned on top, about 8 minutes. Serve hot with melted butter.

ABOUT 3 $\frac{1}{2}$ DOZEN ROLLS

Gingered Rhubarb-Strawberry Fool

Spring is rhubarb time down South, the first fresh strawberries also show up in the markets, and Mother wastes no time combining the two in various pies, puddings, trifles, ice creams, and fools. "Somebody once told me that youngsters won't eat something like tart rhubarb," she relates, "but that's nonsense. Just last year I served this gingered fool at a tassel celebration attended by three teenagers, and they gobbled it up by the spoonfuls. If it's prepared and sweetened correctly, they love it." Do remember, however, that the leaves of field rhubarb are poisonous and must always be clipped off and discarded.

1 pound fresh rhubarb, all leaves removed and stalks carefully trimmed
1½ cups sugar
½ cup water
1 pint ripe strawberries, hulled and halved
1 teaspoon ground ginger
1½ cups heavy cream

Cut the rhubarb stalks into 2-inch pieces, place in a large, stainless steel or enameled saucepan, and add 1 cup of the sugar plus the water. Bring to a boil, reduce the heat to low, cover, and simmer till the rhubarb is very tender, about 40 minutes. Drain in a colander, transfer to a large mixing bowl, add the remaining ½ cup sugar, the strawberries, and the ginger, and toss well. Place the mixture in a blender or food processor, process to a smooth puree, scrape back into the bowl, cover with plastic wrap, and chill for 3 hours.

When ready to serve, whip the cream in a medium-size mixing bowl with an electric mixer at high speed till stiff peaks form, then add to the rhubarb-strawberry mixture, stir till well blended and smooth, and serve in stemmed glasses.

8 SERVINGS

Summer

A Guild Finale Luncheon

A Beach Supper

A Fried Chicken Roost

A Star-Spangled Cookout

A Neighborhood Church Supper

A Carolina Pork Barbecue

An Around-the-Pool Party

To Mother, summer is primarily the season for gathering together groups of people for lots of informal, outdoor fun and celebration. To be sure, she continues on a smaller scale to entertain graciously inside the house those connected with her church and Charity League and members of her book and bridge clubs, but what she really focuses her attention on when the weather turns hot are easygoing cookouts, pool and patio parties, fried chicken roosts, and casual beach lunches and suppers.

Summer is the season for picking plump Southern peaches and all sorts of berries, fetching sackfuls of sweet corn fresh from the field, and utilizing the bounty of huge, thick-skinned tomatoes that have ripened slowly on the vine. It's the time for refreshing fruit punches, large pork barbecues on the deck or in the yard, kettles of aromatic seafood stews, glistening congealed salads, and sumptuous fruit cobblers. And it's when nothing is more in order than a big wooden picnic table, checkered cotton tablecloths, heavy dishcloth or paper napkins, rustic flower arrangements, and washtubs of iced cold beer and wine. As Mother says, "Summer entertaining is generally no time to put on the dog. The weather's usually steamy, people just want to relax out of doors and eat good food, and believe me, this is one season when even I try to stay out of a hot kitchen during most of the day, prepare as many dishes (preferably cold ones) as possible in advance, and really socialize with my guests."

A Guild Finale Luncheon

ONO DOUBT LADIES IN DIFFERENT PARTS OF THE country are keenly active in certain civic, religious, and charity organizations, and Mother is no exception when it comes to her Episcopal Church Guild. Composed of about a dozen members, the guild undertakes any number of projects throughout the year, from doing volunteer work at a home for abused children, to preparing meals for a homeless shelter, to helping execute important church lunches. While each member sponsors a luncheon every month where there's a business meeting followed by a program devoted to Bible study, Mother is always the one selected to host the finale luncheon on the first of June before the ladies disband for the summer months, the sole reason being because they know she'll produce a meal to remember. "Well, that's what they say," Mother remarks modestly, "but the truth is that I love to have this last luncheon, always express my preference at the first of the year, and really go all out to do something special with the food and wine and flowers."

This is when Mother takes out her flowered English plates, Alsatian green-stemmed wineglasses, and hand-embroidered napkins, and it is one of the few times when plates are prepared in the kitchen and guests eat on their laps. "You have to be practical when entertaining this many people inside," she explains, "and with this type of menu, where everything's prepared in advance, it's so easy to assemble everything—dessert included—on the dishes while the girls are sipping fine Gewürztraminer." And what if some of "the girls" are not prone to sip the spicy and delectable wine that Mother so enjoys? "Most do since, after all, we are Episcopalians," she titters, "but I always have iced coffee at this luncheon just in case."

Menu

Gewürztraminer Wine

Cold Dilled Asparagus

Jubilee Congealed Salad

Ribbon Loaf Sandwiches

Butterscotch Delights

Iced Coffee

Cold Dilled Asparagus

Mother and I have certain differences of opinion about preparing fresh asparagus for cooking. She cuts off any white ends, shaves the green bases slightly, and removes all the scales. I simply shave any woody ends till they become soft to preserve as much of the asparagus as possible, and I never shave off the scales. We do agree that far too much of the asparagus is wasted if it is simply snapped at the soft point, and we're both adamant about storing prepared asparagus upright in a container of water in the refrigerator till ready to cook.

2 pounds medium-size fresh asparagus, white bases trimmed and scales removed
2 garlic cloves, minced
1 teaspoon red pepper flakes
12 sprigs fresh dill, chopped
$\frac{1}{2}$ teaspoon mustard seeds
1$\frac{1}{2}$ cups white wine vinegar
3 tablespoons sugar
1 tablespoon salt
1$\frac{1}{2}$ cups water

In a large, deep skillet, arrange the asparagus in about 1 inch of salted water, bring to a boil, reduce the heat to moderate, cover the skillet with a sheet of aluminum foil or the lid, and cook till the asparagus are just tender, 6 to 8 minutes. Drain the water from the skillet, add cold water to refresh the asparagus (stop them from cooking any further), then drain on paper towels. Arrange the asparagus in a long, shallow, heatproof glass dish and add the garlic, pepper flakes, dill, and mustard seeds.

In a stainless steel saucepan, combine the vinegar, sugar, salt, and water, bring to a boil, stirring, and let cool slightly off the heat. Pour the mixture over the asparagus, let cool completely, cover with plastic wrap, and chill overnight. Serve cold.

10 TO 12 SERVINGS

Jubilee Congealed Salad

I think it's safe to say that this very elaborate congealed salad represents the peak of Mother's art. It takes time to make this salad, and careful attention should be paid to each and every procedure, but if you ever wondered what the hoopla over Southern congealed salads is all about (and, admittedly, nothing is worse than a careless congealed salad), this beauty will prove a revelation. Since the juices of the canned apricots and pineapple must be used, don't try substituting fresh fruits. You'll need a 6-cup ring mold for this salad.

One 1-pound can apricot halves, drained and juice reserved

One 8¾-ounce can pineapple pieces, drained and juice reserved

2 tablespoons cider vinegar

1 teaspoon whole cloves

1 medium-size stick cinnamon

Two 3-ounce packages orange-flavored Jell-O

¾ cup water

¾ cup apricot nectar

½ cup sour cream

2 cups mixed fresh blackberries and raspberries, rinsed and patted dry

In a medium-size saucepan, combine the reserved fruit juices, vinegar, cloves, and cinnamon, bring to a boil, reduce the heat to low, and simmer for 10 minutes. Strain the mixture through a fine-mesh strainer into a 2-cup measuring cup and add enough hot water to make 2 cups. Return the mixture to the saucepan and bring to a boil. Remove the pan from the heat, sprinkle one package of the Jell-O over the top, stir till dissolved, let cool, and chill till thickened, 20 to 30 minutes.

Cut the apricot halves in half, then fold them, along with the pineapple, into the thickened Jell-O. Pour the mixture into a 6-cup ring mold and chill till nearly firm, about 2 hours.

In a saucepan, bring the water to a boil, remove from the heat, sprinkle the other package of Jell-O over the top, and stir till dissolved. Add the apricot nectar, mix well, let cool, and chill till partially set, 20 to 30 minutes.

Beat the nectar mixture with an electric mixer till fluffy, add the sour cream, and swirl with a spoon till well blended. Pour the mixture over the already set Jell-O in the mold, cover with plastic wrap, and chill the salad overnight.

To serve, turn the salad out onto a large crystal plate and garnish the center and edges with the mixed berries.

10 TO 12 SERVINGS

Martha Pearl Advises

If I plan to transport a congealed salad that won't be served right away (or when the weather is particularly hot), I add an extra dissolved teaspoon of unflavored gelatin to the mixture to make it firmer.

Ribbon Loaf Sandwiches

If Mother's Jubilee Congealed Salad illustrates the apogee of one refined aspect of her Southern cookery, these composed, exquisite sandwiches demonstrate another. No doubt it takes a bit of time to make all the fillings, which is one reason that Mother does most of the preparation the night before her luncheon—the other reason being that the unfrosted sandwiches really should stand overnight in the refrigerator to mellow. To prevent sogginess, be sure to use day-old bread, and do feel free to experiment with other fillings.

FOR HAM SALAD FILLING

2 cups finely chopped cooked ham

2 celery ribs, finely chopped

¼ cup finely chopped sweet pickles

1 tablespoon Dijon mustard

1 teaspoon prepared horseradish

⅓ cup mayonnaise (Mother prefers Hellmann's)

FOR TOMATO-BACON FILLING

One 8-ounce package cream cheese, softened

2 medium-size ripe tomatoes, finely chopped and drained well on paper towels

4 strips lean bacon, fried crisp, drained on paper towels, and crumbled

1 tablespoon grated onion

½ teaspoon Worcestershire sauce

Salt and black pepper to taste

FOR TUNA-CAPER FILLING

Two 6-ounce cans solid white tuna in vegetable oil, drained

2 celery ribs, finely chopped

2 tablespoons minced capers

2 tablespoons minced fresh chives

¾ cup mayonnaise (Mother prefers Hellmann's)

2 tablespoons fresh lemon juice

Black pepper to taste

1 large, day-old, unsliced loaf sandwich bread

One 3-ounce package cream cheese, softened

¹⁄₃ cup milk

Finely chopped fresh parsley leaves

To make the ham salad filling, combine all the ingredients in a medium-size mixing bowl, mix to a good spreading consistency, and set aside.

To make the tomato-bacon filling, beat the cream cheese in a medium-size mixing bowl with a spoon till fluffy, then add the tomatoes, bacon, onion, and Worcestershire, season with salt and pepper, mix to a good spreading consistency, and set aside.

To make the tuna-caper filling, flake the tuna in a medium-size mixing bowl, add all the remaining ingredients, mix to a good spreading consistency, and set aside.

To make the sandwiches, place the loaf of bread on a large cutting board, trim and discard the crusts, and cut lengthwise into four slices with a sharp knife. Place the first slice on a large sheet of aluminum foil and spread the ham salad filing over the top. Place the second slice of bread on top and spread with the tomato-bacon filling. Place the third slice on top of that and spread with the tuna-caper filling. Top with the last slice of bread, wrap the loaf in the foil, and chill till ready to serve.

When ready to serve, beat the cream cheese and milk together in a small mixing bowl till well blended and smooth, then frost the top and sides of the loaf and sprinkle the parsley all over, pressing it into the frosting. Cut the loaf widthwise into sandwiches.

10 TO 12 SANDWICHES

Martha Pearl Advises

To keep sandwiches from becoming soggy, never cover with a damp towel. Either wrap them in plastic or store them in a tightly covered container.

Butterscotch Delights

The reason Mother created these butterscotch squares was simple enough: she got tired of serving brownies at her guild luncheon and wanted to come up with something like a brownie but with a different flavor and slightly different texture. You can, of course, substitute chocolate chips for the butterscotch ones, but whether for an informal luncheon, picnic, or pool party, these squares do make for a nice change. If the squares are too gummy and awkward to cut, Mother advises dipping the knife in warm water.

FOR THE BOTTOM LAYER

½ cup (1 stick) butter, softened

1 large egg yolk

2 tablespoons water

½ teaspoon pure almond extract

1¼ cups all-purpose flour

1 tablespoon sugar

¼ teaspoon baking powder

One 12-ounce bag butterscotch chips

FOR THE TOP LAYER

2 large eggs

¾ cup sugar

6 tablespoons (¾ stick) butter, melted

1 teaspoon pure vanilla extract

½ teaspoon pure almond extract

1 cup finely ground walnuts

Preheat the oven to 350°F. Grease a large baking pan and set aside.

To make the bottom layer, beat the butter, egg yolk, water, and almond extract with an electric mixer in a medium-size mixing bowl till well blended. Add the flour, sugar, and baking powder and beat till well blended. Scrape the mixture into the prepared pan and pat evenly with your hands across the bottom. Bake for 10 minutes, then scatter the butterscotch chips over the top and bake till the chips melt, about 5 minutes longer. With a spatula, smooth the melted chips over the cake.

To make the top layer, wash and dry the mixer beaters and, in a small mixing bowl, beat the eggs till frothy. Add the sugar, melted butter, and extracts and beat till well blended and smooth.

Pour the mixture over the butterscotch layer, spread evenly, sprinkle the walnuts evenly over the top, and bake till lightly browned, 30 to 45 minutes. Let cool completely, then cut the cake into 1½- to 2-inch squares.

2 TO 3 DOZEN SQUARES

Martha Pearl Advises

I always grease pans and casseroles with vegetable shortening, since it doesn't burn and stick as much as butter.

A Beach Supper

EVER SINCE I WAS A CHILD, IT'S BEEN A RITUAL for our family and other friends to rent oceanfront cottages at one of the North or South Carolina beaches in June for a two-week vacation. We surf and deep-sea fish, go crabbing, shop for rope hammocks and wicker, drive down to Georgetown or McClellanville, South Carolina, to buy huge shrimp off the boat, and visit the old Low Country plantations along the Waccamaw River. But of all the activities, I look forward to none more than the open-air, easygoing suppers that Mother serves the family and guests on the front deck overlooking the sea.

Typically, before dinner, it's the custom to sip mellow peach flips in rocking chairs with our feet propped up on the banister while watching the sun set. Next, the glass-enclosed hurricane lamps are lit, everyone pitches in to anchor sheets of newspaper with large conch shells across the weathered wooden table, more ice is poured into the tub of beer, bowls of butter are placed around the table, and out comes Mother with the big roasting pan full of the most incredible, unpeeled, baked shrimp known to man—plus platters of fresh corn on the cob, cornbread, and whatever else she's decided to serve. This is authentic rustic eating at its best, and if it's messy—and I mean messy!—peeling all the shrimp and dipping cornbread into the herby sauce, so much the better.

Menu

Peach Flips

Beach Shrimp Peel

Bird's-Eye Cornbread

She-Jump-Up Pot

Waccamaw Stuffed Tomatoes

Corn on the Cob

Mixed Berry Cobbler

Beer

Peach Flips

You must use fresh, ripe peaches for these flips. Substitute canned ones, as a foolish acquaintance of Mother's once did, and you'll end up with a thin, almost flavorless mush. Blend the ingredients just till the flips are thickened and smooth. If desired, you can add about 2 tablespoons of sugar to the other ingredients.

7 medium-size ripe peaches
One 6-ounce can frozen lemonade concentrate, thawed
Juice of 1 large lime
5 ounces light rum
5 ounces amber rum
Crushed ice

Peel and pit the peaches and cut the flesh into slices. Place all but 8 slices into a large blender, reserving the 8 slices for garnish. Add the lemonade concentrate, lime juice, rums, and ice to the peaches and blend till thick and smooth. Pour the flips into short glass tumblers, garnish each drink with a peach slice, and serve immediately.

8 FLIPS

Martha Pearl Advises

Many cookbooks call for peeling peaches by first dropping them in boiling water to loosen the skins, then refreshing them in ice water. I find that pretty silly since it softens the flesh too much. Besides, I can peel a peach with a sharp knife much faster than going through all that other unnecessary production.

Beach Shrimp Peel

Much of the wonderful flavor of these shrimp derives from baking them in their shells, and much of the fun and enjoyment of eating them comes from peeling them one by one. Since this is summertime, Mother uses only fresh herbs in the sauce, which should be allowed to meld at least an hour before pouring over the shrimp. We love to dip a peppery cornbread into the sauce, but if you absolutely must have a more sturdy bread that won't crumble, use a dozen hard Italian rolls sliced in half and toasted. And be sure to provide large dishcloth napkins or plenty of sturdy paper ones.

FOR THE SAUCE

1¼ cups olive oil

¾ cup red wine vinegar

1 tablespoon minced fresh tarragon leaves

1 tablespoon minced fresh dill

1 tablespoon minced fresh chives

1 teaspoon salt

¼ teaspoon black pepper

1 garlic clove, peeled and crushed slightly

FOR THE SHRIMP

5 pounds large fresh shrimp in the shells

1 cup fresh lemon juice (about 5 medium-size lemons)

1 cup (2 sticks) butter, cut into small pieces

Freshly ground black pepper to taste

To make the sauce, combine all the ingredients in a large jar with a tight lid, shake vigorously till well blended, and let stand for 1 hour.

Preheat the oven to 350°F.

To prepare the shrimp, rinse them well and spread evenly in a large, deep roasting pan. Pour the lemon juice over the shrimp, then pour on the sauce. Distribute the butter pieces evenly over the top, sprinkle with plenty of ground pepper, and bake, uncovered, till the shrimp are pink and cooked through, 20 to 25 minutes, stirring every 10 minutes.

Serve the shrimp with some of the sauce in large, shallow soup bowls along with Bird's-Eye Cornbread (recipe follows), peeling the shrimp as they're eaten and dipping the bread into the sauce.

6 TO 8 SERVINGS

Martha Pearl Advises

Unless you live near a coastline, most "fresh" shrimp found in markets are actually frozen and thawed. When I buy shrimp, I always sniff them carefully for any offensive odors. Completely immersed in water in plastic cartons, fresh shrimp freeze beautifully up to about two months; thereafter, they tend to smell and taste of ammonia.

Bird's-Eye Cornbread

In homes throughout the South, a common sight in summer is a large pot of tiny, zesty red peppers growing in windowsills. Called "bird's-eye" peppers, they are pickled, used in barbecue sauces, and incorporated in any number of dips, stews, and breads like this tangy skillet cornbread that Mother makes for our beach suppers. When intended to be served with a shrimp peel, I suggest that you heat up two iron skillets and double the recipe.

continued

2 cups yellow cornmeal

1 teaspoon baking powder

1½ teaspoons baking soda

2 teaspoons salt

1½ cups canned cream-style corn

1 cup (¼ pound) grated sharp cheddar cheese

2 to 3 small, red chili peppers, to your taste, seeded and finely chopped

1 cup buttermilk

3 large eggs, beaten

1½ tablespoons corn oil

Preheat the oven to 400°F.

In a large mixing bowl, combine the cornmeal, baking powder, baking soda, and salt and blend well. Add the corn, cheese, chili peppers, buttermilk, and eggs and mix with a wooden spoon till well blended.

Heat the oil in a 12-inch cast-iron skillet till hot, pour the batter into the skillet, smooth with a spatula, and bake till golden brown, about 35 minutes. To serve, cut the cornbread into wedges.

6 TO 8 SERVINGS

She-Jump-Up Pot

Mother remembers distinctly as a young girl with her daddy down in Georgia hearing a lady tell about how the black children on a rice plantation would come screaming, "She-jump-up! She-jump-up!" at the first sight of rice sprouting in the vast water beds. Rice and cotton were the very foundations of this wealthy society till the twentieth century when most of the industries shifted to Louisiana and other states in the Deep South, but to this day there are locals all over the Carolinas and Georgia who still refer to various rice stews, pots, and casseroles as "she-jump-up" this and that.

Mother's not sure, but she thinks it might have been her grandmother, Sweet Maa, who began adding raisins and peanuts to the She-Jump-Up Pot we love to fix at the beach.

¼ cup (½ stick) butter

1 tablespoon bacon grease

1 medium-size onion, finely chopped

1 large celery rib, finely chopped

2 cups long-grain rice

3 cups chicken stock or broth

½ cup chopped golden raisins

½ cup crushed peanuts

1 teaspoon salt

¼ teaspoon cayenne pepper

Preheat the oven to 350°F.

In a medium-size, heavy, flameproof pot, heat together 2 tablespoons of the butter and the bacon grease over moderate heat, then add the onion and celery and stir till soft, about 5 minutes. Reduce the heat to low, add the rice, and stir briefly till the grains are coated. Add the broth, raisins, peanuts, salt, and cayenne, stir well, cover, and bake till the rice is tender, 20 to 25 minutes. Add the remaining 2 tablespoons butter and, using a fork, fluff the rice till the butter has melted. Cover and keep warm till ready to serve.

6 TO 8 SERVINGS

Waccamaw Stuffed Tomatoes

The Waccamaw River, extending roughly from Murrels Inlet down to Georgetown, South Carolina, was the major Low Country waterway used to transport rice from coastal plantations during the eighteenth and nineteenth centuries. On one of our many summer excursions in the area, Mother spotted at a roadside vegetable stand without doubt the most gigantic homegrown tomatoes she'd ever seen, perfect for stuffing with this earthy mixture. And no matter where we travel today in the South, let her see a huge, fresh tomato and she still exclaims, "Looks like a Waccamaw."

8 large, firm, ripe tomatoes
¼ cup (½ stick) butter
2 medium-size onions, finely chopped
1 cup finely chopped country ham
2 tablespoons finely chopped fresh basil leaves
Black pepper to taste
½ cup fine dry bread crumbs
¼ cup (½ stick) butter, melted

Core the tomatoes, carefully scoop out a wide, shallow pocket on the cored end of each, chop the scooped-out flesh, and set aside. Arrange the tomatoes in a large baking dish or on a heavy baking sheet.

Preheat the oven to 400°F. Heat the butter in a medium-size skillet over moderate heat, then add the onions and country ham and cook, stirring, till the onions are very soft but not browned, about 7 minutes. Add the basil, pepper, and reserved tomato pulp and continue to cook, stirring, till the pulp loses most of its liquid, about 7 minutes.

Divide the onion-and-ham mixture evenly among the pockets in the tomatoes and spread it out to the edges with a fork, pressing down slightly. Sprinkle the tops with the bread crumbs, drizzle the melted butter over the crumbs, and bake till the tops are nicely browned, about 20 minutes. Serve hot.

8 SERVINGS

Corn on the Cob

To most people, fresh summer corn is a simple matter of grabbing a few ears in the market, plopping them in boiling water, and letting them cook an indiscriminate amount of time. By contrast, my mother is utterly obsessed with fresh corn, insisting on buying only the sweeter, white-kernel ears (preferably sold within sight of the corn-field), starting the ears in salted cold water that is slowly brought to a simmer ("to maintain as much sugar in the corn as possible before the heat starts to convert it to starch"), and removing them the second the water begins to bubble. So passionate is Mother about great corn, in fact, that, forced to admit that the varieties grown on Long Island are superior even to Southern ones, she loads up the car with no less than five dozen ears when she comes to visit me, dashes back to North Carolina in one day, cuts off the kernels the minute she gets home, and freezes enough to last her at least half the winter. "It's not quite as good as corn cooked the very day it's picked," she affirms, "but I defy anybody to tell the difference."

12 to 16 ears fresh corn, husks and silks removed
2 tablespoons salt
Butter

Place the corn in a large kettle with enough cold water to cover, add the salt, and bring to a roaring boil. With tongs, transfer the corn immediately to a large platter or individual corn dishes and serve with plenty of butter.

12 TO 16 EARS CORN

Martha Pearl Advises

For boiling large quantities of fresh corn on the cob, a stockpot or enameled canner is the ideal vessel.

Mixed Berry Cobbler

Mother calls this the "queen of Southern cobblers" since it includes all the great berries of summer. (If strawberries are still sweet and plump, she might also include these.) Don't fret if every berry happens not to be available; this is Mother's basic berry cobbler recipe and can be used for any combination—or for just a single type of berry. A peach, apricot, plum, or apple cobbler, on the other hand, involves a different cooking principle altogether (see Peach Tree Cobbler, page 299).

Double recipe Basic Pie Shell (page 23), unbaked
2 cups fresh blueberries, stemmed and rinsed
2 cups fresh blackberries, stemmed and rinsed
2 cups fresh raspberries, stemmed and rinsed
1¼ cups sugar
1 cup water
2 tablespoons all-purpose flour
3 tablespoons butter, cut into small bits

Preheat the oven to 375°F.

Divide the pastry dough in half and roll out one half with a lightly floured rolling pin on a lightly floured surface to fit a deep baking dish measuring about 11 by 8 by 2 inches. Roll out the remaining pastry very thin and cut into 1-inch-wide strips. Place one half of the strips on an ungreased baking sheet and bake till just slightly browned.

Increase the oven temperature to 425°F.

In a large saucepan, combine the three berries, 1 cup of the sugar, and the water, bring to a boil, reduce the heat to moderate, and cook just till the berries are soft. In a small bowl, combine the flour and remaining ¼ cup sugar, stir, add to the berry mixture, and cook till the mixture has thickened slightly, stirring constantly. Spoon a layer of berries into the pastry-lined pan, arrange a layer of the browned pastry strips over the berries, and continue layering berries and pastry strips, ending with berries on top. Dot with the butter, arrange the remaining uncooked pastry strips in a lattice formation across the top, and bake till nicely browned, about 25 minutes. Serve hot or at room temperature.

6 TO 8 SERVINGS

Martha Pearl Advises

You can freeze fresh berries, but to keep them from sticking to one another, first freeze them separated on any flat pan, dish, or sheet that will fit in the freezer, then store them in plastic bags.

A Fried
Chicken Roost

IN MUCH OF THE SOUTH, A "ROOST" REFERS TO AN
informal outdoor get-together where any type of chicken in large quantity is
served—a logical expression since, after all, a roost is also (or at least used to be)
the shelf in a henhouse where chickens nest together. Of course, for Mother, a
roost means one thing and one thing only: fried chicken; and if my mother is
known for anything, she's known for her inimitable, sacred, Southern fried
chicken. Even on home territory, neighbors eyeing the big can of Crisco on a
kitchen counter will ask hopefully, "Oh, Martha Pearl, are you cooking fried
chicken?" Ironically, where the pleas for Mother to fry up some chicken and
throw a big roost are most pronounced is at my home in East Hampton. "I tell
my friends," she says playfully, "that I sometimes think I fry more chicken and
make more succotash and biscuits for Yankees than for Southerners."

Traditionally, a roost is always held during the summer months so that
Mother can take full advantage of all the fresh butter beans, okra, corn, tomatoes, and berries that fill the gardens and markets. And never is her entertaining
more casual or the setting less pretentious. So that everybody can sit down
together for this copious supper, she rarely plans the roost for more than eight,
setting the picnic table on the patio with colorful place mats and cloth napkins,
big pitchers of mint lemonade, and, as a fun centerpiece, a big ceramic chicken
surrounded by baby yellow chicks.

Beforehand, pickled oysters are passed while guests lounge leisurely in chairs on the lawn with planter's punches in hand, and when it finally comes time to eat, every item except dessert is placed family-style on the table. Before everyone digs in, Mother makes her standard proclamation (especially when Northerners are present) that the chicken is to be eaten with the fingers. "I mean," she almost whispers in exasperation, "who ever saw or heard of a real Southerner cutting fried chicken with a knife and fork!"

Menu

Planter's Punches

Pickled Oysters

Mother's Sacred Southern Fried Chicken

Creamed Succotash

Okra and Tomato Mull

Redneck Biscuits

Blackberry Crackle

Mint Lemonade

Planter's Punches

Mother once launched her fried chicken roosts with classic mint juleps served in frosted silver julep cups, but so taken was she with a planter's punch she was served a few years ago in New Orleans that she gradually changed the tradition in favor of the potent rum drink—and guests love it. Mother typically prepares a big pitcher of the mixed fruit juices and grenadine in advance and keeps it in the refrigerator till she is ready to make the individual punches. "Why the drinks never come out right when all the rums are simply added to the pitcher of juice I can't figure out," she warns, "but that's just the way it is."

16 ounces pineapple juice
16 ounces orange juice
12 ounces bottled lime juice
$\frac{1}{2}$ cup grenadine
8 ounces light rum
8 ounces amber rum
8 ounces dark rum
Ice cubes

In a large pitcher, combine the three fruit juices, add the grenadine, and stir till well blended. Pour 1 ounce of each rum into each of 8 tall, narrow highball glasses and fill each glass with ice cubes. Fill each glass to the top with the fruit juice mixture, stir well, and serve immediately.

8 DRINKS

Pickled Oysters

Since well before the Civil War (when Union troops in Savannah devoured local oysters by the bucketful), Chincoteague, Kent Island, Gulf, Apalachicola, and Virginia oysters have been one of the most prized food commodities on the Southern table. Mother began pickling oysters when my sister lived in Wilmington, North Carolina, and we were exposed to a bounty of Chincoteagues harvested from local waters. While Mother regrets no longer being able to find loose oysters in different sizes at her fish market, at least the ones now packaged in cans are impeccably fresh. To prevent discoloration, be sure to use white vinegar for this recipe, and Mother always serves toast points (see page 38) on which to balance the oysters.

2 pints fresh shucked oysters (liquor included)
1½ cups white vinegar
1 large onion, chopped
2 garlic cloves, crushed
6 sprigs fresh parsley
2 teaspoons mixed pickling spices
1 bay leaf
¼ cup olive oil
1 lemon, cut into quarters and seeded
Salt and freshly ground black pepper to taste

In a large, stainless steel or enameled saucepan, combine the oysters and their liquor, bring to a brisk simmer, and cook just till their edges begin to curl, about 5 minutes. With a slotted spoon, transfer the oysters to a large bowl of cold water to stand for 5 minutes, reserving the liquor in the pan. Drain the oysters, arrange in a large, shallow glass or ceramic baking dish, and put in the refrigerator.

Add the remaining ingredients to the liquor in the pan, bring to a boil, reduce the heat to low, and simmer for 30 minutes. Strain the liquid through a fine-mesh strainer into a small mixing bowl, let cool to room temperature, then pour over the refrigerated oysters. Cover with plastic wrap and chill overnight.

Remove the oysters from their marinade and serve cold with small oyster forks.

8 SERVINGS

Mother's Sacred Southern Fried Chicken

"The problem," Mother pronounces firmly, "is that most folks have no real respect for fried chicken." And with that she begins her eternal diatribe on why people's fried chicken never turns out like her perfect pieces, and how the first cardinal rule is to cut up the whole chicken yourself, and what's important about using only Crisco shortening with a little bacon grease added to the fat, not turning the chicken but once (with tongs so that the meat is never pierced), draining the pieces only on brown paper bags, and more. "The point is that great Southern fried chicken is easy as pie to produce," she assures, "so long as you really watch what you're doing and use a little common sense—like not undercooking the chicken the way some of today's trendy hotshot chefs do." Follow her directions to the letter, and I can almost promise that you'll end up with crisp, juicy, full-flavored fried chicken equal to Martha Pearl's finest.

Two 3-pound chicken fryers
2 cups all-purpose flour
Salt and black pepper to taste
1 cup milk
Crisco vegetable shortening
1 tablespoon bacon grease

Cut the chicken carefully and evenly into serving pieces, taking great care to keep the skin of each piece intact, and rinse under cold running water. Do not pat dry.

In a heavy brown paper bag, combine the flour and salt and pepper and shake till well blended. Pour the milk into a soup bowl.

Set an electric fry pan at 375°F or place a large cast-iron skillet over moderate heat, fill either half full of melted Crisco, and add the bacon grease. When a drop of water flipped into the fat sputters, dip some of the chicken pieces into the milk, then place in the bag. Shake vigorously to coat evenly, tap the excess flour off each piece back into the bag, and arrange the pieces in the fat, making sure not to overcrowd the pan. Fry the chicken till golden brown and crisp, 15 to 20 minutes, turn with tongs, reduce the heat to 350°F, and fry till golden brown, about 15 minutes longer. (Turn the chicken only once.) Drain on another brown paper bag and repeat the procedure with the remaining chicken, adding a little more shortening and bacon grease if necessary and returning the heat to 375°F or moderate.

Transfer the chicken to a large serving platter and do not cover (otherwise your crispy fried chicken will get soggy). Serve warm or at room temperature.

8 SERVINGS

Martha Pearl Advises

I cut up every one of my chickens. Not only are the pieces cleaner and more uniform when carefully separated at the joints instead of being quickly hacked to death at the supermarket, but I'm able to cut a wishbone from the breast. And don't forget that you're paying for lots of waste with packaged chicken parts.

Creamed Succotash

Ordinary, uncreamed succotash can be a delicious Southern dish in itself, but when Mother adds half-and-half, it becomes truly sensuous. Unlike many other cooks, she simply won't make succotash without all fresh ingredients, going so far as to carefully scrape all the milk from the corncobs into the pot after she's cut off the kernels. While the succotash is thickening over heat, be sure to stir fairly steadily to prevent sticking.

2½ cups fresh lima beans
6 strips bacon, cut into dice
2 large onions, finely chopped
2½ cups fresh corn kernels
2 cups peeled and chopped ripe tomatoes, with their juices
¾ cup half-and-half
Salt and black pepper to taste
Tabasco Sauce to taste

Place the lima beans in a medium-size saucepan with enough salted water to cover, bring to a moderate simmer, cover, cook till tender, about 15 minutes, and drain.

Meanwhile, in a large, heavy pot, fry the bacon over moderate heat till crisp and pour off all but about 3 tablespoons of the bacon grease. Add the onions and stir till softened, about 2 minutes. Add the lima beans, corn, tomatoes and juices, and half-and-half, stir well, and continue to cook another 5 minutes. Season with salt, pepper, and Tabasco and continue to cook, stirring, till the mixture has thickened slightly. Transfer the succotash to an earthenware tureen or deep serving dish and serve hot.

8 SERVINGS

Okra and Tomato Mull

Of all the Southern produce available in abundance during the summer months, I suppose the only items that Mother loves more than fresh corn and peaches are okra and tomatoes. And never is she so fastidious as when selecting okra that are small, dark green, slightly fuzzy, and soft enough "to insert your fingernail in the pods." She boils, steams, and bakes okra, she fries it, she incorporates it into salads and gumbos, but never is the vegetable so palatable as when she mulls (or slowly simmers) it in an iron skillet with homegrown tomatoes and onions, a little bacon grease, and one or two fresh herbs. Anybody who complains that okra is slimy just doesn't know how to prepare it correctly for cooking. The trick is to trim off the stems without cutting at all into the pods.

2 pounds fresh small okra, washed and stems removed
6 strips lean bacon, cut into small pieces
2 medium-size onions, chopped
6 large, ripe tomatoes, peeled and chopped
1 tablespoon fresh thyme leaves
2 teaspoon salt
Black pepper and Tabasco Sauce to taste

Place the okra in a large saucepan, add enough salted water to cover, bring to a boil, reduce the heat to moderate, and simmer till tender, about 10 minutes. Drain the okra in a colander.

In a large skillet, fry the bacon over moderate heat till crisp and drain on paper towels. Pour off all but 2 tablespoons of the bacon grease, add the onions, and stir for about 10 minutes. Add the tomatoes, thyme, and salt, season with pepper and Tabasco, stir well, reduce the heat to low, and simmer till the tomatoes are soft, about 20 minutes. Add the okra and bacon, stir gently, and simmer about 10 minutes longer before serving.

8 SERVINGS

To keep fresh okra from "weeping," never cut into the pod itself, trimming off the stems just above where they connect to the pod.

Redneck Biscuits

Mother was not being derogatory when she named these unusual biscuits; the "redneck" is simply her way of referring to the bits of earthy, reddish country ham that, along with the grits, give them their distinction. Actually, the biscuits originally came about as a way to use up a mess of leftover country ham grits, and to lighten the texture, she decided to use lard instead of vegetable shortening or butter. Suffice it that these biscuits are utterly scrumptious.

1¾ cups all-purpose flour
3½ teaspoons baking powder
½ teaspoon salt
3 tablespoons lard
½ cup milk, or as needed
½ cup plain grits cooked according to package directions, at room temperature
¼ cup finely diced cured country ham

Preheat the oven to 400°F.

In a large mixing bowl, combine the flour, baking powder, and salt and mix till well blended. Add the lard and work it in with your fingertips till the mixture is mealy. Stir in the milk, then beat in the grits and ham with a wooden spoon till well blended, adding more milk if necessary for a smooth dough.

continued

On a lightly floured work surface, knead the dough *briefly* with your fingers, then press it out ½ inch thick. Cut the dough into rounds with a 2-inch biscuit cutter and place on an ungreased baking sheet. Gather up the scraps of dough and repeat the procedure. Bake the biscuits till golden brown, 10 to 12 minutes, checking to make sure the bottoms don't over-brown. Serve hot.

18 TO 20 BISCUITS

Martha Pearl Advises

No matter the style of biscuit, never mix or handle the dough too much to prevent toughness. Same for cookie dough.

Blackberry Crackle

What's different about Mother's berry crackles and crumbles is that she uses oats (old-fashioned rolled oats, not instant) instead of bread or cookie crumbs to produce a crunchier and more flavorful topping. This crackle can also be made with another fresh berry or combination of berries, as well as with about 4 cups chopped ripe but firm fresh peaches or apricots.

1 cup all-purpose flour
½ cup old-fashioned rolled oats (not instant)
½ cup finely ground almonds
1 cup firmly packed dark brown sugar
¾ cup (1½ sticks) cold butter, cut into pieces
2 pints fresh blackberries, stemmed, rinsed, and patted dry
1 cup granulated sugar
3 tablespoons cornstarch

Preheat the oven to 350°F. Grease a large pie plate and set aside.

In a large mixing bowl, combine the flour, oats, almonds, brown sugar, and butter and work the mixture together with your fingers till crumbly. Press one-half the crumb mixture against the bottom and sides of the prepared pie plate and set aside.

In another large mixing bowl, combine the blackberries, granulated sugar, and cornstarch and stir till well blended. Spoon the berry mixture into the pie plate, sprinkle the remaining crumb mixture evenly over the top, and bake till golden, about 30 minutes. Let the crumble cool slightly and serve warm.

8 SERVINGS

Mint Lemonade

Fresh summer mint grows in profusion in Southern gardens, a key ingredient in minted sweet peas and rice, certain jellies and cookies, our famous juleps, and all sorts of refreshing drinks. The secret to this flavorful lemonade is to allow the mint leaves and lemon to fuse for a full 45 minutes.

6 to 8 large, soft lemons
12 fresh mint leaves
1 cup sugar
3 cups boiling water
5 cups cold water
8 small mint leaves for garnish

Slice the lemons thinly, seed them, and place in a large mixing bowl. Add the mint, sprinkle on the sugar, pour the boiling water over the top, and let the mixture fuse for 45 minutes at room temperature, pressing the lemons and mint with a heavy spoon from time to time. Strain the liquid through a fine-mesh strainer into a glass punch bowl and add the cold water, stirring well. Add ice cubes, stir rapidly, ladle the lemonade and a few ice cubes into glasses, and garnish each with a mint leaf.

ABOUT 2 QUARTS LEMONADE

A Star-Spangled Cookout

NO MATTER WHERE MOTHER MIGHT BE FOR THE Fourth of July—at home, in a beach cottage, or at my house in East Hampton—she couldn't conceive of celebrating Independence Day without inviting at least ten old friends, new neighbors, and even virtual strangers for a real midday outdoor blast complete with flags and streamers and paper horns and patriotic music playing in the background—including "Dixie." Her setting on the deck, in the yard, or on the porch looks and sounds like any other elsewhere in the country with one major exception: like any arch-Southerner, she proudly flies the Confederate flag along-side Old Glory, commenting simply that "it's an important part of our history."

As for her menu, Mother decided some years ago that she'd had her fill of July Fourth cookouts with the same old hot dogs and hamburgers and grilled chicken and the like, and Rebel that she is, decided to feature an elaborate fresh seafood stew that could be made in advance and served in her enormous, trea-sured Jugtown pottery casserole made in the sand hills of North Carolina. With it she served only a salad and cornbread, followed by her spectacular strawberry shortcake, and the guests raved so that she determined then and there to make the muddle a tradition on this joyous holiday. "I just wish I could find a practical way to cook the muddle outside in a big kettle over an open fire the way they do on the Outer Banks and further up the coast in Virginia," she almost laments, adding, "Now, *that* would be what I call dramatic entertaining!" Knowing Mother, I wouldn't be at all surprised to learn one day that she'd somehow overcome this slight problem.

Martha Pearl Advises

For large neighborhood parties and cookouts when I'm never sure just how many guests might show up, I usually double most of my recipes to play it safe.

Menu

Jugtown Seafood Muddle

Silver Queen Corn and Black-Eyed Pea Salad

Cracklin' Cornbread

Cottle Farm Strawberry Shortcake

Washtub Beer and White Wine

Jugtown Seafood Muddle

On the Outer Banks of North Carolina and all along the Virginia coast, a muddle is simply a "mess of fish" composed of whatever seafood is freshest and most readily available. It's country cooking at its best, a dish that Mother would never prepare out of season due to her conviction that all major ingredients must be impeccably fresh. It's strategic with this stew that the seafood not be added till the last few minutes. Mother serves her muddle in a large, beautifully glazed Jugtown pottery casserole, but there's certainly nothing wrong about serving it in the kettle in which it's cooked.

8 strips bacon, cut into small pieces

3 large leeks (including about 1 inch of the green leaves), split, rinsed well, and chopped

3 large celery ribs, chopped

2 medium-size carrots, scraped and chopped

1 medium-size green bell pepper, seeded and chopped

2 garlic cloves, finely chopped

2 cups dry white wine

6 large, ripe tomatoes, seeded, chopped, and juices included

2 large red potatoes, peeled and cut into small cubes

1 tablespoon fresh thyme leaves or 1 teaspoon dried thyme

1 tablespoon finely chopped fresh basil leaves or 1 teaspoon dried basil

½ teaspoon red pepper flakes

Salt and black pepper to taste

Bottled clam juice as needed

4 pounds skinless, boneless, nonoily fish (cod, grouper, halibut, monkfish, red snapper), cut into 1-inch cubes

1 pound medium-size fresh shrimp, shelled and deveined

1 pound sea scallops, quartered

½ cup chopped fresh parsley leaves

In a large, heavy kettle, fry the bacon over moderate heat till crisp, drain on paper towels, crumble, and set aside.

continued

Add the leeks, celery, carrots, bell pepper, and garlic to the fat in the kettle and cook, stirring, till the vegetables are soft, about 10 minutes. Add the wine, tomatoes plus their juices, potatoes, thyme, basil, and pepper flakes, season with salt and black pepper, and add enough clam juice to cover. Bring to a simmer, stir well, and let cook till the potatoes are just tender, about 15 minutes. Increase the heat to moderate, add the fish, and cook for 5 minutes. Add the shrimp, scallops, and parsley, stir well, and cook 5 minutes longer. Stir in the reserved bacon and serve hot.

10 TO 12 SERVINGS

Martha Pearl Advises

When chopping fresh herbs, make sure they are completely dried after washing.

Silver Queen Corn and Black-Eyed Pea Salad

Although this quintessential Southern summer salad is ideal with Mother's seafood muddle, I serve it also as a main-course luncheon dish with no more than celery stuffed with pimento cheese and country ham biscuits. Convinced that it's sweeter and milkier than other varieties, Mother uses only Silver Queen white corn in her salad, and she insists that the fresh black-eyed peas be cooked at least an hour or till fully tender without being mushy. If you must use frozen peas, the cooking time will be about 30 minutes.

1 pound fresh black-eyed peas
2 tablespoons bacon grease
12 ears very fresh white corn, husks and silks removed
1 medium-size red bell pepper, seeded and finely chopped

4 green onions (whites and part of green leaves included), finely chopped

½ cup chopped fresh parsley leaves

¼ cup cider vinegar

2 teaspoons Dijon mustard

Salt and black pepper to taste

½ cup olive oil

In a large saucepan, combine the peas and bacon grease with enough salted water to cover, bring to a boil, reduce the heat to low, cover, and cook till just tender, about 1 hour. Drain the peas in a colander and let cool.

Arrange the corn in a large pot with enough cold water to cover, bring to a boil, remove from the heat, and let stand for 1 minute. Drain the corn and, when cool enough to handle, cut off the kernels with a sharp knife onto a cutting board or large plate.

In a large salad bowl, combine the peas, corn, bell pepper, onions, and parsley and toss till well blended. In a small mixing bowl, whisk together the vinegar, mustard, and salt and pepper till well blended, add the olive oil, and whisk till emulsified. Pour the dressing over the salad and toss till the ingredients are well coated. Chill the salad for 1 to 2 hours before serving.

10 TO 12 SERVINGS

Cracklin' Cornbread

Historically in the South, cracklin's are the bits of crisp skin left over from the lard-rendering process after hog-killing in the fall, as well as the brittle, succulent skin produced when a pig is barbecued over hickory embers in an open pit. Today, cracklin' is any form of pork fat that is rendered slowly in a skillet till crisp, and it is used to enhance everything from mashed potatoes to grits to scrambled eggs to black-eyed peas. When the tasty bits are incorporated into biscuits and cornbread, you can almost hear Southerners wax ecstatically. (One of the few restaurants left in the South to serve "cracklin' bread" is Mary Mac's Tea Room in Atlanta.) Do note that this cornbread does not freeze well.

2 cups diced fresh pork fat or lean salt pork with rind removed
4 cups yellow cornmeal
4 teaspoons baking powder
1 teaspoon salt
4 large eggs, beaten
4 cups milk
¼ cup vegetable oil
⅛ teaspoon cayenne pepper

In a medium-size heavy skillet, fry the pork fat over moderately low heat till fully rendered and crisp, about 45 minutes, turning frequently. Drain the cracklin's on paper towels and set aside.

Preheat the oven to 425°F. Grease a 13 by 8½ by 2-inch baking pan and set aside.

In a large mixing bowl, combine the cornmeal, baking powder, and salt and stir well. Add the eggs, milk, vegetable oil, and cayenne and stir with a wooden spoon till the batter is well blended and smooth. Add the cracklin's to the batter and stir till they' are well distributed.

Scrape the batter into the prepared pan and bake till a straw inserted in the center comes out clean, 25 to 30 minutes. Cut the cornbread into squares.

AT LEAST 10 SERVINGS

Cottle Farm Strawberry Shortcake

Mother picks or buys her fresh, plump strawberries exclusively at a large spread in Weddington, North Carolina, called Cottle Farm, hence the name of this eponymous strawberry shortcake always featured at her star-spangled cookout. "If you pick your own, it's five dollars for a gallon tub and seven if the owners do the picking," she informs, "but however I get them, I've rarely ever had a single bad berry." Suffice it that Mother loathes this dessert when made with commercial sponge cake ("That's Yankee," she huffs), and don't even bring up the topic of substituting something like Cool Whip for fresh whipped cream. Rest assured that once you've tasted this authentic Southern strawberry shortcake made with fresh split biscuits, other versions will seem almost inedible.

4 cups all-purpose flour

6 tablespoons sugar

2 tablespoons baking powder

$\frac{1}{2}$ teaspoon salt

1 cup (2 sticks) butter, softened

2 large eggs, beaten

$1\frac{1}{2}$ cups half-and-half

Butter for spreading

8 cups ripe strawberries, rinsed, hulled, sliced in half, and sugared to taste

2 cups heavy cream, whipped to stiff peaks

Preheat the oven to 450°F.

In a large mixing bowl, combine the flour, sugar, baking powder, and salt and mix well. Add the butter and, using a pastry cutter or two knives, cut the butter into the mixture till crumbly. In a small mixing bowl, combine the eggs and half-and-half and mix till well blended, then add to the flour mixture and stir till the mixture is thoroughly moist. Turn the dough out onto a lightly floured work surface and knead *very* briefly. With your hands, pat out the dough to about a $\frac{1}{2}$-inch thickness, then, using a floured 3-inch biscuit cutter, cut out 12 biscuits. Gather up the scraps of dough and repeat the procedure. Place the biscuits on an ungreased baking sheet and bake on the upper rack of the oven till slightly browned on top, about 10 minutes.

While they're still hot, split open the biscuits, spread lightly with butter, and arrange close together on a large crystal cake plate. Spoon the berries and whipped cream onto the biscuits and serve while still warm.

1 2   S E R V I N G S

A Neighborhood
Church Supper

SINCE ATTENDANCE DURING THE SUMMER MONTHS
tends to slack off at Mother's Episcopal church (as it does, no doubt, at most
churches), there is a long-standing and unique tradition of individual lady com-
municants in various neighborhoods sponsoring large get-together suppers every
July or August for church members residing in the respective neighborhoods.
Notices are mailed out weeks in advance for RSVPs, all the clergy are invited,
and while the lady in charge prepares most of the food herself, menus are discussed and people do often volunteer to bring extra dishes to fill out the buffet.
"Don't ask me why," Mother says, "but Episcopalians have always been as good
cooks as they are hearty drinkers, meaning that when I'm responsible for the
supper, I really have to watch my p's and q's with the dishes."

This is strictly an adult social affair, and even with priests in attendance,
there's never so much as a mention of church business. Mother decorates her
home with little more than a huge bouquet of mixed fresh flowers in the center
of the buffet table; she sets up the punch bowl in the sunroom; and since guests
tend to roam around, she places small odd tables to eat on throughout the house.
Generally, even the dessert is included on the main buffet table, but when friends
bring extra dishes ("and you can almost bet it'll be a dessert," Mother laughs),

nothing is more dramatic than to see an array of tempting Southern cakes and pies and puddings lined up on a separate sideboard.

Menu

Sparkling Fruit Punch

Hot Sausage Dip

Turkey and Ham Bake Supreme

Congealed Pineapple, Pimento, and Horseradish Salad

Peach Chutney

Fearrington House Angel Biscuits

Lemon-Glazed Almond Pound Cake

Sparkling Fruit Punch

Mother serves this all-purpose punch at any number of large summer gatherings, always making fairly considerable quantities since she knows how Southerners will drink a good, sturdy punch throughout an entire meal. Here she uses strawberries and peaches, but virtually any fresh summer fruit could be substituted or added.

1 cup water

1 cup sugar

$\frac{2}{3}$ cup fresh lemon juice

One 6-ounce can frozen orange juice concentrate, thawed

2 cups pineapple juice

2 cups apple juice

Two 1-litter bottles ginger ale

Two 750-ml bottles champagne

1 cup light rum

1 cup hulled and sliced fresh strawberries

1 cup peeled, pitted, and sliced ripe peaches

In a large, nonreactive kettle, combine the water, sugar, and lemon juice over low heat, stir till the sugar dissolves completely, and let cool. Add the concentrate and fruit juices, stir till well blended, and pour over a block of ice in a large punch bowl. Add the ginger ale, champagne, rum, strawberries, and peaches and stir gently.

Serve the punch in punch cups or glasses.

ABOUT 6 QUARTS PUNCH

Hot Sausage Dip

This is another typical Southern dip created by Mother's close Mississippi friend, Ann Scarborough, and while it is hearty and rich for an appetizer, I noticed at the last church supper I attended that not a trace was left in the baking dish—and that a certain priest in particular didn't seem to be able to scoop up enough.

1 pound bulk pork sausage
One 8-ounce package cream cheese, softened
One 7-ounce can Rotel tomatoes and chilies (available in most supermarkets), drained
½ pound sharp cheddar cheese, grated

In a large skillet, fry the sausage over moderate heat, breaking it up with a fork, till well cooked, then drain on paper towels.

Preheat the oven to 350°F.

In a large mixing bowl, combine the sausage, cream cheese, and tomatoes and chilies and mix till well blended. Spread the mixture evenly in a large glass baking dish, sprinkle the cheddar cheese over the top, and bake till bubbly and the cheese has melted completely.

Serve the dip hot with a bowl of Fritos or tortilla chips.

1 0 T O 1 2 S E R V I N G S

Turkey and Ham Bake Supreme

Yes, indeed, this is still another example of how Southerners are so adept at turning leftover meat and poultry into an elaborate casserole capable of feeding a large crowd. Turkey and ham is the most amenable combination, but Mother might also use leftover pork, chicken, or even roasted lamb, just as sometimes she substitutes sharp cheddar cheese or ½ cup of grated real Parmesan for the Swiss.

6 tablespoons (¾ stick) butter

1 cup finely chopped onions

6 tablespoons all-purpose flour

1 teaspoon salt

½ teaspoon black pepper

2½ cups milk

½ pound fresh mushrooms, sliced

5 tablespoons dry sherry

5 cups chopped cooked turkey breast

2 cups chopped cooked ham

Two 5-ounce cans water chestnuts, drained and sliced

1 cup shredded Swiss cheese

2 cups fresh bread crumbs

6 tablespoons (¾ stick) butter, melted

Preheat the oven to 400°F. Grease a large, shallow baking dish and set aside.

In a large, heavy skillet, melt 4 tablespoons of the butter over moderate heat, then add the onions and cook, stirring, till soft but not browned, about 5 minutes. Sprinkle the flour, salt, and pepper over the onions and stir for 2 minutes. Reduce the heat to low and gradually add the milk, stirring constantly till the mixture is thickened and smooth. Remove the pan from the heat.

In a small skillet, melt the remaining 2 tablespoons butter over moderate heat, add the mushrooms, and cook, stirring, till golden, about 5 minutes. Add the mushrooms, to the milk mixture, then add the sherry, turkey, ham, and water chestnuts and stir till well blended. Spoon the mixture into the prepared baking dish and sprinkle the cheese over the top. In a small mixing bowl, combine the bread crumbs and melted butter, spoon the mixture evenly over the cheese, and bake till the casserole is lightly browned, about 35 minutes. Serve hot.

1 2   T O   1 4   S E R V I N G S

Congealed Pineapple, Pimento, and Horseradish Salad

What makes this congealed salad so distinctive is Mother's addition of horseradish, an ingredient that nobody will identify but one that enhances the overall flavor, much as it does when added to any seafood salad.

2 cups water
One 3-ounce package lemon-flavored Jell-O
One 3-ounce package lime-flavored Jell-O
One 20-ounce can crushed pineapple (juice included)
One-half 4-ounce jar pimentos (see Martha Pearl Advises, page 205), drained and chopped
1 heaping tablespoon prepared hot horseradish
1 cup mayonnaise (Mother prefers Hellmann's)
One 12-ounce container small-curd cottage cheese
1/2 cup chopped pecans
Bibb lettuce leaves

In a large saucepan, bring the water to a boil, remove from the heat, add the two Jell-Os, stir till dissolved, and let cool. Add the pineapple plus its juice, the pimentos, horseradish, mayonnaise, cottage cheese, and pecans, stir till well blended, and pour into a 9 by 13-inch pan. Cover with plastic wrap and chill till firm, at least 4 hours.

Cut the salad into squares and serve on lettuce leaves on salad plates.

1 2   T O   1 4   S E R V I N G S

Martha Pearl Advises

Congealed salads containing solid foods require about four hours to firm up properly. To reduce that time by about an hour, one trick is to dissolve one envelope of gelatin or a 3-ounce package of Jell-O in 1 cup of boiling water, add 6 to 8 ice cubes, stir till the cubes have melted, and add no more water.

Peach Chutney

Mother utilizes the summer bounty of fresh mangoes, nectarines, apricots, and melons to make all sorts of preserves, pickles, and chutneys, but nothing equals what she does with the luscious peaches that she drives regularly down to an orchard in South Carolina to select so fastidiously. "Just remember that a great peach is large, fully tree-ripened but slightly firm, and fuzzy all over," she advises. "If they're not ripe enough, set them out on a paper bag—never in the refrigerator—just till they begin to soften but have no dark spots." Needless to say, Mother always doubles or triples this recipe in order to can a few jars of chutney for future use.

1 quart peeled, pitted, and coarsely chopped ripe, firm peaches

1 cup seedless dark raisins

$\frac{1}{2}$ cup finely chopped onions

1 small garlic clove, minced

1$\frac{3}{4}$ cups firmly packed dark brown sugar

1 teaspoon ground cinnamon

1 teaspoon ground cloves

1 teaspoon dry mustard

1 teaspoon salt

1 cup cider vinegar

In a large stainless steel or enameled pot, combine all the ingredients and stir well. Bring slowly to a boil, reduce the heat to low, and simmer, uncovered, till nicely thickened, 1$\frac{1}{4}$ to 1$\frac{1}{2}$ hours, stirring from time to time to prevent scorching. Ladle the chutney into a large serving bowl, cover with plastic wrap, and chill overnight. Serve chilled. (The chutney keeps in tightly sealed jars in the refrigerator up to 3 months.)

2 PINTS CHUTNEY

Fearrington House Angel Biscuits

One of Mother's favorite haunts anywhere is Fearrington House in Fearrington Village just outside Chapel Hill, North Carolina, without doubt one of the most distinguished restaurants in all the South—created, incidentally, by the same Jenny Finch with whom I went to high school in Charlotte. Mother loves virtually all the refined Southern food served there, but "I'd make the trip just to eat the angel biscuits they serve at every meal." High praise from a lady who's always said that no biscuit dough should ever be kneaded or contain a trace of sugar! Do note that this dough can be chilled in a greased, covered bowl up to four or five days.

1½ tablespoons active dry yeast
1 cup warm water
5 cups all-purpose flour
1 tablespoon baking powder
1 teaspoon baking soda
¼ cup sugar
1 tablespoon salt
2 cups Crisco vegetable shortening
2 cups buttermilk

In a small bowl, sprinkle the yeast over the water and let proof.

Sift together the flour, baking powder, baking soda, sugar, and salt into a large mixing bowl, then add the shortening and work the mixture with your fingertips till it resembles coarse meal. Add the yeast mixture and buttermilk and stir with a wooden spoon till the dough is smooth.

On a lightly floured work surface, knead the dough for 2 to 3 minutes, then roll out ½ inch thick. Cut out biscuits with a 2½-inch biscuit cutter, place on one or two ungreased baking sheets, gather up the excess dough, and repeat the procedure. Cover the biscuits with a clean kitchen towel and let rise for 30 minutes.

Meanwhile, preheat the oven to 450°F. When the biscuits have risen, bake them till golden brown, about 12 minutes. Serve hot.

ABOUT 60 BISCUITS

Martha Pearl Advises

When making biscuits, never add liquid to the flour mixture till you are ready to mix, since it activates the leavening. If you do so in advance, the biscuits will not be very fluffy.

Lemon-Glazed Almond Pound Cake

"But Missy," I question Mother, "how can this be a pound cake with that baking powder included?" She glares at me. "That just shows how much you really know about Southern cooking. True, most pound cakes don't have any leavening—which is why they're pretty heavy—but some do, and with just that little bit of rising, they can be the lightest, most delicious cakes in the world." And, uh, as usual, she's right.

FOR THE CAKE

1 cup all-purpose flour

2 teaspoons baking powder

1 teaspoon salt

1 cup (2 sticks) butter, softened

1 cup granulated sugar

1 cup ground almonds

4 large eggs

¾ cup fresh lemon juice

1 tablespoon grated lemon rind

FOR THE GLAZE

¼ cup fresh lemon juice

2 cups confectioners' sugar

Preheat the oven to 350°F. Grease and flour a 10-inch Bundt or tube pan and set aside. Sift together the flour, baking powder, and salt into a small mixing bowl and set aside.

In a large mixing bowl, cream together with an electric mixer the butter, granulated sugar, and almonds till well blended, then add the eggs one at a time, beating after each addition till the mixture is smooth. Add the sifted dry ingredients alternately with the lemon juice and rind, beating till the mixture is well blended and smooth. Scrape the batter into the prepared pan and bake till a cake tester comes out clean, 45 to 50 minutes. Let the cake cool completely on a wire rack, then turn out onto a cake plate.

continued

To make the glaze, combine the lemon juice and confectioners' sugar in a medium-size mixing bowl, stir till well blended and thickened, and drizzle the glaze all over the cooled cake. Let the cake stand about 1 hour before cutting into thin slices.

ONE 10-INCH CAKE; 12 TO 14 SERVINGS

Martha Pearl Advises

When a frosting (icing) made with confectioners' sugar and a liquid is intended to be drizzled, it may be necessary to add a little more sugar or liquid for just the right consistency.

A Carolina
Pork Barbecue

AS ANY SOUTHERNER WHO KNOWS ANYTHING ABOUT
barbecue will admit (all but Texans, that is, and they're not really Southerners),
North Carolina pork barbecue (chopped, sliced, or simply picked or pulled from
the bone) is the greatest barbecue on earth. Period. No argument. We in the
Tarheel State were virtually weaned on pig cooked in open pits over hickory
coals for hours and hours and slathered with spicy vinegar basting sauce, a ritual
that goes back to plantation days and is still observed throughout the summer
and early fall at church benefits, political rallies, wedding celebrations, and large
backyard cookouts. Travel anywhere in the state and you're bound to find barbecue houses scattered along the highways and in towns, each with its own special
style of roasting whole pigs (and the debates can be heated) but all respectful of a
classic tradition that is as sacred as the curing and aging of genuine country hams.

For years, Mother was convinced that authentic Carolina pork barbecue
could be produced only in an open pit like the one her daddy once constructed
not far from his vegetable garden. Then, about fifteen years ago, she and I
decided to experiment with an ordinary kettle grill on my deck in East Hampton, slowly cooking two hefty shoulders over charcoal and hickory chips for eight
to nine hours. Suffice it that the entire house had to be closed off to the smoke
and every stitch of clothing tossed in the washing machine, but so successful was

the barbecue that none other than Craig Claiborne pronounced it equal to anything he'd tasted in Lexington or Goldsboro, North Carolina—while to Yankee guests the experience was a revelation. Ever since, Mother and I both have been throwing elaborate barbecues such as this at our respective homes, the only difference being that if she runs out of meat in Carolina, all she has to do is dash over to Spoon's or Bubba's Barbecue for extra containers.

Except for Mother's crabmeat and olive dip, this menu (which rarely changes) is exactly what you'd find at a big Carolina church barbecue or at any respectable barbecue house in the eastern part of the state.

Menu

Crabmeat and Olive Dip

Authentic Carolina Pork Barbecue

Brunswick Stew

Creamy Coleslaw

Soused Red Onions

Onion Hush Puppies

Peach Tree Cobbler

Beer

Crabmeat and Olive Dip

Mother's only comment about this exceptional dip is the same she makes regarding any crab preparation: "Never, repeat never, even think of using canned or frozen crabmeat unless you want a dry, stringy, tasteless mess."

⅔ **cup mayonnaise (Mother prefers Hellmann's)**

2 teaspoons fresh lemon juice

2 teaspoons Worcestershire sauce

1 teaspoon prepared horseradish

½ **cup finely chopped green olives**

2 large hard-boiled eggs, shelled and finely chopped

2 tablespoons finely chopped fresh parsley leaves

Freshly ground black pepper to taste

1 pound fresh lump crabmeat (see Martha Pearl Advises, page 52), picked over for shells and cartilage

In a medium-size mixing bowl, combine the mayonnaise, lemon juice, Worcestershire, and horseradish and stir till well blended. Add the olives, chopped eggs, and parsley, season with pepper, and stir till well blended, then fold in the crabmeat till well incorporated. Keep refrigerated till ready to serve.

Serve the dip with crackers or small Melba toast rounds.

ABOUT 3 CUPS DIP

Martha Pearl Advises

Southerners love dips with cocktails, and it's not unusual for me to fix four or five different ones for large cocktail parties or suppers made with everything from crabmeat or shrimp to spinach to sausage to pineapple. What I truly loathe, however, are potato chips served with dips. Toast, crackers, Fritos, yes, but never potato chips.

Authentic Carolina Pork Barbecue

Let's not beat around the bush: Texans, Kansas Citians, and Tennesseans might think they know a thing or two about great barbecue, but nothing holds a candle to the pit-cooked, hickory-smoked, slightly vinegary, moist, incredibly succulent, inimitable chopped pork barbecue that, over the centuries, has been a North Carolina culinary hallmark. Ideally, you should have an outdoor pit, but trust me, you can produce genuine Carolina pork barbecue on an ordinary kettle grill if you follow our directions to the letter. Use only fresh pork shoulder (which has sufficient fat) and hickory chips, make sure the coals are not directly under the meat and remain gray throughout the process, turn and baste the meat at regular intervals, and above all, be patient. And if you're smart, you'll cook two shoulders since the chopped barbecue freezes beautifully up to about four months without losing its savor and moisture. This barbecue is served either by itself with extra sauce on the side or (as Mother and I and millions of other Tarheels prefer) topped with slaw inside a hamburger roll.

FOR THE BARBECUE

1 small bag hickory chips (available at nurseries and hardware stores)

One 10-pound bag charcoal briquets

One 8-pound boneless fresh pork shoulder

FOR THE SAUCE

4 cups cider vinegar

¼ cup Worcestershire sauce

1 cup catsup

2 tablespoons prepared mustard

2 tablespoons firmly packed brown sugar

2 tablespoons salt

Black pepper to taste

1 tablespoon red pepper flakes

Soak 6 handfuls of hickory chips in water to cover for 30 minutes. Drain.

Open one bottom and one top vent on a kettle grill. Place a small drip pan in the bottom of the grill, stack charcoal briquets evenly around the pan (not in the center), and ignite. When the coals are gray on one side (after about 30 minutes), turn them and sprinkle 2 handfuls of the soaked chips evenly over the hot coals.

Position the pork shoulder skin side up in the center of the grill directly over the drip pan (*not* over the hot coals), lower the lid, and cook for 4 hours, replenishing the coals and chips as they burn up. Turn the pork, lower the lid, and cook 2 hours longer.

Meanwhile, prepare the sauce by combining all the ingredients in a large saucepan. Stir well, bring to a simmer over moderate heat, and cook for 5 minutes. Remove from the heat and let stand for 2 hours.

Transfer the pork to a platter, make deep gashes in the meat with a sharp knife, and baste liberally with the sauce. Replenish the coals and chips as needed, replace the pork skin side down on the grill, and cook 3 hours longer, basting with the sauce from time to time.

Transfer the pork to a chopping board, remove and discard most (but not all) of the crisp skin and excess fat, and chop the meat coarsely with an impeccably clean hatchet, Chinese cleaver, or large, heavy chef's knife. Add just enough sauce to moisten the meat, toss till well blended, and either serve the barbecue immediately with the remaining sauce on the side or refrigerate and reheat in the top of a double boiler over simmering water when ready to serve. (The barbecue can be frozen up to 4 months.)

10 TO 12 SERVINGS

Brunswick Stew

Carolina barbecue without small bowls of thick Brunswick stew on the side? Almost as unimaginable as barbecue without coleslaw and hush puppies. Did the stew originate in Brunswick County, North Carolina, Brunswick County, Virginia, or Brunswick, Georgia? Who cares? What matters is that this phenomenal stew is one of the true superlatives of Southern cookery, so much so that Mother—and I—have been known to throw Brunswick stew suppers featuring nothing more than the stew, a salad, cornbread, and beer. Since the stew freezes well, you really should double the recipe and have plenty available for cold winter nights.

½ cup vegetable oil

One 4-pound chicken (preferably a hen), quartered

1 cup chopped onions

1 cup chopped celery (leaves included)

1 medium-size ham hock, trimmed

3 large ripe tomatoes, chopped

1 small red chili pepper, seeded and minced

Salt and black pepper to taste

2½ quarts water

1½ cups fresh or frozen corn kernels

1½ cups fresh or frozen sliced okra

1½ cups fresh or frozen lima beans

1½ cups mashed cooked potatoes

In a large, heavy skillet, heat ¼ cup of the vegetable oil over moderate heat, then add the chicken, brown on all sides, and transfer to a large plate. In a large stew pot, heat the remaining ¼ cup oil over moderate heat, then add the onions and celery and cook for 2 minutes, stirring. Add the browned chicken, ham hock, tomatoes, chili pepper, salt, black pepper, and water, bring to a boil, reduce the heat to low, cover, and simmer for 1 hour. Remove the chicken with a slotted spoon and simmer the mixture for 1 hour longer. When the chicken has cooled, skin, bone, and shred the meat and set aside.

Bring the mixture in the pot to a boil, add the corn, okra, and lima beans, and cook over moderate heat for 30 minutes. Remove the ham hock with a slotted spoon and, when cool enough to handle, bone, shred the meat, and return the meat to the casserole along with the reserved chicken. Add the mashed potatoes, stir well, and continue to cook till nicely thickened, about 15 minutes.

Serve the stew in small bowls as a side dish to pork barbecue.

10 TO 12 SERVINGS

Creamy Coleslaw

In the South, coleslaw is to pork barbecue what vanilla ice cream is to peach cobbler. Deriving from the Old English word for cabbage ("cole"), "cole slaugh" was mentioned as early as 1839 in Lettice Bryan's Kentucky Housewife, *and in the old days it was almost always made with a boiled dressing (as my grandmother Maw Maw did). Mother's everyday coleslaw is made with lots of vinegar and only a touch of mayonnaise, but when she's planning to serve slaw with pork barbecue, she prefers this much creamier version. Do note that virtually any coleslaw becomes watery if kept in the refrigerator for more than about two days.*

continued

1 large, firm head green cabbage (about 2 pounds)

2 large carrots, scraped

1 medium-size onion, peeled

3 tablespoons cider vinegar

3 teaspoons granulated sugar

1 teaspoon celery seeds

Salt and black pepper to taste

½ cup mayonnaise (Mother prefers Hellmann's)

½ cup sour cream

Remove and discard the outer loose leaves of the cabbage, cut the head into quarters, cut out and discard the hard center core, and shred the quarters into a large glass bowl. Shred the carrots into the bowl, then the onion, and stir to mix.

In a small mixing bowl, combine the remaining ingredients and mix till well blended and smooth. Pour the dressing over the cabbage mixture, toss till well blended, cover the bowl with plastic wrap, and chill about 2 hours before serving.

10 TO 12 SERVINGS

Martha Pearl Advises

When making ordinary coleslaw, I usually grate (not shred) my cabbage, onions, and carrots for a more refined texture. Slaw needs a little sugar to neutralize any bitterness, as well as a few celery seeds to combat blandness. I bind the ingredients with both cider vinegar and mayonnaise—but not so much vinegar as to make the slaw soggy.

Soused Red Onions

Okay, so Mother got the idea of serving simple soused red onions with our pork barbe-cue when they were served at a Texas barbecue we once attended. Not, mind you, that she cared much for the mesquite-smoked beef brisket, but she did have to admit that these sweet-sour onions do complement any smoked meat.

4 large red onions, peeled
2½ cups cider vinegar
¼ cup sugar
2 teaspoons salt
Freshly ground black pepper to taste

Cut the onions into rings and spread them out in a large, shallow serving dish. In a medium-size mixing bowl, combine the vinegar, sugar, salt, and pepper, mix till well blended, and pour over the onions. Cover with plastic wrap and let stand for at least 4 hours before serving.

10 TO 12 SERVINGS

Martha Pearl Advises

When cooking, pickling, or sousing any light fruits, vegetables, or seafood such as peaches, watermelon rind, cabbage, and shrimp, use white vinegar to prevent discol-oration. For dark fruits and vegetables like cherries, beets, and greens, cider vinegar or red wine vinegar is preferable.

Onion Hush Puppies

Almost indigenous to the Carolina coastal areas, hush puppies are traditionally served not only with fried seafood but with pork barbecue as well. For years, Mother refused to add onions to her hush puppies (just as she'd never dream of distorting the flavor of her cornbread), but after a cook at the Center Pier restaurant in Carolina Beach, North Carolina, clued us in on the secret of the sublime oblong dodgers we were raving about, Mother was forced to relent. Hush puppies are easy to make, the only cardinal rule being that they must be served piping hot. This means, of course, staying in the kitchen till the last minute, but rest assured, the pups are worth the inconvenience—and guests at the barbecue gobble them down as fast as they appear in the wicker basket.

2 cups all-purpose flour
1½ cups yellow cornmeal
2 tablespoons sugar
1 teaspoon baking powder
1 teaspoon salt
½ cup finely minced onions
2⅓ cups milk
⅓ cup vegetable oil
1 large egg, beaten
Corn or vegetable oil for deep frying

Into a large mixing bowl, sift together the flour, cornmeal, sugar, baking powder, and salt and stir to blend thoroughly. Add the onions, milk, vegetable oil, and egg and stir with a wooden spoon long enough just to blend well.

In a deep-fat fryer or deep cast-iron skillet, heat about 2½ inches of oil to 375°F on a thermometer, then drop the batter in batches by tablespoons into the fat and fry till the hush puppies are golden brown and crisp, about 3 minutes. Drain on paper towels and serve immediately.

ABOUT 40 HUSH PUPPIES

Peach Tree Cobbler

Throughout most of the year, Mother demonstrates patience with the arrival of fresh produce in the markets, but come early June, she simply can't restrain herself from getting into the car and driving down to The Peach Tree orchard in Filbert, South Carolina, in hopes of finding the first cling peaches of the season. Thereafter, she awaits the Elbertas, Red Glows, Georgia Belles, and other sweet, juicy, preferred freestone varieties, all intended for preserves, pickles, compotes, ice creams, pies, and, above all, her sumptuous cobblers. "Lord, I've been discussing peach cobbler with the owner, Mrs. Smith, for at least twenty years," she relates, "and what's so interesting is that, after trying every technique and variation and modification imaginable, we both come back to this simple, time-tested, traditional method." It is important to pick out soft peaches if you want to make the cobbler Southerners really love, and remember to check the cobbler while baking to make sure a little juice remains on the bottom.

6 pounds ripe peaches, peeled, pitted, and cut into ½-inch-thick slices

1½ cups plus 2 tablespoons sugar

¼ cup (½ stick) butter, cut into small pieces

2 cups all-purpose flour

1 tablespoon baking powder

1 teaspoon salt

¼ cup Crisco vegetable shortening

1 cup heavy cream

Vanilla ice cream

Preheat the oven to 400°F. Grease a 9 by 13-inch baking dish and set aside.

In a large mixing bowl, combine the peaches with 1½ cups of the sugar and toss well. Spoon the fruit into the baking dish and dot with the butter.

Sift together the flour, baking powder, salt, and the remaining 2 tablespoons sugar into a large mixing bowl, then cut in the shortening with a pastry cutter or two knives till the mixture resembles coarse meal. Add the heavy cream and stir till the dough forms a ball. Turn the dough out onto a lightly floured work surface, roll out ¼ inch thick, and trim as necessary to fit the baking dish. Place the dough over the fruit, crimp the edges, and bake till the pastry is golden brown and the peaches are still slightly juicy, about 30 minutes. Let the cobbler cool for about 15 minutes and serve warm topped with ice cream.

10 TO 12 SERVINGS

Martha Pearl Advises

If the fruit used for cobblers is extremely juicy and looks like it may make the cobbler too runny, I add about an extra tablespoon of flour or cornstarch to the sugared fruit before cooking.

An Around-the-Pool Party

THIS WEEKEND PARTY, WHICH HAS BECOME AN annual summer event by the pool at Mother's clubhouse in Charlotte, actually originated some years ago by sheer accident at my house in East Hampton. Having invited a few friends over for a late-morning swim in my pool on a scorching August day and trying to come up with something to offer them for lunch, Mother remembered some baked ham and soused shrimp left over from the night before in the refrigerator, then spotted a couple of avocados that were just ripe enough, then eyed a basket of fat homegrown tomatoes and a half-loaf of casserole bread on the counter and . . . "Honey," she directed me, "run up to the seafood shop and get some crabmeat, and we'll just fix a couple of pretty salads and serve this bread and . . ." Suffice it that by the time she'd finished throwing various ingredients together, our guests not only ended up with three of the most exquisite cold summer salads they'd ever tasted but Mother conceived the idea of doing another salad party at a future date—topped off by a churn of fresh peach ice cream and a few homemade cookies.

Today, guests arrive with bathing suits at the pool for a swim about ten o'clock in the morning, and in good old decadent Southern style, begin sipping chilled Riesling packed in a washtub full of ice around eleven. Mother sets two tables under umbrellas around the pool with paper cloths and napkins, plastic mugs for iced tea, and disposable knives and forks—nothing fancy, nothing complicated, and a minimum to clean up. Between twelve-thirty and one, the chilled salads, bread, and maybe some nicely aged cheese are brought to a narrow buffet table, people help themselves, and last but not least is the fresh peach ice cream scooped directly from the churn's canister into plastic bowls—and washed down perhaps with more Riesling. After all the food and wine, the hardy might take another dip, while the less vigorous simply settle for a short nap in a pool chair.

Menu

Chilled Riesling Wine

Soused Shrimp and Avocado Salad

Ham and Macaroni Salad

Tomatoes Stuffed with Herbed Crab Salad

Casserole Cheese Bread

Churned Fresh Peach and Mango Ice Cream

Orange Iced Tea

Soused Shrimp and Avocado Salad

*Although this salad must be started a day ahead, I consider it to be the most refined
and delicious of all Mother's shrimp salads, a preparation that's ideal for outdoor,
informal summer entertaining but also one that might grace a formal dinner buffet.
Generally, Mother uses highly acidic white vinegar only for canning, but here it's
called for to prevent the ingredients from possibly discoloring. Remembering the way
guests usually devour this salad at pool parties, I strongly suggest that you double the
recipe to play it safe—and to have some left over for another meal.*

2½ cups white vinegar

2 large onions, sliced

1 large celery rib, broken into thirds

1½ tablespoons sugar

10 whole cloves

1 tablespoon salt

1 teaspoon cracked black peppercorns

2½ pounds large fresh shrimp, shelled and deveined

2 large, ripe avocados

3 tablespoons capers, drained

Red-tipped leaf lettuce

3 tablespoons chopped fresh chives

In a large enameled or stainless steel saucepan, combine the vinegar, onions, celery, sugar,
cloves, salt, and peppercorns, bring to a boil, reduce the heat to low, and simmer for 15 minutes. Add the shrimp, return the liquid to a boil, reduce the heat to moderate, cover, and simmer the shrimp for 1 minute. Remove the pan from the heat and let the shrimp cool in the
liquid. Pour the mixture into a large glass bowl, cover with plastic wrap, and chill overnight.

When ready to serve, peel and pit the avocados, cut into 1-inch cubes, add to the shrimp
along with the capers, and toss gently. Drain the liquid from the bowl, line a large serving
platter with lettuce leaves, spoon the salad in the center, and sprinkle the chives over the top.
Serve chilled or at room temperature.

8 SERVINGS

If your lettuce is not crisp enough for salads, place the head in a bowl of cold water with a slice or two of fresh lemon, let stand for about an hour, then pat the leaves completely dry with paper towels.

Ham and Macaroni Salad

Mother remains a little baffled over why everybody seems to adore this salad, and the truth is that even two renowned cookbook authors have come begging for the recipe to publish. "Lord," she shakes her head, "it's just plain old ham and macaroni salad—the same my mama and aunt used to make and the one I've been taking to outdoor get-togethers for years." Well, the dish might be ordinary to Mother, but take my word that it's the first item to disappear at her salad parties.

FOR THE SALAD

4 cups cooked elbow macaroni

$1\frac{1}{4}$ pounds lean cooked ham, cut into $\frac{1}{2}$-inch cubes

$\frac{1}{2}$ pound Swiss cheese, cut into $\frac{1}{2}$-inch cubes

3 large hard-boiled eggs, shelled and chopped

1 medium-size onion, chopped

2 large celery ribs, chopped

$\frac{3}{4}$ cup chopped sweet pickles

$\frac{1}{2}$ cup chopped fresh parsley leaves

Romaine lettuce leaves

¾ cup mayonnaise (Mother prefers Hellmann's)

½ cup buttermilk

1 tablespoon Dijon mustard

¼ teaspoon Worcestershire sauce

Black pepper to taste

In a large mixing bowl, combine all the salad ingredients except the lettuce leaves and toss to mix well. In a small mixing bowl, combine all the dressing ingredients, stir till well blended, and pour over the salad. Toss the salad well, cover with plastic wrap, and chill at least 1 hour before serving in a large salad bowl lined with lettuce leaves.

8 SERVINGS

Tomatoes Stuffed with Herbed Crab Salad

With wonderful homegrown tomatoes, a bounty of sweet blue Carolina crabs, and easy access to fresh garden herbs, Mother considers these stuffed tomatoes to be the quintessential summer dish for outdoor entertaining. Needless to say, she uses only pristine lump crabmeat and would never dream of substituting the dreadful canned or frozen product. Be sure to leach out excess liquid from the scooped tomatoes by salting them and letting them drain, and do remember to keep the tomatoes well chilled till just ready to serve—especially in scorching weather. Mother purposefully makes more salad than is needed to stuff the tomatoes since "people always ask for a little extra."

continued

8 large ripe tomatoes

Salt

1 pound fresh lump crabmeat (see Martha Pearl Advises, page 52), picked over for shells or
    cartilage

2 large hard-boiled eggs, shelled and chopped

2 tablespoons minced fresh chives

1 tablespoon finely chopped fresh parsley leaves

1 tablespoon finely chopped fresh basil leaves

1 tablespoon finely chopped fresh tarragon leaves

1 teaspoon minced garlic

Freshly ground black pepper to taste

1 cup mayonnaise (Mother prefers Hellmann's)

Watercress for garnish

Cut off about ½ inch of the core ends of the tomatoes and, with a spoon, carefully scoop out
and discard about three-quarters of the pulp to form a wide, deep cavity. Salt the inside of the
tomatoes and turn them upside down on paper towels to drain, about 20 minutes.

In a large mixing bowl, combine all the remaining ingredients except the watercress, mix till
well blended, and when the tomatoes have drained, stuff them with equal amounts of the
crab mixture. Arrange the stuffed tomatoes on a large serving platter, garnish the edges with
watercress, and chill till ready to serve.

8 SERVINGS

Casserole Cheese Bread

*I know absolutely nothing about the origins of casserole bread, only that it was popu-
lar in the South during the last century and gradually began to disappear when more
modern breadmaking methods were developed. "My grandmama made it strictly by
hand with cheese and herbs and ham and heaven knows what else," Mother remembers,*

"and I have no idea when people began using an electric mixer to beat the batter for an almost cakelike texture." Mother has experimented with the bread for years, and all I can say is that I find it extraordinary—light, subtly flavorful, mysterious, and utterly delicious for any and all occasions. (I love it especially toasted for breakfast.) One warning: for truly distinctive flavor, the bread must have the oregano—or another similar herb.

2 envelopes active dry yeast

2 cups warm water

1 tablespoon sugar

2 tablespoons salt

2 tablespoons butter, softened

$^1\!/_2$ cup finely grated sharp cheddar cheese

$^1\!/_2$ cup freshly grated Parmesan cheese

2 tablespoons finely chopped fresh oregano leaves or 1$^1\!/_2$ teaspoons dried oregano

4$^1\!/_2$ cups all-purpose flour, sifted

In a large mixing bowl, sprinkle the yeast over the warm water, let proof for 5 minutes, and stir till dissolved completely. Add the sugar, salt, butter, the two cheeses, oregano, and 3 cups of the flour and beat with an electric mixer at low speed till well blended. Increase the speed to medium and beat till smooth, about 2 minutes. Scrape the batter off the beaters back into the bowl and, using a wooden spoon, beat in the remaining 1 $^1\!/_2$ cups flour till the batter is smooth. Cover with a sheet of waxed paper and a clean kitchen towel and let rise in a warm draft-free area till double in bulk, about 45 minutes.

Preheat the oven to 375°F. Grease a 2-quart casserole and set aside.

With a wooden spoon, beat the batter in the mixing bowl vigorously for 30 seconds, scrape it into the prepared casserole, and bake till lightly browned, about 1 hour. Turn the bread out onto a wire rack, let cool completely, and cut into wedges.

1 LARGE LOAF; 8 SERVINGS

Churned Fresh Peach and Mango Ice Cream

Succinctly, there is simply no ice cream on earth to equal the fresh churned peach ambrosia that Mother makes throughout the summer with the large, juicy, unblemished, fuzzy Elbertas she gets at an orchard in Filbert, South Carolina. And when she adds a couple of ripe mangoes, the result is nothing less than celestial. As a child, it was my duty to turn the crank on our old wooden peach churn till my arms almost dropped off; today, we use a nifty electric model that produces a thick, nicely frozen, luscious ice cream in about thirty minutes. Just make sure to buy plenty of cracked ice and a big box or tub of rock salt, and remember to let the churned ice cream mellow a couple of hours before serving. Stored in plastic containers, the ice cream can be kept frozen in the refrigerator up to a month without losing its savor.

6 large, ripe peaches
2 ripe mangoes
1½ cups sugar
3 large eggs
2 cups half-and-half
2 tablespoons cornstarch
Dash of salt
2 cups heavy cream
2 tablespoons pure vanilla extract

Peel and pit the peaches, cut them into small pieces, and place half the pieces in a medium-size mixing bowl. Peel the mangoes, cut the flesh from the pits in small pieces, and add to the peaches. Add 1 cup of the sugar and stir till the sugar is dissolved. Cover the peaches and mangoes tightly with plastic wrap and let stand in the refrigerator for at least 2 hours. In a medium-size mixing bowl, mash the remaining peaches with a heavy fork and refrigerate, covered, with the peach and mango pieces.

In a large, heavy saucepan, whisk the eggs till frothy, add the half-and-half, and whisk till well blended. In a small mixing bowl, combine the cornstarch, the remaining ½ cup sugar, and the salt, mix till well blended, and gradually whisk this into the egg mixture. Cook the mixture over low heat, stirring constantly, till the custard thickens slightly. Remove the pan from the heat, let cool, cover, and chill for 2 hours.

Combine the mashed peaches, heavy cream, and vanilla, add this to the cold custard, and stir till well blended. Pour the mixture into the canister of an electric ice cream freezer and freeze according to the manufacturer's directions. When the ice cream is frozen (it will still be slightly soft), remove the dasher and stir the peach and mango pieces and any juice into the ice cream. Cover the canister, pack more ice and rock salt around the canister, and allow the ice cream to mellow for 2 to 3 hours before serving.

ABOUT ¾ GALLON ICE CREAM;
AT LEAST 12 SERVINGS

Martha Pearl Advises

When churning real ice cream, never substitute plain milk for real cream if you want a truly creamy and not icy texture.

To ripen mangoes quickly, place them in a paper bag with a very ripe banana and check them periodically till they're soft.

Orange Iced Tea

Iced tea is the sacred beverage of the South, and its variations are endless. While most Southerners like both sugar (lots of sugar) and lemon juice in their iced tea, as in this fizzy version, let it go on record that Mother never adds either to her personal brews. "I know to sweeten any pitcher of iced tea when I'm entertaining—and people always love it," she states with a slight frown, "but as far as I myself am concerned, I just don't like sugar in any tea—or coffee." And that's that.

2 large tea bags
4 cups water
1 cup sugar
2 cups orange juice
2 cups club soda water
¼ cup fresh lemon juice

In a large saucepan, drop the tea bags into the water, bring to a boil, remove the pan from the heat, and let steep for 20 minutes. Remove the tea bags, pour the tea into a large pitcher, add the sugar, stir, and let cool completely. Add the orange juice, soda water, and lemon juice, stir till well blended, and serve the tea over ice cubes in tall glasses.

8 DRINKS

Index

corn (*continued*)

    Silver Queen, and black-eyed pea salad, 272–73

    sticks, onion, 42

cornbread:

    Ann's skillet, 136

    bird's-eye, 249–50

    cheddar pimento, 31–32

    cracklin', 274

    Greek, 156–57

Cottle Farm strawberry shortcake, 275–76

crab:

    and olive dip, 291

    salad, tomatoes stuffed with herbed, 305–6

    and shrimp chowder, 225–26

    soup, easy she-, 185–86

cracklin biscuits, 10

cracklin' cornbread, 274

cracklin' roast fresh ham with cider mustard gravy, 131–32

cranberry:

    and apple tart, glazed, 97–98

    grapefruit, and orange salad, gingered, 41

    orange, and pineapple salad, congealed, 57

    relish, 45

    upside-down cake, 147

cream cheese sandwiches, fruity, 116

creamed succotash, 263

creamy coleslaw, 295–96

Creole shrimp and oyster gumbo, 17–18

crusted grits soufflé, 106

curried shrimp paste, 184–85

D

date-nut bread, 116–17

desserts:

    blackberry crackle, 267

butterscotch delights, 242–43

chocolate, walnut, and raspberry torte, 210–11

churned fresh peach and mango ice cream, 308–9

Cottle Farm strawberry shortcake, 275–76

frozen fruit salad, 197–98

fudgy coconut biddy nests, 169–70

gingerbread men, 47

gingered rhubarb-strawberry fool, 232

glazed cranberry and apple tart, 97–98

grasshopper squares, 120

Jefferson Davis pie, 22–23

mixed berry cobbler, 254–55

peach brown Betty, 11–12

peach tree cobbler, 299–300

pecan coconut brownies, 67

raspberry meringue nests, 198–99

Southern Comfort ambrosia, 59

see also cakes; pies

deviled tarragon eggs, 167–68

dilled beet, feta, and onion salad, 156

dips, *see* appetizers

dressings:

    horseradish, shrimp, avocado, and potato salad with, 164–65

    poppy seed, autumn seafood salad with, 82–83

E

easy she-crab soup, 185–86

eggplant and red onions, herbed, 166

eggs:

    deviled tarragon, 167–68

    sausage-apple ring with scrambled, 104–5

F

fancy Parmesan-cheddar straws, 215
Fearrington House angel biscuits, 285–86
frozen fruit salad, 197–98
fruity cream cheese sandwiches, 116
fudgy coconut biddy nests, 169–70

G

get-together vegetable finger sandwiches,
        80–81
ginger(ed):
    cake with lemon raisin sauce, hot,
        137–38
    grapefruit, orange, and cranberry salad,
        41
    pear, raisin, and walnut conserve, 146
    rhubarb-strawberry fool, 232
gingerbread men, 47
glazed cranberry and apple tart, 97–98
goalpost punch, 141
grand slam creamed chicken on toast points,
        195–96
grape, mango, and grapefruit compote, 177
grapefruit:
    mango, and grape compote, 177
    orange, and cranberry salad, gingered,
        41
grasshopper squares, 120
gravies:
    cider mustard, cracklin' roast fresh ham with,
        131–32
    for roast turkey with oyster and almond
        stuffing, 53–54
Greek beans and tomatoes, 155
Greek cornbread, 156–57
Greek-style roast leg of lamb with potatoes,
        153–54
green beans and tomatoes, Greek, 155

H

grits:
    and shrimp, 173–74
    soufflé, crusted, 106
ground chicken and almond sandwiches, 118
gumbos:
    chicken and ham perloo, 186–87
    Creole shrimp and oyster, 17–18

Halloween spiders, 46
ham:
    -and-cheese pizza, 124
    and chicken perloo, 186–87
    country, braised in cider and molasses,
        92–93
    country, spoonbread, 40
    cracklin' roast fresh, with cider mustard gravy,
        131–32
    hock, with turnip and mustard greens combo,
        133–34
    and macaroni salad, 304–5
    minced country, biscuits, 114–15
    and turkey bake supreme, 281–82
herbed eggplant and red onions, 166
holiday bourbon cake, 60
holiday seven-layer salad, 96
holy fried Creole oysters, 142
hoppin' John, smoky, 134
horseradish:
    dressing, shrimp, avocado, and potato salad
        with, 164–65
    pineapple, and pimento salad, congealed,
        283
hot cross buns, 178–79
hot ginger cake with lemon raisin sauce, 137–38
hot sausage dip, 280
hot seafood dip, 51–52
hush puppies, onion, 298

I

ice cream, churned fresh peach and mango,
    308–9

J

Jefferson Davis pie, 22–23
Jezebel, 91
Joseph's hoecakes, 189
jubilee congealed salad, 238–39
Jugtown seafood muddle, 271–72

K

Kentucky beer cheese, 37
kumquat and apple chutney, 9

L

lamb, Greek-style roast leg of, with potatoes,
    153–54
last-minute chicken pâté, 71–72
leeks and baked country sausage supreme,
    143–44
lemon:
    -glazed almond pound cake, 287–88
    raisin sauce with hot ginger cake, 137–38
lemonade, mint, 268

M

macaroni and ham salad, 304–5
M&M's holiday wreaths, 128
mango(es):
    and churned fresh peach ice cream,
        308–9

grapefruit, and grape compote, 177
Maw Maw's stewed tomatoes, 135
mayonnaise, molded avocado salad with herb,
    30–31
meat loaf, company, 6–7
milk punches, 103
minced country ham biscuits,
    114–15
mint lemonade, 268
Miss Ella's Sazeracs, 15
Missy's buttermilk biscuits,
    98–99
mixed berry cobbler, 254–55
molasses, country ham braised in cider and,
    92–93
molded avocado salad with herb mayonnaise,
    30–31
molded salmon salad, 72–73
Mother's sacred Southern fried chicken,
    261–62
muffin(s):
    banana buttermilk, 66
    biscuit, 108
    sandwiches, chicken sour cream,
        123
mulled apple cider, 39
mushroom(s):
    bacon-stuffed, 119
    and pecan wild rice, 218–19
    and sausage strata, 64
mustard cider gravy, cracklin' roast fresh ham
    with, 131–32
mustard and turnip greens combo with ham
    hock, 133–34

N

nuts, see almond; pecan(s); walnuts
nutty collard greens, 11

T

tangy pimento cheese dip, 16
tidewater pickled shrimp, 63
toasted orange pecans, 90
toast points, 38
tomato(es):
    and beans, Greek, 155
    Maw Maw's stewed, 135
    and okra mull, 264–65
    plantation baked, 188
    in ribbon loaf sandwiches, 240–41
    stuffed with herbed crab salad, 305–6
    Waccamaw stuffed, 252
top-hat walnut shortbreads, 221–22
turkey:
    and ham bake supreme, 282–82
    roast, with oyster and almond stuffing,
        53–54
turnip and mustard greens combo with ham
        hock, 133–34
twice-stuffed baked potatoes, 5

V

Virginia peanut soup, 79

W

Waccamaw stuffed tomatoes, 252
waffles, pecan, with orange syrup, 175–76
walnut:
    chocolate, and raspberry torte, 210–11
    pear, and raisin conserve, gingered, 146
    shortbreads, top-hat, 221–22
watercress and shrimp paste rolled sandwiches,
        112–13
white turnip and onion soufflé, 8
winter squash casserole, 94–95

Y

yogurt-almond cake, 157–58